SPOON RIVER ANTHOLOGY

Edgar Lee Masters

SPOON RIVER ANTHOLOGY

AN ANNOTATED EDITION

Edited and with an Introduction
and Annotations by
John E. Hallwas

UNIVERSITY OF ILLINOIS PRESS
Urbana and Chicago

Introduction and Notes to the Poems © 1992
by the Board of Trustees of the University of Illinois
Manufactured in the United States of America
P 12 11 10 9 8

This book is printed on acid-free paper.

Library of Congress Cataloging-in-Publication Data

Masters, Edgar Lee, 1868–1950.
    Spoon River anthology / by Edgar Lee Masters.—An annotated ed.
/ edited and with an introduction and annotations by John E.
Hallwas.
        p.   cm.
ISBN 0-252-06363-6 (alk. paper) / ISBN 978-0-252-06363-3 (alk. paper)
    I. Hallwas, John E. II. Title.
    PS3525.A83S5   1992
811'.52—dc20   91-16968
                                                          CIP

CONTENTS

ACKNOWLEDGMENTS

Many people and institutions contributed to this annotated edition. First of all, I am indebted to Western Illinois University for a sabbatical leave that allowed me to visit several libraries and complete the project sooner than I otherwise could have. I am also grateful to the following libraries for access to their collections: Alderman Library at the University of Virginia, Dartmouth College Library, Georgetown University Library, the Illinois State Historical Library, the Newberry Library, Petersburg Public Library, Parlin-Ingersoll Library at Canton, Seymour Library at Knox College, Van Pelt Library at the University of Pennsylvania, and Western Illinois University Library.

I also want to acknowledge the generous assistance of Fulton County historian Marjorie Turner-Rich Bordner, who provided background information, photographs, and comments on the manuscript, and scholar Charles E. Burgess, who provided much helpful information about the poet and extensive commentary on the introduction and annotations.

Several other scholars read and commented on the manuscript, and their contributions are deeply appreciated: James Hurt, Professor of English at the University of Illinois; Thomas P. Joswick, John Mann, and Charles Mayer, professors of English at Western Illinois University; Gordana Rezab, Archivist at Western Illinois University Library; and Milton R. Stern, Professor of English at the University of Connecticut.

Thanks are also extended to several other individuals who provided information that was useful in annotating the poems: David D. Anderson, Professor of American Thought and Language at Michigan State University; Allie Goudy, Music Librarian at Western Illinois University; Robert Henry, Professor of Biological Sciences at Western Illinois University; John Stierman, Reference Librarian at Western Illinois University; Cindy Sutton, IRAD intern at Western Illinois University; and Douglas Wilson, Professor of English and Library Director at Knox College.

I am also grateful to the following institutions for providing photographs for this edition: Dartmouth College Library, the Edgar Lee Masters Memorial Museum at Petersburg, Georgetown University Library, and the Illinois State Historical Library. Special thanks are due to the *Illinois Historical Journal,* which granted permission to reproduce photographs that appeared in "The Spoon River Country" by Josephine Craven Chandler, vol. 14 (1921-22): 252-329.

I am particularly indebted to Richard L. Wentworth, Director of the University of Illinois Press, whose interest and expertise were indispensable to the completion of this project and the production of this complex edition. My appreciation is also extended to Karen Hewitt of the University of Illinois Press, who handled a variety of matters related to the publication process, and Beth Bower, also of the press, who copyedited the manuscript.

Finally, I want to thank my wife Garnette for her support and patience during this four-year project and my son Darrin for putting my work onto the computer and catching some errors in the process.

John E. Hallwas

INTRODUCTION

Spoon River Anthology (1915; 1916) is widely known but not well understood. No other volume of American poetry made such an immediate impact, and few have been so influential. Composed of monologues spoken by the dead in a midwestern cemetery, it was conceptually stunning; focused on the inner lives of even the violent and the sexually maladjusted, it was shockingly frank; written in flatly realistic and often ironic free verse, it was stylistically innovative; and concerned with frustration, struggle, and conflict in America, it was an ambitious portrayal of cultural decline firmly grounded in the specifics of community life. No volume of poetry since Whitman's *Leaves of Grass* (1855) had attempted so much or had been so original. Masters himself did not fully comprehend the book's uniqueness or the reasons for its powerful impact on American readers. He began it without knowing precisely what he wanted to do; he ended it without clearly realizing what he had done. He thought he could do better work in another, more traditional mode of poetry, but he never did. Of the twenty-two volumes of poetry that followed *Spoon River Anthology,* the most well received was *The New Spoon River* (1924), a less successful continuation of his one famous book. And much of his later poetry was poor indeed—conventional, simplistic, and exhortative. Moreover, as Masters's literary career declined, American poetry went in another direction— toward the Europeanized formalism that T. S. Eliot and Wallace Stevens promoted and away from the American realism (nativistic informalism) that he had championed. *Spoon River Anthology* slowly faded from the canon of significant American literature— before we learned to read it well.

Of course, the book is still regarded as an effective exposé of the small town—a view typified by May Swenson's comment in the introduction to the paperback edition: "the *Anthology* remains

1

fascinating if for nothing else than to untangle the lurid web of small-town scandal provocatively placed before us."[1] As this suggests, readers of American literature continue to associate the book with the so-called "revolt from the village" movement that also produced Sherwood Anderson's *Winesburg, Ohio* (1919) and Sinclair Lewis's *Main Street* (1920). Anthony Channell Hilfer discusses that literary development, which countered the idealization of the American small town, in *The Revolt from the Village, 1915-30* (1969). As he and other scholars acknowledge, Masters's book was of seminal importance in that development. But *Spoon River Anthology* is not recognized for what it more deeply is—a depiction of the struggle for self-realization in a society that has lost contact with the great democratic vision that once gave purpose and meaning to American lives, and an account of the poet's quest to resolve his inner conflicts and to restore that vision.

The Social Background

Fortunately for Masters, one person who did read the *Anthology* very well and immediately recognized its importance was William Marion Reedy, the influential editor who published the serialized version in 1914-15. Reedy not only encouraged the little-known poet and provided an enthusiastic readership for the experimental epitaph-poems, he also wrote the first important evaluation of *Spoon River Anthology*, which appeared in *Reedy's Mirror* on November 20, 1914, while the series was still in progress. In that remarkably perceptive essay, entitled "The Writer of Spoon River," Reedy revealed the identity of Webster Ford, Masters's pseudonym, and asserted that the *Anthology* was "a great work of literary art."[2] More than that, he comprehended the basis for its unique appeal: Spoon River, the village in the book, was a sociological microcosm, effectively portrayed because firmly grounded in the poet's experience:

> The Spoon River country is a composite of several small communities around and about Havana, Illinois. It is a small town populated by the memories of Mr. Masters' youth. The youth . . . was impressed by the life of the people, who were very close together. Everyone knew everyone else and the ram-

ifications of family relationships, the multitudinous drama of neighborhood gossip, the ups and downs, successes and failures of the people. But it was left to Edgar Lee Masters to take all this, or as much of it as suited his purposes, and fuse it and shape it into an artistic creation. . . . He saw and knew his Spoon River so well that when he came to write it out of himself, with his personality added to what he saw and knew, he wrote the life of man everywhere, or at least everywhere in America.

Like a number of others on the literary scene, Reedy had been anxious for authentic American poetry to arise—poetry grounded in the facts of the American experience—so he was quick to recognize that "Masters moves from particulars to universals." In the *Anthology* poems, reality—the truth about life—was clearly based on the details of actuality, the concrete particulars of an American locality. That is precisely what William Carlos Williams advocated after World War I and crystallized in his now-famous poetic dictum, "no ideas but in things." It was this sense of experiential truthfulness that gave *Spoon River Anthology* its impact—and that makes the poet's background so important for a deeper understanding of the work.

The village of Spoon River is, in fact, based on two Illinois communities (not "several") where the poet grew up: Petersburg, on the Sangamon River in Menard County, and Lewistown, forty miles farther north, near the Spoon River in Fulton County. They are on opposite sides of the historic Illinois River, which flows through western Illinois diagonally to the southwest before emptying into the Mississippi River north of Alton and East St. Louis. During the nineteenth century the two communities were also on opposite sides of an Illinois cultural divide.

In the bottom half of the long state, settlers from Kentucky, Tennessee, and Virginia predominated. They were Indian-fighting, game-hunting, story-telling, and whiskey-drinking frontier people who celebrated courage, stressed kinship, prized hospitality, opposed abolitionism, advocated individual rights, idolized Andrew Jackson, and supported the Democratic party—if they participated in politics at all. They were "agrarian traditionalists," as Richard J. Jensen has pointed out.[3] They feared change and maintained intense loyalty to a narrow circle of people: family, kinsfolk, and others like themselves. Petersburg was settled primarily by such southern (or southern upland) people, as was Lincoln's New Salem, only two miles farther south.

In the top half of Illinois, settlers from the East predominated. Always called "Yankees" on the frontier, they were more apt to be community organizers, business founders, churchgoers, school-teachers, and social reformers. They were "modernizers," as Jensen has called them—ambitious, self-confident, upwardly mobile people who advocated and enacted change.[4] Opposed to drinking and slavery, they were not afraid to place limits on individual freedom in order to promote social improvement. Lewistown was dominated by such people. Social clash between southern and Yankee settlers in Illinois fostered the dynamic political atmosphere in which Stephen Douglas and Abraham Lincoln emerged. But ironically, Lincoln, despite his Kentucky background, epitomized and advocated Yankee values, while Douglas, despite his Vermont heritage, became the chief spokesman for agrarian traditionalism.

This cultural divide was still evident after the Civil War, although it diminished as communities became more cosmopolitan, and it had an enormous influence on Masters and *Spoon River Anthology*. First of all, he was a product of both New England and southern pioneer stock. His mother, Emma Dexter Masters, was the daughter of a Methodist minister who lived in Vermont and New Hampshire, while his father, Hardin Wallace Masters, was the son of a Tennessee-raised frontier farmer who had moved to Illinois in about 1830. Masters was very conscious of this split in his family background, which is outlined in the opening pages of his autobiography, *Across Spoon River* (1936). In fact, he attributed the discord that marked his parents' marriage to the "gospel hate" of his mother's New England religious heritage, which focused on "breaking the will" and inevitably clashed with the easygoing "gospel love" that characterized the Tennessee heritage of his father.[5] As this suggests, Masters eventually rejected the eastern values of his mother's family—except for commitment to learning—and celebrated the southern values of his father's family. That response was not so much an intellectual decision as a personal one: he had difficulty getting along with his mother, whose extreme changes in attitude toward him—from affection to scorn—troubled him deeply, but he admired and identified with his father and his paternal grandparents.

The most important figures in his life were those grandparents, Squire Davis and Lucinda Masters, who lived near Petersburg and apparently doted on him when he was a child. He later idealized them as Illinois pioneers and celebrated them in two of his finest *Spoon River Anthology* poems, "Aaron Hatfield" and "Lucinda Matlock." During his early years Masters spent much time at their Menard County farm, located four miles north of town in a rural precinct called Sand Ridge (or "Sandridge," as the poet spelled it). It was a place where gently rolling farmland gave way to an expanse of prairie running north and east to the Sangamon River. Throughout his life, the poet's memories of that area, and of nearby Petersburg, anchored him to the Midwest and influenced his writing.

Masters was born in Garnett, Kansas, on August 23, 1868, while his parents were homesteading there, but they failed to establish a successful farm and soon returned to Sand Ridge. They lived in a cabin at Shipley Hill, near the Masters family farm, so Hardin could work for his father. In 1871, when the poet was three, Squire (which was the grandfather's given name) bought his son a farm near the tiny village of Atterberry, four miles away. The poet's earliest memories were of that place.

Like Lincoln, Hardin Masters was a likable, principled, ambitious man who turned to the law as a means of rising in society. He was elected state's attorney of Menard County in 1872 and, for that reason, moved his family to Petersburg, the county seat. At that time, it was a bustling little town of about two thousand people, with a dozen sizable brick stores and many smaller wooden ones, a woolen factory, two banks, three flour mills, and half a dozen blacksmith shops. In the center of the square was a brick courthouse with limestone columns. Built in 1843, it typified "the old Kentucky tobacco-barn style of architecture," according to an 1879 county history, so it was a visible reminder of the town's southern upland pioneer heritage.[6] Among the Menard County people that young Lee—as his family always called him—saw around the square were Mentor Graham, who had taught Lincoln, and William H. Herndon, who had been Lincoln's law partner. Like many others in the Petersburg area, they had been associated with the pioneer village of New Salem, two miles away, which had ceased to exist in the 1840s, and their recollections contributed to the wealth of Lincoln lore that circulated in the community.

While living in Petersburg, Lee attended school but hated it, and he enjoyed frequent visits to his grandparents' farm. Their place at Sand Ridge offered an escape from the stresses of his parents' home as well as an opportunity to roam the outdoors without much restriction. He eventually developed a deep sense of belonging there, based on his kinship ties to his beloved grandparents and his close acquaintance with the neighboring families, who valued personal relationships and worshipped together at the nearby Concord Church. It is not surprising that he never passed up a chance to travel the few miles north from Petersburg to the old farm. As he says in *Across Spoon River*, "The thrill of the ride out to the farm is unforgettable. To see again the familiar road stretching straight ahead; to see the rims of forestry, and the farmhouses that I knew; to pass into the sweet woods and by the oak tree . . . to pass over the bridge which spanned Concord Creek; to come up the hill, and suddenly to see the beloved barn and house" (p. 10). In the years that followed, the journey to Sand Ridge became longer and longer, as Masters traveled back from Lewistown, from Chicago, from New York, and finally— after his grandparents had died and the farm he remembered had disappeared from the landscape—all the way from the present into the past. Sand Ridge became a region of the mind, a time as well as a place. In *The Sangamon* (1942) Masters depicts it as a beautiful prairie landscape laden with memories of an idyllic agrarian culture, and he remarks, "I am happy that this was my nurturing spot of earth, as it is still my spiritual home."[7] By that time, all of the Menard County area around Petersburg had become for him a kind of lost paradise, and he felt dispossessed by change, like the speaker in his autobiographical poem "Jonathan Houghton." In a 1926 letter to his close friend Edwin P. Reese, the poet indicated that he had made "several trips west" to Menard County, hoping to reestablish relationships there and end his chronic loneliness, but without success: "Like a hawk that circles around the tree, I have circled over the old haunts; and have gone clear around the country without finding any place that I wanted to stay in, or anyone that I wanted to be with." He concluded that "the Petersburg environment is as dead as my grandparents."[8] In one sense *Spoon River Anthology* was a spiritual quest for "the Petersburg environment," an attempt to recover what had vanished—from his life and from American culture—by memorializing it in his poetry. That is, in fact, the key to much of what follows here.

During the 1880s Masters experienced the Yankee side of the Illinois cultural divide, which later represented for him the forces of change that had destroyed "the Petersburg environment." In July of 1880, his father moved the family north to Lewistown, where he hoped to build a thriving law practice with the help of an influential friend, Colonel Lewis Ross, for whom the town had been named. In many ways, Lewistown was similar to Petersburg. A county seat town of about two thousand, it had a courthouse with limestone pillars that had been erected during the pioneer days. Along its dirt streets the village had many brick and wooden stores, several blacksmith shops, a large grist mill, and a woolen factory. Unlike Petersburg, however, Lewistown had a high school, housed in a three-story brick building, which Masters attended.[9] A teacher there, New England-born Mary Fisher, encouraged him to read widely and to write.

In other ways, too, Lewistown provided intellectual stimulation for the promising youth. He joined the Fulton County Scientific Association, a study group headed by Dr. William S. Strode, a physician and amateur naturalist of Pennsylvania background who was later the basis for "William Jones" in the *Anthology*. The organization had about two dozen members—mostly teachers, physicians, and ministers—and although they read and discussed papers on the flora of the prairies, the shells of Spoon River, and similar topics, their interests were not exclusively scientific. For example, Rev. John Hughes spoke on German philosophers; schoolteacher and biologist Homer L. Roberts discussed Huxley and Spencer; teenage poet Margaret George commented on Elizabethan dramatists; and Lee Masters, the youngest member, gave talks on Whitman, clairvoyance, and the imagination. Masters fell in love with Margaret George, a brilliant young woman who was already writing for national publications and who was later the basis for "Caroline Branson," "Amelia Garrick," "Julia Miller," and "Louise Smith" in *Spoon River Anthology*. Her poetic talent and promising career undoubtedly increased his interest in writing poetry. Also, her father, Rev. Benjamin Y. George, was a Princeton-educated man with a large personal library that was made available to Masters. Hence Lewistown contributed significantly to the poet's development, largely because of the town's eastern attitudes toward education and intellectual life.

However, the Masters family had not moved to a thoroughly Yankee community. Lewistown itself was an expression of the Illinois cultural divide, as the poet indicated in a 1927 article for *The Commonweal*:

> My mother, who had come as a girl to Illinois from Marl-boro, New Hampshire, saw at once that she was in a New England atmosphere. Here and there were houses all immac-ulately white . . . with the half-enclosed porch which led to the wood house, which in turn was joined to the barn. Here was the church standing back of an open space and facing the courthouse at the other end of this space. . . .
>
> But right at hand, around the business square, were evidences of a different taste, of a stock that was not of New England. The courthouse itself had its origins in the culture of Tennessee and Kentucky. It was a building of brick and painted gray. Its projecting roof was supported by large limestone pillars which had been brought in 1837 from the quarries along the Illinois river, hauled by oxen under the supervision of Major Walker, a Virginian. . . .
>
> Then in parts of the town a little removed from the square there were houses which showed their southern influ-ence. . . . And further on was the finest house in town, owned by Colonel Ross, who had been in Congress, and whose father had come from Virginia. . . .
>
> In a word, there were two breeds of people in this town, and all these things showed it, as well as the religion and politics which throve here, later to be noted. There were the New Englanders whose leading spirits shared with the prosperous Virginians the wealth of the place. And attached to these New Englanders, as the villeins of old were bound to the feudal lord, were the work-people, whom they controlled in religion and economics. On the other hand, there were the Virginians, whom lesser folk followed and believed in . . . kept faithful by

the lesser ties of sentiment and political faith. Characterized by a word, these groups were republicans on the one hand and democrats on the other; conservatives and liberals; hard, dry, thrifty Calvinists, and believers in a softer evangelism; the rich and the poor; the prudent, and the shiftless and generous. And these two hostile and never-to-be-reconciled kinds of human nature fought each other at every point and all the time.[10]

This conflict in Lewistown was later reflected in *Spoon River Anthology*, but the poet developed that aspect of his literary village by also creating a number of positive characterizations based on Petersburg-area people of southern stock, such as Ann Rutledge, Fiddler Jones, and William H. Herndon.

Masters's dislike of the New Englanders stemmed from his family's first several years in town, when they experienced difficulty in becoming established. Hardin W. Masters was, after all, a Democrat in a strongly Republican community. As the poet later said in *Across Spoon River*, "a cloud had followed him from Petersburg; and at once in Lewistown he was reputed to have been a 'Copperhead.' This made trouble for him, and prevented him from getting business" (p. 56). Soon his father's reserve of money was gone, and the family was caught in "straitened circumstances." Masters was deeply affected: "I was filled with shame because of our deprivation" (p. 56). While his father was struggling for a foothold and his mother was in nervous distress, he felt isolated, and he also had a difficult time getting along at school. Furthermore, Hardin was a drinker and a supporter of saloons in a community marked by increasing temperance activism. As a result, he clashed with William T. Davidson, the anti-liquor editor of *The Fulton Democrat*, who exerted great influence in Fulton County affairs. Young Lee identified closely with his father and soon hated his enemies. In fact, Masters's first published poem was a satirical attack on Davidson, printed as a broadside in the *Lewistown News* office, where the aspiring poet worked as a printer's devil.[11] In the *Anthology*, "Jefferson Howard," based on his father, and "Editor Whedon," based on Davidson, relate directly to this situation in Lewistown during the 1880s, as does the entire "village war" between conservatives and liberals.

By reflecting the Lewistown conflict related to the Illinois cultural divide, Masters focused on the problem of community in

9   *Introduction*

America—a nation of clashing values—and exploded the myth of the small town as cultural idyll.[12] He emphasized that poetic intention in "The Spooniad," the mock-heroic fragment that appeared in *Reedy's Mirror* on December 18, 1914, and which was subsequently employed to close the 1915 book version of *Spoon River Anthology*. In a 1915 letter to H. L. Mencken, he referred to "The Spooniad" as "the epic binding together of the more than two hundred dramatic expressions of the microcosm," but, ironically, the theme that he develops to achieve that "binding together" is conflict.[13] The satirical poem, written in blank verse, depicts an episode in the "village war" between the conservatives (easterners), who support A. D. Blood for mayor, and the liberals (southerners), who support John Cabanis. At issue is the legalization of liquor, which is mentioned in several epitaph-poems. There is violence at the polls on election day, as each side brings in a Homeric champion: "hog-eyed Allen" for the conservatives, and "Bengal Mike" for the liberals. The latter wins, but only after the fight becomes a free-for-all in which "many valiant souls / Went down from clubs and bricks." Further confusion occurs when men bring in the mortally wounded town marshal, who has been shot by Jack Maguire—an event discussed in two epitaph-poems—and amid cries of "Lynch him!" and the sound of running feet, the poem breaks off.

"The Spooniad" is both a parody of Homer's style in *The Iliad* and a mock-heroic satire akin to Pope's *Dunciad*. William Marion Reedy thought it was very effective, as indicated by his headnote to it, reprinted in the annotations to the text in this edition, but most readers have not been impressed by it. Regardless of its literary merit, "The Spooniad" is inappropriate within the context of the *Anthology*. Not only does the mock-heroic style jar against the predominantly serious tone of the epitaph-poems, it undercuts one of the great strengths of *Spoon River Anthology*—the depiction of everyday people as fit subjects for poetic analysis. The poem disparages small-town residents. Worse yet, "The Spooniad" violates Masters's unique poetic form by presenting the actions of people who are already dead and buried, including A. D. Blood and John Cabanis. So, even though it stresses community conflict along the lines that Masters felt revealed a split in the American consciousness, it is not an effective conclusion to the book.

It should be emphasized that Masters's view of both communities where he had lived was highly subjective. Petersburg was not as harmonious and Lewistown was not as conflict-ridden as his prose recollections and *Anthology* poems suggest. They merely seemed so to the poet. As James Hurt pointed out in a very insightful article, Masters was beset with a variety of psychological problems—including conflicts stemming from stressful family relationships—which he "dredged up and confronted through the medium of his art."[14] This analysis is surely correct, for the continuing conflict between his parents apparently caused a painful division of loyalty in the extremely sensitive youth, who identified sometimes with his father (the kin-proud, morally relaxed, nonintellectual, saloon-haunting, religious skeptic) and sometimes with his mother (the socially ambitious, morally strict, intellectually committed, church-going temperance advocate). And he related his inner conflict, and their marital problems, to the social environment in Lewistown, which he therefore both loved and hated. His ambivalence toward his small-town background—the inner tension that produced both his escape to Chicago in 1892 and his lifelong yearning for the people and places of his youth— was eventually "translated into radical conflict, with all the love going to Petersburg and all the hate going to Lewistown."[15] Rather than acknowledge that he was psychologically divided, Masters projected his conflicts into clashing figures outside of himself. Petersburg and Lewistown residents were transmuted into poetic characterizations that symbolized the discordant aspects of his inner life—and expressed his mythic perception of America, as the discussion below reveals. In any case, the two communities— and the two groups in Lewistown—became cultural polarities in the poet's mind, expressions of two "never-to-be-reconciled kinds of human nature." In a deep sense they became *his* towns.

The Poet as Literary Naturalist

Masters's outlook on life was also rooted in his early experience. First of all, he was profoundly troubled by death during his childhood. When he was six or seven years old, he contracted measles, complicated by pneumonia, and he almost died—an event vividly recalled in his autobiography. Of even greater impact

11 *Introduction*

was the death from diphtheria of his younger brother, Alex, in 1878, when Masters was ten. In *Across Spoon River* he comments that his "beautiful little brother took the disease in its most malignant form and died after three weeks of torture" (p. 27). That family tragedy caused Masters considerable anguish and prompted youthful speculation about the nature of death. Later, in the *Anthology,* he reflected on that episode in "Hamlet Micure." Sometime afterward he wrote another poem about his brother's death, which refers to

> ... the long years in which no answers come
> To us who ask why you were born to die
> So soon—where you departed to, and why
> The tomb remains the tomb.[16]

One year after the death of Alex, Masters's closest friend, Mitch Miller, was killed while trying to jump onto a moving train. That event was later depicted in the *Anthology* poem "Johnnie Sayre" and in Masters's first novel, *Mitch Miller* (1920). The poet also had a cousin in Petersburg who was struck by lightning, suffered for months, and later died of croup. Partly as a consequence, Masters became terrified of storms, especially lightning.

Of course, he was exposed to Christianity through his mother, but his father's religious skepticism and dislike of churches undoubtedly prevented him from overcoming his death anxiety through faith. On the contrary, Christian speculations about the approaching end of the world troubled him as well. In his autobiography he sums up one particularly upsetting period of time by saying, "There were deaths about us, and altogether we lived in terror. The revivalist was flourishing on this soil; but somehow I never confessed my sins and took conversion and the church" (*ASR*, p. 32). Clearly, he sometimes felt at risk, terrified by the prospect of death, yet he was unable to achieve the comfort that Christianity provides. It is perhaps not surprising that during his teenage years he "read Poe's tales over and over, and his poems too," or that he wrote an unpublished short story called "The Dance of Death."[17] The story title refers to a medieval tradition in art and literature that depicts the dead, who warn the living of their mortality.

Masters's death anxiety had an influence on *Spoon River An-*

thology, which is a kind of poetic Dance of Death set in a village cemetery. Of course, many of the speakers talk about their own death, and lawyer John M. Church even uses grisly imagery from the Dance of Death tradition when he complains that after he died "the rats devoured my heart / And a snake made a nest in my skull." Here the rats and the snake are indeed symbols of corruption—not just of his corpse but of his moral self, for Church paid off judges and juries to defeat the injured and the poor. But perhaps no figure evokes the author's death-consciousness more effectively than Jennie M'Grew, who has a terrifying vision of "something black" in the midst of a sunny rural scene. What she sees is death, the frightful presence that lies at the heart of life and darkens even our happiest days. It is significant too that the only figure in the *Anthology* who speaks for all humankind, Scholfield Huxley, chronicles humanity's achievements and then expresses his deepest frustration by asking God,

> How would you like to create a sun
> And the next day have the worms
> Slipping in and out between your fingers?

As that poem also suggests, free thought played a very significant role in Masters's intellectual development. His beloved father "had no religion at all except that he always believed in a God" (*ASR,* p. 32), so the elder Masters surely undermined his wife's efforts to get young Lee to attend church and must have openly questioned her Christian beliefs. Also, the poet's favorite high school teacher, Mary Fisher, was a freethinker, committed to individualism and self-development, who introduced her students to Emerson and Ingersoll. It is not surprising that by his early teens Masters "had thrown out the Bible as revelation and the miracles as nonsense" (*ASR,* p. 81). However, he knew the Bible well and had high regard for it as literature, especially the thought-provoking Book of Job. In Lewistown he also had access to the personal library of a freethinker, Judge John Winter, and one of his friends, Homer Roberts, was a freethinker with whom he read Herbert Spencer, A. C. Swinburne, and T. H. Huxley. Furthermore, Masters's first meaningful job, as printer's devil for the *Lewistown News* from 1884 to 1889, placed him under the influence of a religious skeptic and student of Greek literature, editor Lewis C. ("Lute") Breeden, whom he greatly admired. And his participation in the above-mentioned Fulton County Scientific Association brought him into contact with physician-naturalist William S. Strode and teacher Julia Brown, who were both infidels and who probably encouraged him to read Darwin and Whitman. In short, Lewistown had a remarkable number of freethinkers who collectively had an enormous lasting impact on the poet.

It is not surprising that at Knox College Academy in 1889 Masters liked to discuss religious questions and was nicknamed "the atheist" by one of his classmates (*ASR*, p. 115). While there he also intensified his study of Greek literature, which had a major influence on him and undoubtedly strengthened his humanism. He soon read the plays of Sophocles, whose tragic Oedipus, enmeshed by fate and struggling to comprehend his life, must have appealed to him. By that time Masters had read dozens of major British authors, including the great Romantic poets, and he was deeply committed to Shelley, whose philosophical non-conformity, passion for humanity, and radical criticism of society made a lasting impression on him. He also read works by such thinkers as Bacon, Spinoza, Locke, Hume, Kant, Rousseau, Hegel, Schopenhauer, and Mill.[18]

As a result of his religious skepticism, remarkably wide reading, and concern about transience and death, Masters embraced philosophical naturalism. That is, he developed a thoroughly materialistic and ultimately tragic view of the human condition: mankind is the product of natural causes, living in a wholly transient world, where individuals struggle amid forces beyond their control and are finally defeated by death.[19] This outlook was also reflected in the fiction of American literary naturalists like Stephen Crane, Frank Norris, and Theodore Dreiser, who were Masters's contemporaries — and, in Dreiser's case, a good friend and important influence. Their philosophical determinism often prompted them to view life as a trap, and the same was true for Masters. In a 1918 lecture to the St. Louis Art League he used the term "rat trap" to symbolize his perspective in *Spoon River Anthology*. A newspaper reporter provided this summary of his talk:

> Masters' subject had been announced as "The Rat Trap and How to Get Out of It," the rat trap symbolizing the average

human's environment. However, about the only sure way to escape which he suggested in his address is death. He read a number of selections from "Spoon River Anthology," most of them being about people who tried to escape from the "rat trap," but succeeded in fastening themselves in more tightly, where they squirmed and struggled until they reached "the only democracy—the graveyard."[20]

Undoubtedly Masters had referred to "Robert Fulton Tanner," in which the speaker—who was killed by a rat bite while demonstrating his patent trap—views life itself as a gigantic trap. The notion of death as the only escape is suggested by the *Anthology* as a whole since the characters speak from the grave, but that somber view is also shockingly presented in "Plymouth Rock Joe," which portrays the villagers as chickens confined in a barnyard—and destined for the hog trough:

> Be chivalric, heroic, or aspiring,
> Metaphysical, religious, or rebellious,
> You shall never get out of the barnyard
> Except by way of over the fence
> Mixed with potato peelings and such into the trough!

Like the literary naturalists, Masters felt that he was being rigorously objective in portraying people as he did. The newspaper account of his St. Louis lecture adds this remark: "Commenting on the somewhat pessimistic hue of most of the poems, Masters declared that he had repeatedly refused to color them with a more cheerful tinge, because they were largely true characterizations of real persons and would not be accurate if any different." What he did not say, of course, and perhaps did not realize, was that his own experience and outlook prompted him to select those particular "real persons" and interpret their lives as he did.

As with Crane, Norris, and Dreiser, Masters's newspaper background provided a thrust toward the use of factual material in his literary works. From 1884 to 1889 he wrote much copy for the *Lewistown News*—including obituaries, which are, like the *Anthology* poems, brief overviews of lives that have ended. Unfortunately, the issues of that newspaper do not survive. However, he apparently also wrote some letters summarizing local events for the *Fulton County Ledger* at nearby Canton. Those do survive, although he did not sign them, so it is difficult to determine which correspondent letters from the county seat are his.[21] In any case, those letters reflect local politics, murders, fights, accidents, court cases, baseball games, opera house programs, weddings, deaths, and other events in Lewistown, some of which are reflected in the *Anthology*. Without a doubt, the small-town newspaper, with its intimate account of ordinary people and its revelation of countless conflicts and interrelationships, had an enormous influence on the poet. In fact, when Masters left Lewistown for Chicago, he was planning to become a newspaperman, not a lawyer.

In regard to the poet's "pessimistic" view, which pervades much of the *Anthology*, it was indeed based on observations of real people. For example, when he analyzed his father's life in *Across Spoon River*, he clearly portrayed him as a man trapped by his environmental and psychological circumstances and, thus, ultimately defeated: "It was a tragedy that my father became caught in circumstances and among the small-minded people that he did, but it could scarcely have happened otherwise. Born in the country and with no desire for city life . . . a man not fond of books or of the intellectual life . . . a Democrat by nature and conviction . . . the life of Petersburg or Lewistown was his fated lot." Thus, despite his many gifts, "his political ambition was unrealized" (p. 81). That is, Hardin W. Masters was a man fated never to make his mark in life because of inner and outer forces that he could not overcome. As mentioned above, Masters's father inspired "Jefferson Howard," in which the speaker is a heroic struggler against small-town repression who becomes "Tangled with [the] fates" of others, is deserted by his supporters, and eventually dies knowing that his valiant fight will be forgotten.

Likewise, Masters persistently viewed himself as trapped by inner and outer forces, and that is nowhere more apparent than in his comments on relationships with women. When he realized that his engagement to Helen Jenkins was a mistake and asked his father for advice, the elder Masters responded, "The girl is as good as anyone, which is to say that none of 'em are any good. A man has got to have one of 'em. . . . That's the game Nature has laid for us to play. No escape! Besides, it ain't going to do you any good to have it known that you went with a girl for more than a year, and then quit her; and it will come out on you" (*ASR*, p. 244). The poet was ensnared by sexuality and convention. Years afterward he felt that his wife was enervating him, "cutting off my hair, and putting out my eyes." Like a domesticated Samson, he regarded himself as "biologically used and enslaved" (*ASR*, p. 288). However, he also recognized that she was trapped by "the social system" that made her fear divorce. Masters's unhappy first marriage is reflected in "Benjamin Pantier" and "Mrs. Benjamin Pantier," whose fundamentally opposed natures reflect the easygoing and repressive qualities that he regarded as southern and eastern. Pantier feels that he was "snared" by his wife, who broke his will, but she was equally ensnared by a social system that confined her sexual life to a man who disgusted her. For that matter, Ollie McGee and Fletcher McGee were the victims of a relationship that became increasingly hateful and destroyed both of them, and it is perhaps not accidental that their monologues are followed by Robert Fulton Tanner's assertion that life is a trap.

As James Hurt has pointed out, Masters had a long series of difficult relationships with women, whom he alternately idealized and blamed for his psychological problems.[22] As a result, he apparently developed considerable sympathy for men and women caught in relationships that damage or destroy their lives, and he realized that people are often the victims of their own attitudes, desires, and impulses. His views were probably influenced by the realistic plays of Henrik Ibsen, such as *A Doll's House* (1879) and *Ghosts* (1881), which portray people as victims of narrow social attitudes and assert the importance of self-realization. In his autobiography Masters mentions that during the early years of the century he read Ibsen's plays, "all of them" (p. 260).

Perhaps the most insightful commentary on *Spoon River Anthology* that the poet ever provided views the book as an inquiry into the factors and forces that ensnare people—and defeat most of them. In a manuscript copy of "The Genesis of Spoon River," which Masters wrote for the *American Mercury,* he asserts that the *Anthology*'s influence on American literature lies "in the impulse it gave to bring forth from human lives the secret things that form and fate them." He reveals that he strove to convey the hidden force or factor in each character's life—"something in the human heart which gnaws without ceasing, and affects all the acts of the person; [or] something which happens and causes the person acted upon to change his attitude, his life." Masters realized that he was not the first author to drag forth "such soul secrets, diseases, faults, and tragedies from the hidden hearts of human beings," but he was the first to create "a whole community civically and ecologically related and intertwined," in which such hidden factors were exposed.[23]

Certainly the revelation of concealed values, motives, and actions that have decisively affected people's lives is central to the impact of the *Anthology*—and it also has a clear parallel in Ibsen's plays of social realism. This revelatory technique is evident in even the earliest poems written for *Reedy's Mirror,* such as "Ollie McGee," "Serepta Mason," and "Cassius Hueffer." In fact, Serepta Mason explicitly refers to those hidden factors as "the unseen forces / That govern the processes of life." As these poems and others in the book so clearly show, such "unseen forces" commonly result in the disintegration of values, personalities, and hopes.

Masters was, then, a kind of literary naturalist who worked in poetry instead of prose, and who analyzed not just one individual who was trapped and defeated, but a deeply interrelated community of people, "Caught in the jungle of life where many are lost," as speaker Harmon Whitney puts it. These people are not only acted upon but are themselves part of the trap, the jungle, the social environment. Operating within that environment are biological, economic, political, religious, and social forces that limit human freedom and sometimes destroy individuals. *Spoon River Anthology* deeply shocked people because Americans were supposed to be free and happy, but the speakers in the epitaph-poems often were neither. The book is an inquiry into the complexities that condition human fate, complexities from which Americans are not exempt.

This is made clear in "The Hill," which opens the book. It is not just a variation of the traditional *ubi sunt* motif, asserting that many who once lived are now dead. Rather, by referring to the ways that people died, it suggests the enormous variety of inner and outer factors that impinged upon those lives:

Where are Ella, Kate, Mag, Lizzie and Edith,
. . . .
One died in shameful childbirth,
One of a thwarted love,
One at the hands of a brute in a brothel,
One of a broken pride, in search for heart's desire;
One after life in far-away London and Paris
Was brought to this little space. . . .

It is evident that sexuality was a factor in some of these deaths, an emphasis that prepares the reader for the extensive examination of sexual life in the *Anthology*. That motif also links Masters to the literary naturalists, who viewed the sex drive as a powerful, disturbing force.

Masters again emphasized the many factors that condition human fate in the "Epilogue," which he wrote for the expanded, 1916 version of the *Anthology*. It is a somewhat confusing and altogether unnecessary poetic drama that attempts to place the village of Spoon River, and all human life, in cosmic perspective. In the middle of it, Loki, the Norse god of mischief and destruction, lists some of the factors that bring people into his "web":

> Passion, reason, custom, rules,
> Creeds of the churches, lore of the schools,
> Taint in the blood and strength of soul,
> Flesh too weak for the will's control;
> Poverty, riches, pride of birth. . . .

And Beelzebub, in the process of resurrecting the dead, defines mankind in the materialistic and tragic terms that formed the essence of Masters's vision:

> Out of the mold, out of the rocks,
> Wonder, mockery, paradox!
> Soaring spirit, groveling flesh,
> Bait the trap, and spread the mesh.
> Give him hunger, lure him with truth,
> Give him the iris hopes of Youth.
> Starve him, shame him, fling him down,
> Whirled in the vortex of the town.

Although the "Epilogue" opens in "The Graveyard of Spoon River" and Beelzebub here refers to "the vortex of the town," the play does not relate to community life, so it seems utterly foreign to the rest of the *Anthology*. Moreover, the play's central point—that humanity is trapped in an indifferent cosmos, where life is a "hell-born tangle" that leads to death—unfortunately denies what the *Anthology* most deeply affirms: that life has significance because, despite humanity's predicament, individuals struggle for self-realization and, successful or not, learn from their experience. As Reedy said in his 1914 article, "In these ashes are fierce, unquenchable fires," and "In each auto-analysis there is a . . . touch of sympathy or, oftener, of irony. These dead see themselves, not as others see them, yet with a larger, more penetrating comprehension of their lives as a whole." Hence the closing play views humanity from the outside, from the perspective of cosmic and cultural forces personified, while the epitaph-poems examine people from within, engaging our sympathy and enlarging our comprehension. In *Spoon River Anthology* life may be frustrating and ultimately tragic, but it is not meaningless—which the "Epilogue" implies.

On the contrary, the *Anthology* dramatizes the struggle for meaning—244 times—and in the process, it reveals that everyone's outlook is but a reflection of one life lived amid the infinite complexity of multiple experience. The great enemy of deeper comprehension is psychological isolation, or as Masters put it in a 1922 poem called "Worlds,"

> . . . every soul is a world to itself,
> Making its own murmurous music night and day,
> And having its realest world in itself,
> And knowing none of the other worlds.[24]

But the *Anthology* is designed to penetrate our isolation. As Reedy put it, "All Spoon River comes to confession to us, and—they are our *doppelgangers*." As we read the book, we are prompted to see our lives reflected in the fabric of the community and, hence, to initiate our own, more enlightened self-analysis, which comprehends our deep relationship to those "other worlds."

The Influence of Spinoza

The poet's deterministic emphasis on the forces that govern life and his effort to help the reader see more deeply into the human condition point to the most important philosophical influence on the *Anthology*: Benedict de Spinoza. The great Dutch thinker of the seventeenth century asserted that all reality is one substance, God-as-Nature, or the infinite, of which the finite is a manifestation. Hence the individual is a fragment of primal reality, and the great secret of life is that we are all deeply connected to one another. However, every person is inclined to view the world from his or her own limited perspective, seeing the self in social terms as a whole in opposition to other wholes rather than as a fragment of the ultimate whole—the Spinozistic God. Confused by this partial perspective, individuals are in bondage to external and internal forces that are aspects of primal reality, but they can free themselves—and realize their individuality— by identifying with the divine intellect. In short, salvation for Spinoza is a matter of deepened understanding, or seeing things "under the aspect of eternity." Immortality is, then, not a post-death condition but a sense of union with God (primal reality, or the infinite), and it is achieved by intellectual effort. In a sense, it is a kind of self-knowledge because the better we understand our own essential nature, the more firmly we unite ourselves with the primal reality of which we are an expression. The struggle for salvation is, then, a search for truth as well as freedom, and it is an arduous intellectual ascent.[25]

In a 1926 interview Masters asserted his debt to Spinoza: "I have been called an atheist . . . but my atheism is that of Spinoza, in whom I find my profoundest satisfaction—and he was an all-God man, not an atheist."[26] By way of explanation, the poet summarized his monistic view of things: "I see just one force in the world, in the universe, and everything from chemical activity to spiritual aspiration is a manifestation of it." Within such a context, man struggles to comprehend "the world becoming" and hence to know "what he is, why he is, and what his destiny is." Such intellectual striving is precisely what Spinoza advocated as a means of freeing the self and achieving salvation.

The influence of Spinoza on Masters is sometimes difficult to pin down because he also had an impact on Goethe and Shelley— not to mention other Romantic poets—who in turn had an enormous influence on Masters.[27] For example, a poem called "Nature," which appeared in *The Open Sea* (1921), is similar in some respects to Shelley's "Mont Blanc," but Masters is not concerned about spiritual communion with an indwelling power that can be sensed in wild nature. He sees Nature as "all," the complex of forces that "rules throughout," and in which man struggles for intellectual dominion:

> This is the dole
> And tragedy of man: He has outgrown
> His kinship with the beasts that kept him whole
> Through thought. . . .
> He sinks
> In tangled madness, anger, railing speech,
> Below the ape, or else he rises, links
> His being to a life to which he climbs,
> A realm of thought harmonious, while he thinks.[28]

Masters was obviously influenced by evolution as well, but the emphasis here on the mind's effort to control the passions and unite humanity with an underlying, harmonious, intellectual realm is Spinozistic. The Dutch thinker harmonized well with Darwin, for he viewed humanity as mentally ascending, or passing from lesser to greater perfection.

The influence of Spinoza is also evident in the "Epilogue" of *Spoon River Anthology*. At the end of that strange work the Third Voice attempts to find the essence of life, only to be told by the Second Voice, who embodies it, "Nay, child, I am God." The entire closing movement of the "Epilogue" is an effort to portray the infinite—or Spinoza's primal reality—within nature, and the poem closes with the revelation of "Infinite Law, / Infinite Life." Also, another figure, called simply A Voice, asserts that salvation comes only through intellectual aspiration: "Sleep not but strive, / So shalt thou live."

The *Anthology* as a whole dramatizes the difference between a limited, self-bound comprehension, which results in bondage to the passions, and the freedom and triumph that result from a deeper perspective. The most troubled and unhappy speakers have a view that does not transcend their immediate situation. For example, Ollie and Fletcher McGee, at the very outset, have no mutual sympathy but, instead, view each other as purely oppressive, destructive forces. They are in bondage to their emotions and have no inner peace or sense of relatedness. They are alienated, like Kinsey Keene, Benjamin Pantier, "Indignation" Jones, and so many others. In Spinozistic terms they are fragments of primal reality who mistakenly see themselves as wholes, or separated entities, in desperate opposition to one another. Their confused focus on an external cause must be replaced by comprehension of the underlying reality that unites them and others. Their spiritual opposites in the *Anthology* are William and Emily, who recognize "a power of unison between souls." For them, death is not perpetual isolation but a kind of consummate togetherness, "Like love itself," which is why they speak in unison of their relationship.

As the *Anthology* progresses, many references to "seeing" and "vision" help to convey the importance of a deeper perspective — and reveal the influence of Spinoza. For example, "Faith Matheny" refers to "sudden flashes in your soul," or "visions," through which people can see "the Mystery" or "the secret" in each other — that is, the primal reality of which they are manifestations. When those intuitions occur, the speaker says, "You're catching a little whiff of the ether / Reserved for God Himself." Indeed, Spinoza posited a level of intuitive understanding beyond discursive reason, so the "sudden flashes" here reveal that the mind is moving toward union with the Spinozistic immanent God. Because such insight, such recognition of the truths of human nature, leads to happiness in life and individual salvation, Jeremy Carlisle says,

> Passer-by, sin beyond any sin
> Is the sin of blindness of souls to other souls.
> And joy beyond any joy is the joy
> Of having the good in you seen, and seeing the good. . . .

This philosophical perspective also explains one of the most puzzling poems in the *Anthology*, "Willie Metcalf." The speaker often felt that he "was not a separate thing from the earth." In fact, he talked with animals — "Anything that had an eye to look into" — for they gave him a sense of relatedness to the primal reality beneath everything. And in these otherwise incomprehensible lines he expresses the universal striving of all things (fragments) to feel integrated with that reality: "Once I saw a stone in the sunshine / Trying to turn into jelly." Spinoza was a pan-psychist. He believed that mind is not just found in humans but everywhere—even in stones. Because the speaker is illegitimate, he is a "natural" child, in turn-of-the-century social terms, so he possesses an unusual sense of relatedness to God-as-Nature.

The influence of Spinoza is also evident in the several poems about freethinkers. The frustration of humankind is expressed by the speaker in "Scholfield Huxley," who has employed his mind in an intellectual effort to find God—and indeed, to become God-like—but is troubled by his mortality. That is exactly how Spinoza viewed humanity—striving to escape finitude through a search for truth that led to God. Indeed, the Village Atheist proclaims that "Immortality is an achievement," and that "only those who strive mightily / Shall possess it." In other words, immortality is the result of intellectual effort—precisely what Spinoza, whom many regarded as an atheist, had asserted. Immanuel Ehrenhardt conducts an intellectual search for "the ultimate secret," which leads him into cosmic speculation, but he does not achieve success until he sees "a letter of [naturalist] John Muir"—which implies that God is in nature. That is also what his first name means: Immanuel, or "God with us," does not refer to Christ but to the Spinozistic immanent God. Also, as Alfonso Churchill says, the important thing is to see humanity as "part of the scheme of things" and discover "what the drama means." Churchill's lectures on the stars symbolize the poet's Spinozistic effort to see man "under the aspect of eternity."

Spinoza's influence also explains "Thomas Rhodes." The speaker is the great self-serving materialist of the *Anthology,* and the failure of his bank causes hardship that is mentioned in other poems, yet he does not seem to be condemned. Instead, he portrays Spoon River's liberals and intellectuals as "Blown about by erratic currents, tumbling into air pockets," while "Getters and hoarders of gold" like himself "Are self-contained, compact, harmonized, / Even to the end." But Rhodes is condemned, for the poem is deeply ironic from a Spinozistic perspective. The questing liberals and intellectuals are tumbling into the air and splitting into atoms because they are becoming free from bondage to the self and unified with God-as-Nature, while Rhodes is still imprisoned in his self-bound perspective. He is a superb example of the confused human fragment of primal reality whose inner wholeness is a delusion—which has indeed brought him to "the end," or the spiritual death of isolation.

A number of other poems reflect Spinoza's thought. Among them are two important but seldom-discussed accounts of spiritual triumph. The point of "Judson Stoddard," which depicts various mountain peaks as "the thought of Buddha," "the prayer of Jesus," "the dream of Plato," "the song of Dante," and so on, is that those great figures succeeded in achieving immortality through the power of the intellect, through deepened insight into the truth. The peaks that rise "almost to heaven" symbolize the eternal community of such individuals. Included among them is "the hope of the Mother Church" because, as Lydia Humphrey realized, the church "was the vision, vision, vision of the poets / Democratized!" That is, it represents insight into primal reality that has been made available to everyday people, who have far less intellectual ability. The mountain peaks are excellent symbols of the almost unlimited perspectives of those great minds, their success in achieving union with God, and hence their preservation of individuality. They are indeed immortals—and by implication, so is the speaker, who symbolizes the poet's sense of intellectual relationship to those figures.

And what they have achieved is dramatized in "Elijah Browning," the penultimate and, in some ways, most revealing poem of the *Anthology*. It symbolically portrays the poet's successful intellectual effort to see deeply into himself and his past, control his psychological discord, and hence unite his mind with God (primal reality). The speaker recalls that he found himself "among multitudes of children" who were dancing at the foot of a mountain—a reference to Masters's childhood days of inner harmony and happiness. Later the speaker was "amid multitudes who were wrangling," which surely refers to the poet's emotional problems, and perhaps to his intellectual uncertainty as he struggled for self-realization. Then Elijah Browning was seduced by a temptress, who symbolizes the impediments to Masters's intellectual struggle—not only his sexual involvement (which is discussed below), but also probably his law career, since justice is often personified as a woman. Despite those problems the speaker made a painful, isolated ascent through the clouds—a Shelleyan symbol of mental activity that also suggests the confusion of a limited perspective, as outlined by Spinoza. At the mountain's pinnacle he attained self-knowledge, achieved freedom, touched a solitary star, and became one with "Infinite Truth." That is, his mind was united with primal reality, which is why he vanished:

> I touched that star
> With my outstretched hand.
> I vanished utterly.
> For the mountain delivers to Infinite Truth
> Whosoever touches the star!

The star above the clouds symbolizes poetic achievement, which was Masters's means of approaching infinite truth. At the close of his autobiography, he uses similar imagery to convey the inner process of "thought and reflection" that leads to "vision," or poetic insight: "the clouds lifted, the star came forth, and I arose and climbed the hill before me, carrying my poems" (*ASR,* pp. 414-16).

In any case, the speaker in "Elijah Browning" did not die; he conquered his inner problems by intellectual effort and thus transcended temporality. He realized and preserved his self. In a discussion of Spinoza's thought, John Wild describes the achievement of this kind of intellectual salvation in terms that clearly illuminate the poem:

> Such then is the hard and lonely way which the soul must take in order to loose itself from the trammels of finitude which bind it to the body, in order to realize its own essential nature and find its place in the eternal community of rational intellects which make up God. The person whose self is most real, whose eternal individuality is most concrete and valuable, is he who devotes himself most thoroughly and unswervingly to the search for truth — not mere theory but the knowledge that vitalizes conduct. . . . Such a mind which thinks truly becomes one with the real which it thinks. It does not lose itself in the absolute, but through its intimate relations with the rest of reality becomes more uniquely itself. [29]

A close parallel to the experience of Elijah Browning is found in Goethe's poem "One and All," which begins with this stanza:

How yearns the solitary soul
To melt into the boundless whole,
  And find itself again in peace!
The blind desire, the impatient will,
The restless thoughts and plans are still;
  We yield ourselves—and wake in bliss.[30]

Spinoza was the most important influence on the great German poet, which would have been reason enough for Masters, who revered Goethe above all modern poets, to become thoroughly acquainted with Spinoza too. And no doubt both poets were profoundly influenced by the great philosopher because, like them, he was a deeply divided person. He wanted to be part of the human world and improve it and, at the same time, yearned to escape his finitude and touch being itself. It is not accidental that all three men were involved in politics and yet devoted themselves to a search for truth that had the wholehearted commitment of a religious quest for the meaning of life.

Because "Elijah Browning" comes at the end of the *Anthology,* it suggests that the entire work is a Spinozistic quest for salvation. That is, in fact, true. Spinoza not only provided a philosophical basis for Masters's determinism, he showed the troubled American poet an intellectually satisfying means of escaping "the rat-trap" of life and helped to direct his poetic search for truth in the writing of *Spoon River Anthology.* The literary and cultural terms in which that search was conducted are discussed below.

The Struggle for Self-realization

Spoon River Anthology not only relates to Masters's early life, expresses his view of the human predicament, and symbolizes his Spinozistic intellectual struggle to comprehend himself, it reflects the formation of his literary identity. Not that it focuses directly on such matters as his wide reading in British poetry, his enthusiasm for Whitman, Shelley, Browning, and Goethe, or his early newspaper poems, but it depicts symbolically his struggle for self-realization as a poet despite what he called the "adverse conditions" of his youth (*ASR*, p. 114). Many poems in the *Anthology* portray individuals who were frustrated in their quest for self-realization, and several of those are about writers or artists: "Minerva Jones," "Margaret Fuller Slack," "John Horace Burleson," "Petit, the Poet," "Penniwit, the Artist," "Jonathan Swift Somers," "Voltaire Johnson," and "Archibald Higbie." Perhaps no other group of characterizations so readily reminds us that most of the *Anthology* poems are masks for the poet.

The last of these, "Archibald Higbie," focuses on the central problem that Masters felt he faced—creating significant literary art in spite of his limited cultural background. He always believed that his experience in the culturally disadvantaged communities of central Illinois was a limitation that had to be overcome by his dogged determination to educate himself and to deepen his perspective. As Archibald Higbie says,

> There was no culture, you know, in Spoon River,
> And I burned with shame and held my peace.
> And what could I do, all covered over
> And weighted down with western soil,
> Except aspire, and pray for another
> Birth in the world, with all of Spoon River
> Rooted out of my soul?

Masters's struggle for self-realization as a poet is clearly reflected here, and, as the text reveals, he tried to accomplish his new "birth" by rejecting his past. His first volume of poetry, *A Book of Verses* (1898), is characterized by highly imitative poems that show very little relationship to his downstate experience. The same can be said of his poems in *The Blood of the Prophets* (1905), *Songs and Sonnets* (1910), and *Songs and Sonnets, Second Series* (1912). All but the first of these books were written in Chicago, where Masters established a successful law career—after his escape from, and hence rejection of, his past.

Several factors finally prompted him to write about the small-town world that was such an important part of his life—and, in fact, was the repressed foundation of his identity. One was the influence of Theodore Dreiser.[31] In *Across Spoon River* Masters mentions that he was so impressed by the realism of *Sister Carrie* (1900) that he wrote a letter of congratulation to the novelist, which started their friendship (p. 284). Apparently Masters wrote that letter in 1906. Soon afterward he visited Petersburg to see his grandmother and, at that time, mentioned to his father that he hoped to write a novel about many kinds of people—an idea that was "the germ of *Spoon River Anthology*" (*ASR*, p. 286). Some early letters to Dreiser reveal other aspects of his influence. Upon reading *The Financier* (1912) shortly after it appeared, Masters told the novelist, "your 'sceptical daring' is immense. Your treatment of evil and sin and such things is such an unmasking of the passing show."[32] A week later he remarked, "You are helping to rid us of the Presbyterians and the cock-sure moralists."[33] These comments also relate to Masters's purpose in *Spoon River Anthology*, which he began less than eighteen months later. Moreover, his poetics—which commonly prompted him to work "from particulars to universals," as Reedy said in 1914—were undoubtedly influenced by Dreiser. In the second letter quoted above, Masters told him, "You have such a capacity for detail and for the pure fact from which truth is secreted," and he was soon providing Dreiser with information about Chicago for use in writing *The Titan* (1914). So it is hardly surprising that Masters thought increasingly about basing his own writing on the details of small-town life. Indeed, he took Dreiser for a visit to Menard County in 1913, and his first attempt to exploit his background was a short, comic prose piece in dialect called "The Oakford Derby," which he sent to Dreiser later that year.[34]

By the spring of 1914 Masters's plan to write a realistic novel of small-town life had changed, and he had embarked on the *Anthology*, a series of poetic character sketches. One of them, which appeared the following July, was inspired by Dreiser, and it was apparently Masters's way of paying tribute to the writer who had influenced him. In an August 20 letter to the famous novelist he commented, "I have you pickled in my Anthology as 'Theodore the Poet,'" and he sent the poem along.[35] "Theodore the Poet" is not a monologue, and there is no indication that the man who sat and examined life "On the shore of the turbid Spoon" is dead, so the poem violates the epitaphic conventions of the *Anthology*. Nevertheless, Masters was by then writing poetry that was specific, based on people he knew, and related to his downstate Illinois background—and he undoubtedly hoped to become the Dreiser of "the turbid Spoon." Hence, "Theodore the Poet" testifies to the influence of the great American novelist, who prompted Masters's poetic realism.

During this period Masters also became impressed with the free verse that was appearing in *Poetry* magazine, especially Carl Sandburg's, which often focused on life in Chicago and exhibited "a refreshing realism" (*ASR*, p. 335). He developed a friendship with the journalist-poet, who also had a downstate Illinois background and a love for Whitman, and when the *Anthology* poems were being written, Sandburg often dropped by to read them in typescript and comment on them (*ASR*, p. 339). Masters later denied that Sandburg had been an influence, but that was simply a jealous reaction to a rival poet and Lincoln biographer whose writing continued to receive acclaim.[36]

Reedy was also urging Masters to avoid conventional verse and write about what he knew from experience. More important, the well-known editor referred to *The Greek Anthology* in his magazine and recommended that Masters read it. The latter did so in 1909. That book is a collection of epigrammatic poems by many hands, produced over several centuries. Primarily written in first person, they succinctly sum up human lives, often in frank terms and from the vantage point of the grave. *The Greek Anthology* prompted the poet to compose his short, free-verse epitaphs, as he later indicated.[37] Of course, the "anthology" concept, signifying a collection of related poems, was also derived from *The Greek Anthology*. Although written by many people, the Greek poems are culturally related, and some of the speakers address or refer to one another. The first *Spoon River Anthology* poems that Masters sent to Reedy were quite brief and clearly showed the Greek epigrammatic influence: "Hod Putt," "Ollie McGee," "The Unknown," "Cassius" (later "Cassius Hueffer"), "Serepta the Scold" (later "Serepta Mason"), "Amanda" (later "Amanda Barker"), and "Chase Henry." They appeared on May 29, 1914, along with "The Hill," which has no parallel in *The Greek Anthology*.

Of those early poems, none is more revealing or important than "The Hill," in which the poet-speaker's visit to a cemetery prompts his reflections on the dead, whom he imaginatively brings to life in the epitaph-poems that follow. One poem that may have contributed to that idea is Goethe's "The Dance of Death," in which a cemetery caretaker looks "On the graves where the dead were sleeping," and suddenly the spirits of the dead arise and dance.[38] But a much more interesting parallel occurs in "Earth" by William Cullen Bryant. In that long lyric the speaker hears the voices of the dead telling about their broken and frustrated lives:

> The forgotten graves
> Of the heart-broken utter forth their plaint.
> The dust of her who loved and was betrayed,
> And him who died neglected in his age;
> The sepulchres of those who for mankind
> Labored, and earned the recompense of scorn;
> Ashes of martyrs for the truth, and bones
> Of those who, in the strife for liberty,
> Were beaten down, their corses given to dogs,
> Their names to infamy, all find a voice.[39]

This description of the dead who start to speak continues for another fifteen lines, but the specifics are not as important as the idea—that the dead comment on their substantially unhappy lives. Masters had read Bryant's poetry while in Lewistown, and since he had great anxiety about death, he must have been impressed with the famous poet's emphasis on that theme. Of course, in "The Hill" Masters is not making a generalized comment on life but questing into the small-town world that he had left behind, calling up the ghosts of Major Walker, Fiddler Jones, and others that he had known. And the epitaph-poems that followed it were deeply referential to his own experience, as the annotations to this edition demonstrate.

In *Across Spoon River* the poet says that a visit from his mother in May of 1914, during which they discussed "the whole past of Lewistown and Petersburg," inspired him to write "The Hill" and the first few epitaph-poems (pp. 338-39), but it is likely that his inquiry into the past of those communities was not limited to their discussion. During the years that preceded *Spoon River Anthology,* the poet may well have been influenced by others who focused on the people that he had known or heard about. For example, he may have read R. D. Miller's *Past and Present of Menard County, Illinois* (1905), which sketches the lives of many Petersburg-area people, praises the pioneers, and includes this suggestive comment: "If some of those early settlers could rise from the grave and come back to their haunts of eighty years ago, their surprise would be far greater than that of Rip Van

Winkle."[40] Here is the theme of extensive cultural change that is central to the *Anthology*, and it is expressed in terms of dead residents rising from the grave. Also, Masters probably continued to receive the Lewistown newspaper in Chicago, or at least to read it now and again, and William T. Davidson's *Fulton Democrat* carried a page-one column called "Old Days in Fulton County" during the 1890s and early twentieth century. That newspaper consistently celebrated the pioneer heritage of the county, which may have contributed to Masters's conviction that midwestern culture had degenerated since the frontier. Davidson's long obituary of Major Newton Walker—a Virginian of "lofty integrity and worthy family pride," a vigorous pioneer who "despised wealth" and served the community, a patriot whose father fought in the Revolutionary War—is similar in tone to such *Anthology* poems as "John Wasson" and "Rebecca Wasson," which celebrate pioneers.[41] In writing the obituary, Davidson was clearly setting the life of the old pioneer before his readers as a model for themselves to emulate, just as Masters does in the Wasson poems and "Lucinda Matlock." However, celebration of local pioneers such as Davidson engaged in, which implied criticism of more recent residents for failing to measure up, was common throughout the Midwest in the later nineteenth century.

In any case, the writing of *Spoon River Anthology* represented a turning away from conventional poetic themes and forms and an embracing of the original subject matter that Masters's small-town experience provided. "Petit, the Poet" reflects that new direction. Obviously autobiographical, it is an epitaph for his early career as a poet:

> Life all around me here in the village:
> Tragedy, comedy, valor and truth,
> Courage, constancy, heroism, failure—
> All in the loom, and oh what patterns!
> Woodlands, meadows, streams and rivers—
> Blind to all of it all my life long.

The entire writing process was an excursion into the self—the true source of all distinctive poetry. Masters realized that his past experience was bound up with his identity and, hence, with his literary art. The "Spoon River" that Archibald Higbie tried to root out of his soul was not only inescapable, it was essential.

Samuel Gardner's image of an "umbrageous elm," which depended on its roots to create the extensive branches and leaves "Wherefrom the breeze took life and sang" in "sweet aeolian whispers," expresses, through an Americanized version of the Romantic aeolian harp metaphor, the poet's new comprehension of the relationship between background, self, and art. It is not accidental that the poet's initials spell the name of the tree: E. L. M.

After years of frustration, Masters was very gratified by the reception of his *Anthology* series in *Reedy's Mirror*, and he undoubtedly felt a sense of triumph over his limited, repressive background. He had faced his past, come to terms with his problems, and created what he hoped was imperishable poetry. "Elijah Browning," discussed above in reference to Spinoza, symbolizes the poet's view of his struggle and achievement. In fact, it recapitulates the process of self-analysis and poetic self-realization that is symbolized by the entire *Anthology*. That is, aside from the poems about writers and artists, which are clearly self-referential, "Hare Drummer," "Johnnie Sayre," "Dillard Sissman," "Jonathan Houghton," and others reflect the alternating security, anxiety, and yearning of his childhood; "Frank Drummer," "Emily Sparks," "Alfred Moir," "Immanuel Ehrenhardt," and others are based on his reading and educational experience; "Caroline Branson," "Herbert Marshall," "Daniel M'Cumber," "Lucius Atherton," and others relate to his idealized females, love affairs, and sexual frustration; "John Cabanis," "English Thornton," "Hiram Scates," "Magrady Graham" and others are based on his political partisanship and hope for America; "Father Malloy," "Scholfield Huxley," "The Village Atheist," "Le Roy Goldman," and others reflect his philosophical-religious questioning—and so on. Some of these are discussed below. The point here is that the yearning, frustration, anguish, hope, and triumph in *Spoon River Anthology* are reflections of the poet's inner life, and all of that is the equivalent of Elijah Browning's ascent of the mountain.

Masters believed that poetry was the greatest means of attaining truth, as Elijah Browning's prophet-poet name suggests. In fact, that poem and the *Anthology* as a whole were influenced by the search for truth in Robert Browning's "Pauline" (1833), "Paracelsus" (1835), and "Sordello" (1840).[42] In the first of those romantic poems of psychological analysis the troubled speaker pursues truth, experiences God's love, and finally affirms, "I believe in God and truth / And love."[43] In "Paracelsus," which is a poetic drama, the protagonist commits himself to a search for the truth, especially for knowledge of God, and he eventually finds that "Truth is within ourselves."[44] And in "Sordello," which is directly related to "Elijah Browning," the central figure is a poet who ascends a mountain that symbolizes deeper understanding, and at the summit "he felt himself alone, / Quite out of Time and this world: all was known."[45] Cloud and star imagery also connect the two poems, as does an important line, "Sordello vanished utterly," which is similar to the climactic line in Masters's poem, "I vanished utterly."[46] More important, Sordello is the champion of the masses, a bard who is the "incarnation of the People's hope," and who dreams of restoring Rome as a city devoted to the rights of humanity.[47] Replace Rome with America and that is precisely how Masters viewed himself, as the discussion below demonstrates.

The symbolic reflection of the poet's struggle for self-realization emerged in *Spoon River Anthology* because of the way in which the book was written—serially, for a weekly magazine—and because of the self-examination that Masters carried out by confronting the past that had troubled him so deeply. But he did not fully recognize the symbolic power of his book, despite the fact that he once said, " 'Spoon River' is my life, since it came from me as my summation of what I had seen and lived."[48] He thought that its effectiveness lay solely in its authentic portrayal of community life—as a microcosm that expressed the spiritual condition of America. Hence he says in "The Genesis of Spoon River" that, were it not for his declining health, he would have "made the Anthology fuller and richer and longer" by adding other characterizations based on people he had known or known about.[49] Nevertheless, the *Anthology* is, in fact, a complex work of Romantic self-creation, which lies within the naturalistic framework that governs the lives of the Spoon River villagers. It is a kind of twentieth-century "Song of Myself," a single poem about the making of a poet in which the characterizations are a multifaceted mask for the poet's discordant and struggling literary mind, which eventually does assert its dominion, creating his new identity. Hence the book has a profound wholeness, and Masters deserves recognition as a literary innovator for his use of poetry to explore the fragmented, searching, twentieth-century self.

The final poem in the *Reedy's Mirror* series, which is also the last epitaph-poem in the book version of the *Anthology*, contributes much to the motif of poetic self-realization. In "Webster Ford"—an epitaph for the pseudonym Masters had used in two previous books and while writing the series—he fashioned his life into a myth. As the speaker says, Apollo, the god of poetry, had called him during his youth to a life of song, but, fearful of the world's ridicule, he had rejected the call, concealing his vision. The word "vision" refers to both his mystical experience of the god and, metaphorically, his vision as a poet. The only other person who saw Apollo, Mickey M'Grew, died by falling down into the darkness of the water tower. Based on Mickey McFall of Lewistown, who was the poet's boyhood friend, M'Grew is a psychological double whose death symbolizes the fate from which the speaker narrowly escaped—not the fate of death only, but of death without self-realization, for "The vision . . . perished with him." Meanwhile, the speaker endured a long spiritual struggle— dying but "fighting the numbness"—until he "seemed to be turned into a tree with trunk and branches / Growing indurate, turning to stone, yet burgeoning / In laurel leaves." This passage reflects the myth of Apollo and Daphne, in which the water nymph fled from the god and was turned into a laurel tree, whereupon the laurel became Apollo's favorite tree and its leaves were used in wreaths to signify achievement by poets and others.[50] Hence the speaker is referring to his eventual poetic achievement, which occurred not in his youth but in later years, when he was deeply aware of "the grisly hand" of death. The "laurel leaves" also refer to his poems, which "never cease to flourish [i.e., come forth] until you fall." Webster Ford closes with an apostrophe to them, and to "Delphic [i.e., mysterious, wise] Apollo":

O leaves of me
Too sere for coronal wreaths, and fit alone
For urns of memory, treasured, perhaps, as themes
For hearts heroic, fearless singers and livers—
Delphic Apollo!

As the closing apostrophe suggests, Apollo had become the poet's ideal. That development shows the influence of Browning's "Sordello," for the central figure in that poem struggles, and fails, to embody Apollo. Masters was apparently indicating that he too had failed, but he would no longer. In this poem he conveyed his regret for having repressed his poetic impulse, for as he says in *Across Spoon River* when discussing his law career, "I still kept my passion for poetry, and there was a hurt always in my heart that I was forced to neglect the call I felt" (p. 230). Henceforth he would no longer put poetry second to anything else or conceal his identity with a pseudonym for the sake of his law career. He realized that if he wanted to create "themes / For hearts heroic, fearless singers and livers," he must openly and fully respond to Apollo. By such an act of self-creation, he would become a kind of cultural hero, whose "leaves" (poems) would be fit "For urns of memory." And he would triumph over the small-town repression of his youth — and over death, through "death in the flame" of poetic inspiration.

As this commentary suggests, "Webster Ford" concludes the *Anthology* about as well as one epitaph-poem could be expected to, and in that respect, the series in *Reedy's Mirror* is superior to the book version, which tacks on "The Spooniad" and the "Epilogue." Furthermore, "Webster Ford" relates very well to the cultural meaning of the *Anthology,* discussed below.

Poetics and Myth

The motif of poetic self-realization in *Spoon River Anthology* raises two questions, which are posed symbolically in the climactic autobiographical poems "Elijah Browning" and "Webster Ford": what was the "Infinite Truth" that the poet felt he had finally grasped, and why would his poetry hopefully be treasured by "hearts heroic, fearless singers and livers"? These are, in fact, deeply related questions, for Masters hoped that *Spoon River Anthology* would be treasured because of the truth that it revealed. That truth was his vision of America, which was achieved during the composition of the *Anthology.* Although Masters did not realize it, his vision was mythic.

In his remarkable 1914 essay, William Marion Reedy recognized that the *Anthology* was not just a sociological microcosm but a depiction of American cultural decline. As he said,

> readers of the *Mirror* [have] hailed happily a new light and a new voice in letters. The light and the voice are American—American of the country's declining heroic age, of the age in which came to first acuteness the personal problem of life in multiplying complications. "After the war" the complexities became confusing and the [patriotic] fervor died fitfully down, and materialism came into rule; and more and more idealists in Spoon River and elsewhere went down to dusty defeat. But here, in the "Anthology," they rise again, and even the materialists arise.

Although he did not realize that the *Anthology* reflected a mythic view of America, Reedy did associate it with two other works of "the Lincoln country" that clearly are mythic: *The Valley of Shadows* (1909) by Francis Grierson and *Herndon's Lincoln* (1889) by William H. Herndon and Jesse W. Weik. Both of those works depict the "heroic age" of the Illinois frontier, which is a version of the American pastoral—an image that conveys our civic belief in America's radical innocence and the nation's potential for becoming the Garden of the World. That mythic view derives from our country's sense of uniqueness as a culture committed to the democratic ideal and, hence, to a new and better kind of society, inherently different from all previous societies. America was a new beginning, established on an unspoiled continent traditionally called the New World, and thus Americans are unfallen, innocent, Adamic figures who embody and expound a utopian dream for humanity.[51] It is this mythic vision of America that the pioneers and a few other "idealists" struggle for or evoke and that the "materialists" defeat, and it is this vision that Masters expressed throughout his life, starting with *Spoon River Anthology*.

Readers have missed the book's mythic significance because they have viewed it as a realistic exposé of the small town, steeped in the details of actuality. It is that, but Masters's deep inner conflict extended into his poetics. As he says in *Across Spoon River*, because of his law career and his extensive reading in science, he developed a "Cyclopean eye" that "saw everything with realistic clearness" and "saw through people with penetration," but he always retained his two normal eyes, "which saw

beauty where it was not, and truth where it had never been."
And he remarks that "All through my poems there run the two
streams of realism and mysticism" (p. 318). Although Dreiser,
Ibsen, and others had taught him to use the particulars of ex-
perience to convey reality, Goethe, Shelley, Poe, Browning, and
Whitman—who had influenced him earlier—had taught him that
the touchstone of artistic truth lies within the writer, which is
the poetics of Romanticism. Hence the most inaccurate comment
that Reedy made in his 1914 essay was this: "There be those who
say the Anthology derives from Walt Whitman. Not consciously.
There is little in common between Whitman and Masters except
the freedom. Masters moves from particulars to universals, Whit-
man *vice versa*." In truth, the *Anthology* was deeply influenced
by Whitman, who both reflected the American myth in *Leaves
of Grass,* where he portrayed himself as an Adamic figure, and
criticized the forces that prevented America from living up to its
promise in *Democratic Vistas* (1871). And Masters worked from
universals to particulars when writing at least some of the *An-
thology* poems, especially once he grasped the potential for ex-
pressing his view of America through the characterizations.

The poet asserts his commitment to Romantic poetics—that
is, to the expression of imaginative or inner truth—in *Across
Spoon River* when he says, "the greatest poetry is that which
founds itself upon the truth which is the beautiful and the beau-
tiful which is the truth," and which "proves the laws of the spirit
of man" (p. 413). The poet starts with his imaginative grasp of
the truth about humanity and "proves" it in his literary art. He
does not discover it in his materials. In "The Genesis of Spoon
River" Masters makes it clear that this poetic theory had an impact
on the *Anthology* when he discusses his most famous poem, "Anne
Rutledge":

> But finally, "Anne Rutledge" does not say that the Republic
> will bloom forever; it simply expresses an imploration on the
> part of this obscure voice speaking from beneath the weeds of
> that lonely graveyard, that the Republic will bloom forever
> from the dust of her bosom—something that Ann Rutledge
> never thought of, and never could have thought of in her simple
> heart; but which I, as the creator of the Anthology, did think
> of, and with the fervent hope that the Republic will bloom

forever, nourished by every life that can give it sustenance out of poetry or prose, fact or fiction. . . . As Matthew Arnold said, "poetry attaches its emotion to the idea; the idea is the fact."[52]

In other words, in creating the poem, Masters started with what was to him a great, personally realized truth—that the democratic ideal, embodied in the republic, has been nourished and must be nourished by the lives of ordinary Americans—and he "proved" this truth by creating a beautiful poem that expresses it.

Of course, Arnold's "the idea is the fact" is diametrically opposed to Williams's "no ideas but in things," which expresses the approach used in creating many other *Anthology* poems. Additional poems that start with "the idea," a truth held by the poet, include "Robert Fulton Tanner" (life is a trap), "Scholfield Huxley" (humanity is frustrated by death), "John Wasson" (pioneers embodied the American ideal), and "Elijah Browning" (artists must struggle to achieve their vision). The expression of intense, sometimes exalted, emotion in these and other epitaph-poems also betrays the influence of Romantic poetics. In contrast, *Anthology* poems that are clearly based on specifics from the poet's past include " 'Indignation' Jones," "Doc Hill," "Johnnie Sayre," and "Jack Maguire," to name a few. That Masters wavered between the realistic approach to poetry, influenced by Dreiser and others, and the Romantic, influenced by Browning and others, can be seen throughout the *Anthology*. That is what gives the book its curious texture, which is at once sociological and intensely personal, a recollection of small-town life and an expression of the poet's values and conflicts.

As indicated above, *Spoon River Anthology* as a whole reflects a central idea, a truth that is deeply mythic: the democratic ideal that originated with Jefferson was realized on the Jacksonian frontier in the lives of the uncorrupted (Adamic) pioneers, who held fast to the American vision, but the Civil War destroyed that idyllic agrarian democracy and allowed materialistic and repressive forces to dominate the country. In short, America degenerated from primal innocence. *Spoon River Anthology* is a kind of objective correlative of this idea, a microcosmic reflection of America's spiritual condition after the Edenic culture had been displaced by those subversive forces.

This is the central perspective in all of Masters's poetry and prose, starting with the *Anthology*, and it can be traced to the 1890s, when his father's values, his reading, and his political involvement combined to provide a new purpose for the young writer. As he points out in his autobiography, in 1896 he and his father attended the Democratic convention in Chicago, where he saw and heard William Jennings Bryan. The "Peerless leader" was the champion of agrarian America and of the political myth of the Democratic party, which viewed itself as struggling to return the nation to the simple and noble way of life originated by Jefferson and achieved under Jackson:

> It was a spectacle never to be forgotten. It was the beginning of a changed America. Bryan's voice, so golden and winning, came clearly to my ears as he said, "You shall not press down upon the brow of labor this crown of thorns, you shall not crucify mankind upon a cross of gold." And as the vast crowd rose in ecstasy and cheered, and as the delegates marched about yelling and rejoicing for the good part of an hour, I sat there thinking of what I had read in Milton, in Mill, in More, in Bacon's *New Atlantis*, in Shelley, and resolving that I would throw myself into this new cause, which concerned itself with humanity. . . . A new life had come to me as well as to the Democracy [the Democratic party]. And at night at the apartment my father and I talked. Bryan would sweep the country, and it would be reclaimed from the banks and the syndicates who had robbed the people since 1861 and whose course had made it so impossible for a young man to get along in the world. . . . Andrew Jackson had come back in the person of Bryan! (*ASR*, pp. 209-10)

Masters committed himself to Bryan's presidential campaigns in 1896 and 1900 and to the cause of the Democratic party, which he believed was "trying to hold America to its noble path, its primal vision."[53] And in the same period he was provoked into the role of a writer defending that vision by the coming of the Spanish-American War: "The Phillipine venture filled me with furious championship for America as a republic setting an example to the world by keeping out of the tangles of commercial exploitation and militarism. I determined to master the history that went into the making of the Constitution and our republican system, and plunged myself into Montesquieu, More, Plato, Aristotle, and into histories. . . . I read almost untold books to this end, and began to write articles for the Chicago *Chronicle*" (*ASR*, p. 255). Those articles and others made him well known in Chicago, and he was soon president of the Jefferson Club, which he helped to organize. In 1904 his political articles were collected in *The New Star Chamber and Other Essays,* and in the following year his poetry collection, *The Blood of the Prophets,* included some poems against the war. In 1902 he also published a blank verse drama entitled *Maximilian,* which depicts the struggle for liberty in Mexico. Thus, at the turn of the century Masters was increasingly devoted to the cause of the republic—which is to say, the Jeffersonian tradition of individual rights—and he later said in *Across Spoon River* that his studies and writings of that era "laid the foundation for many things in *Spoon River Anthology*" (p. 405).

As a proponent of the Democratic party, the party that idolized Jefferson and Jackson and claimed the allegiance of his father and grandfather, Masters developed a severely dichotomous view of American politics. As he put it in a later essay, the two major parties are not simply rival approaches to promoting democracy: "The Democratic party serves and expresses America. . . . The Republican party betrays America and has always betrayed it."[54] In his mind the former stood for Jeffersonian individualism and commitment to the people, while the latter stood for Hamiltonian centralism and commitment to money-making. At about the turn of the century Masters began to regard America as composed of two groups locked in a cultural dialectic, of which the major parties were simply one expression. He later described those two groups very succinctly in *The Tale of Chicago* (1933): "There are two strains of blood in America, one that stayed close to the soil and developed character and originality, the other that struggled for riches in the cities and became parasitical."[55]

As this suggests, his view was a response to dramatic cultural change. Between the Civil War and the turn of the century America had been transformed from an agrarian republic with a fairly homogeneous northern European ethnic background to an industrialized, urbanized nation, filled with business entrepreneurs devoted to capitalistic growth and immigrants clinging to Old

World traditions. That enormous change also affected Mark Twain—whose mythic evocations of the Old Republic in *Tom Sawyer* (1876), *Huckleberry Finn* (1884), and *Life on the Mississippi* (1883) influenced Masters—as well as William Dean Howells, Henry Adams, Henry James, Sherwood Anderson, and other writers. However, no American writer was more deeply troubled by that change than the author of *Spoon River Anthology,* who fused his awareness of it with his memories of social conflict in Lewistown, his admiration for the pioneers, his love for his grandparents, and his idealized recollections of the Petersburg area to create his mythic view of conflicting social groups and cultural decline.

In a poem called "I am America," published in 1918, Masters depicts the origin of the good cultural group mentioned above, the real Americans, as a mystical reuniting of divided humanity, accomplished by the spirit of the land. The speaker in the poem is the land itself:

> The secret of my spirit mixes the blood of the races.
> I shall have none for my own but my breed and clan.
> I take the spirits of Babel, the stranger faces,
> And make them into my image, American.[56]

This is a deeply mythic poem, an expression of American civic belief, which has asserted the originality of the American self since the Revolutionary era—and especially since the Age of Jackson. The poem's closest forerunner is Whitman's "Song of Myself," and like that great poet, Masters saw himself as a representative American, one who embodied the basic goodness of the new "breed and clan." Unfortunately, he did not view everyone else in America as spiritually equal and sharing in the same potential, as Whitman had. Instead, his philosophical determinism prompted him to regard human character as substantially fixed by heredity and environment. Those who were fortunate enough to share in the revolutionary and pioneer experiences that had established America, or who were related to those experiences through family background and upbringing, were the real Americans. Those who were unrelated to such culture-making experiences were not apt to share the American vision—and they were on the increase.

In another little-known poem called "The Great Race Passes," published in 1920, Masters complains that

> Crackers and negroes in the South,
> Methodists and prohibitionists,
> Mongrels and pigmies
> Possess the land.[57]

His lament for American cultural decline had led to bigotry. In that same year, he published *Domesday Book*, a narrative poem that assesses America's degenerated spiritual condition, and he dedicated it to his father, "Hardin Wallace Masters / Splendid Individual of / a Passing Species—an American."[58] By that later period of his career, he held out little hope for America. As that dedication and the title of "I am America" also suggest, Masters viewed himself in mythic terms, as a scion of the primal tribe. In a 1942 interview he was asked, "What are your roots?" He replied, "The America of Jefferson—of Jeffersonian democracy. I date back a long time. . . . I have a number of Revolutionary ancestors."[59] He also had a grandfather, Squire Davis Masters, who symbolized George Washington and somehow "belonged to the days of the Revolution"—although he was a Jacksonian pioneer—and about whom Masters also said, "my deepest conviction is that when I am my best self, I am that old gentleman of Virginia stock reincarnated" (*ASR*, pp. 5, 403). No American author had a more profound sense of native roots, except perhaps Henry Adams, who was also troubled by cultural change and felt that he belonged to a tradition that was being abandoned and to a social group that was being overrun by alien masses.

Because of his background, Masters viewed himself as a latter-day prophet of Americanism, uniquely qualified to recall his nation to its "primal vision" in an era of cultural degeneracy. That was his purpose in many later works, including *Domesday Book* (1920), *Lee* (1926), *Jack Kelso* (1928), and *The New World* (1937). As he said in a poem called "Give Us Back Our Country," published in *Invisible Landscapes* (1935),

> Give us back our country, the old land,
> The cities, villages, and measureless fields
> Of toil and song, the just reward and sleep
> That follows after labor performed in hope.

> For this America is not mere earth,
> But living men, the sons of those who shouldered
> A destiny and vision. . . .[60]

To Masters, history became a memory of the "great race," for that race embodied and promoted the American vision (the democratic ideal), which alone could bring cultural renewal.

And poetry became the servant of that mythic perspective, starting with the *Anthology*. In the symbolic terms of "Elijah Browning," that view of America was the "Infinite Truth" achieved by the prophet-poet after a long struggle—the truth to which his soul was united, creating a permanent identity from his discordant inner self. In the symbolic terms of "Webster Ford," that view (poetic vision) had created a poet whose "leaves" were "urns of memory" that might inspire "hearts heroic, fearless singers and livers," and thus restore the Old Republic. In short, Masters became a Whitmanesque bard of democracy, and he later expressed his poetic purpose in just those terms: "I may say that if I had any conscious purpose in writing it [the *Anthology*] and the New Spoon River, it was to awaken that American vision, that love of liberty which the best men of the Republic strove to win for us, and to bequeath to time."[61] However, *Spoon River Anthology* is not an expression of "conscious purpose" with regard to this cultural meaning, but a record of discovery. Masters looked into his personal experience and discovered that his background in Petersburg and Lewistown gave him a perspective on the American vision and what had become of it.

Myth in *The Sangamon* and the *Anthology*

It is easier to recognize the poet's mythic perspective in the *Anthology* if one first reads *The Sangamon* (1942), which is the most obviously mythic work in his canon. Despite its place in the Rivers of America Series, the book is not a history of life along that famous river of the Lincoln country. It is an autobiographical essay, with poetic inclusions, that expresses Masters's roots in "the Petersburg environment"—and hence in the mythic Old Republic. It conveys the basis for his sense of authority as a writer. As he says early in the book, "Let us return to Menard County, to fine hospitality and prairie peace, to the hills about

Petersburg, to New Salem two miles away, to the fiddlers and the lovers of horses" (p. 6). That place-of-the-past was an idyllic world, populated by Americans of natural goodness, who were the spiritual descendants of Jefferson: "They adhered to Virginia, and to Thomas Jefferson. . . . Considering that these folk were shaped by the prairie and by the blood of Virginia, it may be said that no breed of people in the whole land was ever more individual, more distinguished by strength and courage, by good will and hospitality, by industry and the independent spirit" (pp. 14-15). He not only describes those people as "exemplars of Americanism," he also views his grandfather as a paragon of that culture—"a Jeffersonian Democrat, and a devoted adherent to the causes of Jackson" (p. 26). Moreover, both Squire Davis and Lucinda Masters shared with their neighbors a profound natural goodness: "The sky and the meadows inspired them and their neighbors with a goodness and a worship so simple and beautiful that it hurts the heart to think it was ever lost" (p. 30). "Truthtelling, honest dealing, neighborly kindness were their religion" (p. 124). In Masters's view those Petersburg-area people were Adamic figures, innocent Americans. They knew nothing of Bible-based rituals for "the remission of sins" because they were inherently sinless; they "knew nothing of history" because they were exempt from its implications (p. 124); and, as the word "neighborly" suggests, they formed a community, based not on economic enterprise but on shared American values. Thus, unlike their twentieth-century counterparts, they were not alienated.

As this analysis reveals, *The Sangamon* is a version of the American pastoral, an evocation of the New World Eden that embodies the essence of the nation's democratic ideal. It is a social utopia set on American soil. In *The Stubborn Structure* (1970) Northrop Frye describes the origin of pastoral myth in terms that clearly relate to Masters's early experience in Menard County, although he is thinking in general terms: "At the heart of all social mythology lies what may be called . . . a pastoral myth, the vision of a social ideal. The pastoral myth in its most common form is associated with childhood, or with some earlier social condition—pioneer life, the small town, the *habitant* rooted to his land—that can be identified with childhood. The nostalgia for a world of peace and protection, with a spontaneous response to the nature around it [is typical]."[62] Pastoral myth has flourished in America and appeared repeatedly in our literature, in the writings of Crèvecoeur, Bryant, Melville, Whitman, Twain, and many other authors. Masters's reflection of it stands out primarily because of his very clear embodiment of the democratic social ideal.

The mythic American culture in *The Sangamon* is perhaps most explicitly revealed in one of the many poems in the book, "New Salem Hill," which Masters had previously published in *Invisible Landscapes*. It celebrates New Salem as a frontier flowering of the American vision—and ultimately a Jacksonian realization of John Winthrop's "city upon a hill," that earliest social image of the New World utopia:

> Here on this Hill to blossom burst
> A life all new, all pure American.
> In western soil this seed of our loveliest flower,
> Grown in Virginia first,
> And on this hill resown, produced the men
> Made altogether of our original earth,
> . . . .
> This hill is loved, by history is revered
> Because America sees its happiest strains
> Of a people new, who briefly here appeared,
> Simple and virile, joyous, brave, and free,
> Kindly, industrious, full of hardihood,
> And happy in a sylvan democracy,
> And purged of Old World blood.
>
> (pp. 160-61)

Masters's view of the famous village in this poem was probably influenced by historian George Bancroft, whose ten-volume *History of the United States* (1834-74) was the most influential American history of the nineteenth century and was surely read by the poet during his period of constitutional studies. An apologist for Jacksonian democracy, Bancroft asserted that in the Mississippi Valley Americans would achieve an organic relationship to the virgin land and, hence, would be reborn as natural democrats.[63] That view is localized to Menard County in "New Salem Hill." In any case, to Masters that frontier village of the Jacksonian era epitomized the Old Republic, "the America that Thomas Jefferson wanted" (p. 160), and its decline was "a sign and symbol that the American idea was menaced" (p. 194). In all of American literature it would be hard to find a more explicit expression of the American myth of Edenic innocence and utopian community than "New Salem Hill," or a more thorough, personalized evocation of that perspective than *The Sangamon.*

Spoon River Anthology is also deeply infused with the myth. For example, because Ann Rutledge had belonged to that "sylvan democracy" at New Salem, she was an ideal figure to employ for expressing the hope that the Old Republic, which incarnated the American vision, would never fail: "Bloom forever, O Republic, / From the dust of my bosom!" Of course, that poem also expresses the essence of the legendary Lincoln-Rutledge romance—that her importance for the nation resides in the influence she exerted on Lincoln. "Anne Rutledge" asserts, in fact, that the spiritual rebirth of America, accomplished by Lincoln, can be traced to her. But we misread this famous poem unless we recognize what Masters knew so well—that Ann Rutledge was an idealized figure who symbolized the simplicity and goodness of Jacksonian frontier culture. In "The Genesis of Spoon River" the poet mentions that he read and believed William H. Herndon's version of "the Lincoln romance," and she is an exemplar of frontier virtue in that famous biography.[64] Masters also indicates that his deepest spiritual roots were in "the Petersburg–New Salem–Concord–Sandridge country," where his memories of "kind hearts and simple faiths" furnished "the purest springs for the Anthology."[65] In the manuscript version of that essay, which is at the University of Virginia Library, he even explicitly refers to the "Kirbys and Rutledges and Goodpastures" as examples of such people.[66] Although he could not have known Ann Rutledge, he had heard the story of her love for Lincoln from his grandmother, who had taken him to visit her grave, and he was still living in Lewistown in 1890 when her grave was moved from the rural Concord Cemetery to Oakland Cemetery in Petersburg, where it was a historical shrine. So Masters knew that she represented the roots of local people in the Old Republic, the "heroic age" of the Jacksonian frontier. In short, the speaker in "Anne Rutledge" symbolizes that mythic America.

And she is a spiritual model for the modern, alienated Spoon River villagers because her personal relationships in life were irradiated by a deep commitment to the republic—which is why she inspired Lincoln. That commitment is conveyed in the poem through her American idealism and her use of the historically poignant words "union" and "separation" to describe her relationship with Lincoln. Hence, despite being "unworthy and unknown," she deeply belongs, and her life has meaning. Her spiritual opposite in the *Anthology* is Knowlt Hoheimer, whose death in the Civil War seems without purpose and who puzzles over the meaning of *"Pro Patria"* on his tombstone. He is alienated because he has no commitment to the republic.

The myth of America as New World Eden is evident in several other *Anthology* poems, including "Hare Drummer" and "Jonathan Houghton," where it is evoked symbolically by images of the American pastoral ideal. In *The Machine in the Garden* (1965) Leo Marx traces that ideal—which depicts an Edenic rural landscape, free from anxiety, guilt, and conflict—back to Jefferson's *Notes on the State of Virginia* (1785), Crèvecoeur's *Letters from an American Farmer* (1782), and other works. As he points out, "the cardinal image of American aspiration was a rural landscape," a metaphoric garden or "pastoral utopia" that conveyed the American hope of transforming the continent into an idyllic "Garden of the World." As time passed and America changed, that vision of a pastoral utopia shifted its location from the future to the past, and the image evoked "the countryside of the old republic, a chaste, uncomplicated land of rural virtue."[67]

That is precisely what is evoked in "Hare Drummer," which has one of the most effective openings in the *Anthology:*

> Do the boys and girls still go to Siever's
> For cider, after school, in late September?
> Or gather hazel nuts among the thickets
> On Aaron Hatfield's farm when the frosts begin?
> For many times with the laughing girls and boys
> Played I along the road and over the hills
> When the sun was low and the air was cool,
> Stopping to club the walnut tree
> Standing leafless against a flaming west.

This is clearly a symbolic landscape, which conveys a spiritual refuge from the world of frustration, struggle, and conflict that time and change have brought to Spoon River. The subtle irony of the poem is that those idyllic days seemed timeless, patterned by repeated activities, but they were passing, as the images of sunset and fall suggest. This opening section is vividly realized because it is based on Masters's recollections of happy childhood days—at Sand Ridge, where Aaron Hatfield's farm was located, and at Lewistown, where the Siever family had an orchard. The close of the poem, which continues the reminiscent questioning, implies that the pastoral landscape is a unifying factor in the speaker's mind:

> Where are those laughing comrades?
> How many are with me, how many
> In the old orchards along the way to Siever's,
> And in the woods that overlook
> The quiet water?

Living or dead, the "comrades" are together, inseparable from that place, and, hence, not alienated. Masters's use of the word "comrades" also evokes the American myth in Whitman. In his book on the great poet, Masters refers explicitly to "the dear love of comrades, Whitman's dream of America."[68] That dream has become a memory. Moreover, the poem is a stunning evocation of the power of memory—which is, of course, what gives meaning to a place. That is emphasized by the closing image of "The quiet water," metaphorically the recollective mind in which the entire scene is reflected. A finely wrought objectification of a mental state, "Hare Drummer" is one of the best pastoral poems in American literature.

"Jonathan Houghton" also depicts the pastoral ideal through a rural image based on the poet's memories of his grandparents' farm at Sand Ridge:

> There is the caw of a crow,
> And the hesitant song of a thrush.
> There is the tinkle of a cowbell far away,
> And the voice of a plowman on Shipley's hill.
> The forest beyond the orchard is still
> With midsummer stillness;
> And along the road a wagon chuckles,
> Loaded with corn, going to Atterbury.

And an old man sits under a tree asleep,
And an old woman crosses the road,
Coming from the orchard with a bucket of blackberries.
And a boy lies in the grass
Near the feet of the old man,
And looks up at the sailing clouds,
And longs, and longs, and longs
For what, he knows not:
For manhood, for life, for the unknown world!

This beautiful pastoral description evokes a world poised in "midsummer stillness," beyond the reach of time. The old woman and old man are, of course, poetic reflections of the poet's grandparents, and the boy is an image of himself, yearning for self-realization but secure at their farm. As the poem indicates, the boy left that idyllic setting for "the unknown world." Thirty years passed, and then he returned,

And found the orchard vanished,
And the forest gone,
And the house made over,
And the roadway filled with dust from automobiles—
And himself desiring The Hill!

This poem reveals how traumatized Masters was by cultural change. As mentioned above, Sand Ridge gradually became a region of the mind. His memory of it became a refuge from his psychological problems, a counterforce to his sense of alienation in modern America, and a verification of the pastoral utopia of the Old Republic. He knew that Jefferson's America was a historical reality, for it seemed to him that he had once lived there, although he was now dispossessed. Hence Masters symbolized his psychological experience in this tragedy of Adamic innocence: the speaker was raised in an apparently timeless world of pastoral goodness, yearning for self-realization, but the medium of self-realization was time, which destroyed Arcadia. The vanished orchard is an especially fine image of a lost Eden. The exiled American Adam ends up yearning again—but for the timeless world of the cemetery.

That the American Arcadia was threatened by cultural change, especially by the rise of industrialism and cities, is a view that also goes back to Jefferson. In perhaps the most famous section of *Notes on the State of Virginia* he expressed his fears about the decline of democratic America:

> Those who labour in the earth are the chosen people of God, if ever he had chosen people, whose breasts he has made his peculiar deposit for substantial and genuine virtue. It is the focus in which he keeps alive that sacred fire [of liberty], which otherwise might escape from the face of the earth. Corruption of morals in the mass of cultivators is a phaenomenon of which no age nor nature has furnished an example. . . . The mobs of great cities add just so much to the support of pure government, as sores do to the strength of the human body. It is the manners and spirit of a people which preserve a republic in vigour. A degeneracy in these is a canker which soon eats to the heart of its laws and constitution.[69]

This view had an enormous influence on Masters, who was a serious student of Jefferson, his greatest hero. It is the philosophical justification for his idealization of the rural people of Menard County as embodiments of the American democratic vision and for his disparagement of cities and commercialism as inherently opposed to the preservation of the republic. Hence *Spoon River Anthology* is a deeply Jeffersonian work. Indeed, it is Jefferson's vision for which the speaker struggles in "Jefferson Howard," as he recalls "My valiant fight! For I call it valiant, / With my father's beliefs from old Virginia." Certainly Jefferson was the speaker's spiritual father. He also recalls how he opposed the "Republicans, Calvinists, merchants, bankers"—which is to say, the forces that threatened the Jeffersonian ideal. The real-life model for that poem was the poet's father, that "Splendid Individual of a Passing Species," who could be expected to defend the American vision against the forces of degeneracy because of his background.

As "Jefferson Howard" suggests, Masters's family became the synecdoche for America's heroic but eventually defeated culture makers. His father was the last of them, but other, earlier ancestors were also the basis for mythic poems. "John Wasson" and "Rebecca Wasson" were based on the poet's great-great-grandparents and carry their actual names. The speakers are idealized pioneers who helped to create the "Beautiful young republic" (as Rebecca calls it) at the Revolution and then established it in frontier Illinois. They symbolize the entire "heroic age" of American culture—

from the Jeffersonian origination of the American vision to its Jacksonian realization. That is why John Wasson speaks in the plural, extending his family's experience (the first "We") to encompass the accomplishments of all the pioneers:

> We went by oxen to Tennessee,
> Thence after years to Illinois,
> At last to Spoon River.
> We cut the buffalo grass,
> We felled the forests,
> We built the school houses, built the bridges,
> Leveled the roads, and tilled the fields,
> Alone with poverty, scourges, death. . . .

In the same way, Rebecca Wasson's experience encompasses that entire era:

> . . . that stretch of years like a prairie in Illinois
> Through which great figures passed like hurrying horsemen:
> Washington, Jefferson, Jackson, Webster, Clay.

Her recollection of the historical period dominated by those great figures dramatizes the notion that, like all the pioneers of the "heroic age," she carried the American vision within herself— for that vision is precisely what those leaders symbolize. The Wassons provide a standard of energetic devotion to the republic by which America's cultural decline can be measured.

So does the speaker in "Lucinda Matlock." That poem was based on the poet's grandmother, whom he also regarded as a pioneer. The speaker's natural goodness and energy make her a kind of spiritual mother of the race, who indeed "made the garden"—symbolically, the American Eden—and went forth "Shouting to the wooded hills, singing to the green valleys." In that remarkable poem Masters worked from the actual details of his grandmother's life to create an American Eve, an idealized mother figure. After shedding her spirit upon the land, she does not even suffer death but just passes "to a sweet repose" and becomes a cultural memory. As the spiritual mother of all Americans, she upbraids her "Degenerate sons and daughters"—all the later generations—for their inner weakness, which has resulted in the cultural decline that Spoon River epitomizes.

In contrast to the "Anger, discontent, and drooping hopes"

that Lucinda Matlock complains of are the sturdy values of the pioneers in "Aaron Hatfield," based on the poet's grandfather. The poem depicts the pioneers as true apostles of Christ, virtuous workers in an agrarian culture who gather at Concord Church to mourn "the peasant youth / Of Galilee who went to the city / And was killed by bankers and lawyers," and who receive "the consolation of tongues of flame!" "Aaron Hatfield" symbolizes Jefferson's perception of rural Americans as "the chosen people of God," in whom the "sacred fire" of liberty is kept alive, as he put it in *Notes on the State of Virginia*. The speaker's biblical first name reflects his role as the leader of those people. Because they embody the American democratic ideal, the humble worshipers at Concord Church are not alienated, but deeply unified — hence the repeated plural pronoun "Us" toward the end of the poem. As that pronoun also reveals, in writing "Aaron Hatfield" Masters expressed his sense of spiritual communion with the heroic figures of his grandfather's generation. That is, by celebrating them he shared their devotion to the transcendent myth of America. To him they were people of biblical stature, apostles of the gospel of Americanism, who therefore triumphed over death — not only the death of family members whose lives were sacrificed in the sacred, culture-making cause, but the eventual death of their spiritually infused, highly unified culture. Spoon River's "memory picture" of Aaron Hatfield standing before the virtuous pioneers at the symbolically named Concord Church is "better than granite"; hence that culture is a lasting inspiration to an America in conflict and decline. Hatfield and the other pioneers reveal the direction that America was going before it got off the right track. Of course, Masters fails to show here, or anywhere in his writings, how the agrarian society of the Jacksonian era could be a viable model for modern America, but he created a fine poem that reflects the mythic Old Republic.

The Spiritual Quest

"Aaron Hatfield" is the climactic poem of *Spoon River Anthology*, which is symbolically an archetypal quest for psychological unity in which the poet moves inward, to his spiritual home, and achieves the poetic vision that will allow him to inspire cultural restoration.

The cemetery that surrounds Concord Church and the speaker's lament for "the sons killed in battle and the daughters / And little children who vanished in life's morning" recall the opening poem of the book, where the quest begins. The poet-speaker in "The Hill"—perhaps the most misunderstood poem in the *Anthology*— is questing among the dead for some comprehension of the human predicament. In all the book, from "The Hill" to "Webster Ford," his action alone is in the present. Like T. S. Eliot's famous J. Alfred Prufrock, he is a divided modern person, and despite his repeated inquiries, his inner self keeps telling him that the dead can reveal nothing, can provide no answers: "All, all are sleeping on the hill." That refrain also expresses his sense of alienation from the community that he remembers—and reminds him of his own forthcoming death, for the meaning of every *ubi sunt* poem is just such a reminder. When he recalls the pioneers, like Towny Kincaid and Major Walker, he realizes that they faced the tragedy of apparently meaningless death—which was, as indicated above, a major cause of anxiety for Masters:

> They brought them dead sons from the war,
> And daughters whom life had crushed,
> And their children fatherless, crying—
> All, all are sleeping, sleeping, sleeping on the hill.

The word "They" has no referent, so it evokes the impersonal forces that assaulted the pioneers—and now oppress the speaker. At this psychological low point he recalls Old Fiddler Jones, a pioneer whose life was so triumphant, so spiritually fulfilling, that he "played with life all his ninety years," and suddenly the poet-speaker's inner voice responds, not with the expected refrain but with a recollection of the dead man's voice:

> Lo! he babbles of the fish-frys of long ago,
> Of the horse-races of long ago at Clary's Grove,
> Of what Abe Lincoln said
> One time at Springfield.

Masters regarded Jones and other old-time fiddlers—who were also dance-callers and tale-tellers—as bardic figures who expressed and interpreted American culture. That is why the fiddler Blind Jack is portrayed in the *Anthology* as sitting at the feet of Homer. He is a kind of American Homer. So it is not surprising that the voice of Fiddler Jones, as recalled by the speaker, evokes life in the Old Republic, which somehow holds the key to the human predicament, and to the poet-speaker's inner turmoil. That voice launches him on a spiritual quest to reunify himself and establish his identity as a poet, a quest that leads to Arcadia-incarnate-in-America, which lies in the past—and ultimately in himself, as an unrealized vision.

Although Browning's "Sordello," discussed above, was influential, the central inspiration for the poet's quest surely came from Whitman. After all, it was he who said in the "Preface to *Leaves of Grass*" that "a bard is to be commensurate with a people" so he can create "the great psalm of the republic."[70] Hence an American bardic poet must take the people into himself, as Whitman did through sympathetic identification with scores of typical Americans in "Song of Myself." And, according to Whitman, the vision that needed to be poetically realized was "the idea of political liberty."[71] Masters agreed, but for him that lay in the past, and it had to be sought there and brought to light as an inspiration for twentieth-century America. Whitman's description of the bardic poet's approach includes these suggestive comments: "He drags the dead out of their coffins and stands them again on their feet. . . . he says to the past, Rise and walk before me that I may realize you."[72] And that is precisely what Masters did.

The poet's quest among the spirits of the dead, who are the ghosts of his past and symbols of his discordant self, is emphasized throughout the *Anthology* by the myriad references to "seeing," especially to comprehending the pattern or meaning of life. Hence it is a Spinozistic struggle to discern the truth and achieve salvation. For example, Widow McFarlane asserts that "A pattern you never see" is hidden under the loom of life and is visible only after you die, and the visionary Zilpha Marsh sees spirits with messages but cannot communicate "What it is I see!" Those two poems surely provide symbolic parallels to the poet's struggle to both discern and communicate the meaning of his life. Likewise, one of the most deeply frustrated figures in the *Anthology* is Petit, the poet, who laments that there was "Life all around me here in the village, / All in the loom, and oh what patterns!," but he was "Blind to all of it all my life long." His was the tragedy of a poet without vision—without insight into his culture or himself. So he recognizes that he will not be an immortal embodiment of truth like Homer and Whitman.

Many other poems refer to "vision," often in the context of a search. For example, Alexander Throckmorton feels that he is too old to "follow my vision," and Marie Bateson urges people to "Find the goal or lose it, according to your vision." Also, various epitaphs dramatize spiritual vision, including "Jacob Goodpasture," "Dillard Sissman," and "Isaiah Beethoven." One speaker, William Goode, even portrays himself as a man searching in the dark, guided by inner sight like a bat, and he sums up his life by saying, "all my wanderings / Were wanderings in the quest." It could hardly be more clear that the poet behind the masks was on a sometimes frustrating spiritual quest. And his anxiety about following (or developing) his own poetic vision, and hence realizing his potential, is perhaps nowhere more effectively symbolized than in "Jonathan Swift Somers." The speaker is a writer whose "soul takes fire" but who also cautions, "Be thankful if in that hour of supreme vision / Life does not fiddle."

The poet's spiritual quest begins with the expression of his inner conflict through the portrayal of such deeply discordant figures as the McGees, who hate and destroy each other, and Cassius Hueffer, whose inner turmoil destroys him. It continues through a vast number of personae who can be traced directly to Masters's own life or to the people he knew, as the annotations to this edition reveal, and through whole categories of people— battling lawyers, frustrated writers, unhappy spouses, regretful conformists, aspiring intellectuals—who clearly relate to his sense of identity. And it leads to the achievement of intellectual control over his discordant inner self through the truth-seeking process advocated by Spinoza and to the assumption of his bardic role through the mythic quest inspired by Whitman.

A good example of how the poems function as imaginatively constructed personae in a spiritual quest is "Lucius Atherton," in which the speaker is a "Toothless, discarded, rural Don Juan." The poem reflects the life of Lewistown resident Lewis C. ("Lute") Ross, who was apparently a woman chaser, but it also symbolizes an important conflict in Masters. In *Across Spoon River* he says, "I longed for a woman who was beautiful of person and gifted of mind"—an idealized female figure—but he also indicates that he strove to seduce "Anne" (Margaret George), who first embodied that ideal, and that he was regarded in Lewistown as a "Lothario" (pp. 88, 101, 105). After Masters broke off the relationship with Margaret George to woo a more sexually attractive young woman, his sense of guilt—and perhaps the feeling that he had betrayed his ideals—nearly led to a nervous breakdown (*ASR*, pp. 106-7). Later he had numerous affairs, which are also referred to in his autobiography, and he rationalized those as resulting from his fated "pursuit of the eternal feminine" (pp. 170-71, 250-51, 406-8), but they obviously led to psychological stress as well. As this evidence suggests, Masters was troubled by his sexuality, which always betrayed or compromised his ideal female and caused disillusionment—an experience symbolized in "Caroline Branson." Lucius Atherton mentions Dante's love for his idealized Beatrice and says, "I see now that the force that made him great / Drove me to the dregs of life." That is, Masters felt guilty that his search for an idealized, inspirational female was abortive because his sex drive always led him to the bedroom, where he "took many a trick." Hence "Lucius Atherton" symbolizes his sense of self-disgust as a betrayer of the idealized female: he was indeed "a heartless devil" who destroyed innocence and, in the process, subverted both his quest for the lost paradise—connected in his mind with his Edenic, presexual boyhood—and his search for poetic inspiration. By writing the poem, Masters confronted that inner problem, which had impaired his sense of wholeness, and he exorcised it—at least temporarily. But since it was such a severe, deeply rooted discordance, it later surfaced in another form.[73]

The poet's slow reunifying of himself by creating figures based on memory or local tradition who externalized his inner problems, and his consequent achievement of a new, nonalienated spiritual life, is symbolically presented toward the end of the book in "Jeremy Carlisle." The speaker regrets his former "blindness" to other souls and then reveals his increasing sense of wholeness and feeling of community as he reconciles himself to his own past:

> . . . do you remember the liquid that Penniwit
> Poured on tintypes, making them blue

Introduction

With a mist like hickory smoke?
Then how the picture began to clear
Till the face came forth like life?
So you appeared to me, neglected ones,
And enemies too, as I went along
With my face growing clearer to you as yours
Grew clearer to me.
We were ready then to walk together
And sing the chorus and chant the dawn
Of life that is wholly life.

This poem clearly relates to the ubiquitous "seeing" and "vision" imagery that conveys the poet's spiritual quest, even as it reveals the deepest truth embodied in the *Anthology*—that the harmonious self is a product of sympathetic identification with others.

The poet's quest leads to such autobiographical evocations of the American pastoral as "Hare Drummer" and "Jonathan Houghton," to the celebration of his Jeffersonian and Jacksonian roots in "John Wasson," "Rebecca Wasson," and "Lucinda Matlock," and to the reassuring voice of Anne Rutledge, who surely symbolizes Masters's own hope that "Out of me, unworthy and unknown" might come "vibrations of deathless music" to help restore the "Republic." Ultimately the poet's yearning for wholeness and struggle for a restorative vision leads to "Aaron Hatfield." In that climactic poem the poet-hero accomplishes his spiritual quest. That is, he imaginatively identifies with the pioneers, achieves a sense of unity and confidence in the face of death, verifies that the Jeffersonian ideal existed on the Jacksonian frontier, and secures the vision that his culture needs for spiritual regeneration.

"Aaron Hatfield" does more than any other epitaph-poem to enact the mythic pattern of return to a lost paradise that unifies the book, and it is immediately preceded by "Russell Kincaid," which emphasizes the need for such a return. In that highly mythic and symbolic poem the speaker recalls sitting in "the forsaken orchard" (the ruined republic) with his "spirit girded," like a dying tree, "thinking of youth, and the earth in youth" (his idyllic boyhood, and the Edenic Old Republic). And he laments the "cyclone" (cultural change) that swept him out of "the soul's suspense" (Edenic innocence and the timeless pastoral world). Both the man and the place are in need of restoration, and "Aaron

Hatfield" then supplies the vision that restores his Adamic innocence and holds the promise of cultural renewal. Both poems were written at the end of the serialized *Anthology,* just before "Webster Ford," in which the speaker casts his life into a myth of spiritual rebirth and the poet casts off his pseudonym—a symbol of his divided self. Thus the Adamic poet-hero is born (Masters is reunified), and he can now strive in the present to restore the "wasted garden," as Conrad Siever calls the spiritually dead cemetery-community of Spoon River—which is, symbolically, America.

Furthermore, between "Aaron Hatfield" and "Webster Ford" in the *Anthology* are "Isaiah Beethoven" and "Elijah Browning." Also written late in the serialized version, those poems express spiritual-artistic triumph and prophetic purpose. That is, they indicate that the poet achieved the spiritual quest that he had undertaken in "The Hill." He completed his Spinozistic search for the truth about human life, so poignantly initiated by his double-voiced inquiry about the dead; for he looked within his own experience and found it, as "Elijah Browning" effectively reveals. And the achieving of truth brought a sense of transfiguration, a spiritualizing of the poet's identity. He became what Sacvan Bercovitch has called an "American Jeremiah," a writer "simultaneously lamenting a declension and celebrating a national dream."[74] And he moved beyond the boundary of threatening time, so vividly evoked by his death-consciousness at the cemetery. He entered into the timeless world of poetic vision, which is symbolized by the triumph of Isaiah Beethoven, who took the soul of Spoon River into himself and lifted it "Above the battlements over Time!" Like his poetic hero in *Leaves of Grass,* Masters had become his book—which is to say, his poem. And as all of these closing poems reveal, Whitman's poet-seer, "a man cohered out of tumult and chaos," who incarnates America and who is committed to "the idea of political liberty," has finally arrived.[75]

Oddly enough, the other important influence on the creation of a spiritual quest in the *Anthology* was not an American work, but Goethe's *Faust* (1808; 1831). In *Across Spoon River* Masters indicates that he bought a copy of the great poetic drama while in Lewistown and was enthralled with it. Later, at Knox College

Academy, he studied German and read *Faust* in the original (*ASR,* pp. 97, 111, 117). The famous Romantic play made a lasting impression on him, and he regarded Goethe as the greatest writer of the modern world. Like Masters, Goethe had deep inner con-flicts—related to sexuality—and a gift for transmuting them into literary art. In his play Faust represents the idealistic, searching, but frustrated and death-conscious human mind; and the cynical, realistic Mephistopheles represents the self-defeating impulses in humanity that are associated with the body. The two character-izations are contradictory but inseparable aspects of the human self. The questing hero, Faust, finally dies, but not before achieving a vision of paradise for his people:

> I work that millions may possess this space,
> If not secure, a free and active race.
> Here man and beast, in green and fertile fields,
> Will know the joys that new-won region yields,
> Will settle on the firm slopes of a hill,
> Raised by a bold and zealous people's skill.
> A paradise our closed-in land provides. . . .[76]

That Masters saw himself as a kind of Goethean split-self is evident at the end of his autobiography, where he quotes from *Faust,* refers to the "delusion I had of being two persons" while writing the *Anthology,* and views his inner life as a troubled imaginative quest: "my thinking seems to be lighted along the dark corridors of thought by the circling and holding aloft of the flashlight of imagination. Some secrets seem thereby revealed, but often that light has blinded me to pitfalls right beneath my feet" (*ASR,* pp. 398-99). Also, in a 1942 interview for the *New York Times Book Review,* Masters referred to reading *Faust* while writ-ing the *Anthology* and described the creative experience in this way: "For a time it was as though I was living two lives. The life in the [law] courts and the life in the poems. . . . All through that Summer and Fall I carried on the two lives and felt, after a time, that I was outside the world."[77] He was outside the world because he was inside the *Anthology.* That Masters understood *Faust* as a purgation of inner conflict and an achievement of redemptive vision is clear from a comment in his introduction to *The Living Thoughts of Emerson* (1940): "[Byron] had no point of view save that of the pessimist, the suffering objector to life and the world as he found it. Goethe expended all such reactions in the portrait of Mephistopheles, and then wrote the exalted poetry which Faust uttered at death."[78] The phrase "exalted poetry" refers to Faust's utopian cultural vision, part of which is quoted above. Masters quotes from that same speech by Faust at the end of his auto-biographcial novel, *Skeeters Kirby* (1923), after the title character finishes writing his book, which was a purgation of "the passions which scar, depress, sear and weaken and embitter."[79] Masters did not try to imitate *Faust,* but he reflected the great play unconsciously as he worked his way through his own inner conflicts and achieved the redemptive cultural vision depicted in "Aaron Hatfield." Later he consciously drew upon the famous Walpurgis Night section of Goethe's play to create the "Epilogue," which has similar diabolical spirits and disembodied voices, the same kind of seriocomic tone and mixture of verse forms, and even a phantasmagoric play within it, akin to the "Walpurgis Night's Dream."

Of course, in *Spoon River Anthology* the polarity between opposing forces is not embodied in two great figures, but in the New England and southern cultural groups that Masters felt represented "two hostile and never-to-be-reconciled kinds of human nature" — yet they relate just as deeply to his inner conflicts as Faust and Mephistopheles did to Goethe's. As he examined his past experience, or quested within himself, he came to view eastern-dominated Lewistown as characteristic of what had destroyed the Old Republic and had prevented the restoration of the "primal vision" under Bryan. The community became the symbolic opposite of the southern-dominated Sand Ridge–Petersburg–New Salem country in Menard County. Although he does not deal with Lewistown extensively in nonfiction, he refers to that area in *The Sangamon* as "a different country . . . alien to New Salem and Sand Ridge," where violence was common and spirituality did not flourish (pp. 33, 239-40). In *Across Spoon River* he supports that perspective with a hellish description of violent, disease-ridden people from the Spoon River bottoms, who came into town on Saturdays: "These creatures at Lewistown howled in their insane cups, they fought with knives and guns and knucks" (p. 411). Masters asserts that the cultural environment in Lewistown was "calculated to poison, to pervert, and even to kill a sensitive nature," so "no poet in English or American history ever had a harder life than mine was in the beginning at Lewistown" (p. 410). Because his psychologically stressful, conflict-ridden experience at Lewistown made the community seem like an inversion of the Sand Ridge–Petersburg–New Salem country, the Lewistown people he recalled embodied the corruption, materialism, selfishness, and repression that had destroyed the Jacksonian Republic. That explains the severely negative portrayals of "Editor Whedon," "Thomas Rhodes," "The Town Marshal," and others. They are akin to the Snopses in Faulkner's fiction, who are in perpetual and inevitable conflict with the Sartorises. (Faulkner's characters, too, are ultimately mythological, and for precisely the same reason.)

"Editor Whedon," for example, is the polar opposite of the humble, spiritually infused, community-oriented Aaron Hatfield. He is corruption and selfishness incarnate because he uses the "great feelings and passions of the human family / For base designs." His life is not irradiated by a commitment to the people or a spiritual response to the democratic ideal, so he betrays the community, increases its discord, and ends up forgotten. His burial location where the sewage flows and the garbage is dumped symbolizes his alienation from the community, which was a self-created condition.

Although based on a Lewistown editor whom Masters hated, Editor Whedon is clearly a reflection of the *Anthology's* mythic polarity. In fact, the real-life editor was a highly principled man whose praise of Major Newton Walker's integrity and service to the community was described above. William T. Davidson was, in fact, a public-spirited, reformist editor. And far from being an enemy of the American vision, Davidson was a very patriotic individual. In July of 1891 he even showered high praise on the poet's father for delivering an outstanding Fourth of July oration to the community.[80] Yet he was transmuted by the poet's mythic vision into Editor Whedon, who is "demoniac" because he symbolizes the evil motives that have destroyed the Old Republic.

This transmutation occurred not only because Davidson was a political opponent of Masters's father and the journalistic rival of Masters's boss, Lute Breeden of the *Lewistown News,* but also because, like the poet, Davidson had been born and partly raised in Petersburg and had a family background that extended to Virginia during the Revolutionary War era. In short, to the poet Davidson was a scion of the "great race" who had betrayed it and the democratic ideal that it embodied. Similar reasoning would eventually cause Masters to depict Lincoln as an egotistical, hypocritical, and tyrannical figure in his debunking biography, *Lincoln, the Man* (1931). In other words, both Davidson and Lincoln were the focus of obsessive hatred because of Masters's mythic perspective.

Moreover, "Editor Whedon" may be a symbolic reflection of the poet's self-hatred because, despite what he says in his autobiography, he did not always support his father's liberal values. He sometimes sided with his mother. After his developing law career and emerging political views caused him to idolize his father, Masters's failure to support him at times during the 1880s probably caused self-loathing, which he exorcised through the depiction of Editor Whedon. If this assessment of one facet of the poet's inner discord is correct, it would explain why the poem begins with this curious reference to inconsistency: "To be able to see every side of every question; / To be on every side." Masters became a very opinionated man who could not stand ideological inconsistency because, in his early life, he had been so deeply and painfully divided between two sets of parental values.

Since Editor Whedon and others like him dominate the once-Arcadian Spoon River established by the Wassons, Lucinda Matlock, and Aaron Hatfield, the *Anthology* is a kind of tragic pastoral, like Fitzgerald's *The Great Gatsby* (1925). Perhaps no epitaph-poem reflects that sense of cultural decline as clearly as "Rutherford McDowell," in which the speaker laments that "the strong men / And the strong women are gone and forgotten," those who "from the womb of the world / Tore the Republic." Only their degenerated descendants remain,

> With so much of the old strength gone,
> And the old faith gone,
> And the old mastery of life gone,
> And the old courage gone,
> Which labors and loves and suffers and sings
> Under the sun!

But unlike *The Great Gatsby,* the *Anthology* closes with the promise of restoration through the questing poet-hero's return to the lost paradise and his consequent spiritual rebirth.

Our New Poet

As this discussion reveals, Masters recast his personal experience as public experience through the focusing and intensifying power of myth. His Midwest was a New World Eden that had degenerated under the influence of a corrupt, materialistic group that, since the time of Alexander Hamilton (Jefferson's political enemy), had not worked for the democratic ideal. He later depicted that historical process in *The New World,* but he expressed that mythic view for the first time in *Spoon River Anthology.* Masters created the series of epitaph-poems to clarify the American cultural dialectic that he had internalized, just as Faulkner created a myth of the South for the same purpose. In the process, Masters brought the unpoetic lives of everyday Americans into poetry for the first time and used his characterizations to symbolize his mythic vision—without realizing, of course, that it was mythic. *Spoon River Anthology* is, then, not only a kind of fragmented "Song of Myself," it is a more pessimistic version of Whitman's *Democratic Vistas,* focused on the triumph of the forces of disorder and decline in turn-of-the-century America. But within that account of a discordant, aimless, corrupted—and, hence, degenerated—society, the poet-hero struggles to secure the Jeffersonian vision and to place it in poetic "urns of memory," as Webster Ford says, where it may yet inspire cultural restoration. Once Masters's purpose and perspective are recognized, everything in the *Anthology* is absorbed into his powerful mythic image, and the book has remarkable wholeness and significance.

Indeed, *Spoon River Anthology* is culturally important because it reveals the inherent contradictions in the myth of America and the potentials for good and evil that such a cultural myth contains.[81] First of all, the Adamic American is an isolated, self-dependent figure who has no place in the Garden of the World, the social utopia that America is devoted to establishing. Hence the triumphant Elijah Browning, who creates himself in his own image as prophet-poet, achieves that identity by escaping from society. His New World Eden is the mountaintop, where he stands alone before the universe, responds to "the symphony of freedom," and achieves transcendence. As he says, "I could not return to the slopes— / Nay, I wished not to return." But the slopes, which represent his discarded past, are also where everyone else is—and where people like Jeremy Carlisle hope "to walk together / And sing in chorus and chant the dawn / Of life that is wholly life." In other words, the myth of America reflects an ambivalent national spirit, with contradictory thrusts toward individualism and community.

The unfortunate results of that ambivalence are seen throughout the *Anthology,* as individualism brings isolation from the community and the desire for social unity leads to the repression of nonconformists. This problem is symbolized by the experience of Julian Scott, who was alienated precisely because he was an individualist with an Adamic sense of his own rightness:

> The truth of others was untruth to me,
> The justice of others was injustice to me;
> Their reason for death, reasons with me for life;
> Their reasons for life, reasons with me for death;
> I would have killed those they saved,
> And saved those they killed.
> And I saw how a god, if brought to earth,
> Must act out what he saw and thought,
> And could not live in this world of men. . . .

Such a figure must either die, as Julian Scott did, in an act of social repudiation or escape, as Huckleberry Finn hoped to, by lighting out for the Territory.

Moreover, while Jeremy Carlisle depicts the joyful progress of "the good" toward an emerging great society, English Thornton reveals the intolerance that results when people who see themselves as inherently good confront others who are apparent obstacles to their sacred purpose:

> Here! You sons of the men
> Who fought with Washington at Valley Forge,
> And whipped Black Hawk at Starved Rock,
> . . . .
> Arise! Do battle with the fops and bluffs,
> The pretenders and figurantes of the society column,

And the yokel souls whose daughters marry counts;
And the parasites on great ideas,
And the noisy riders of great causes,
And the heirs of ancient thefts.
. . . .
By God! If you do not destroy these vermin
My avenging ghost will wipe out
Your city and your state.

He speaks like an angry prophet and, in fact, symbolizes Masters's new sense of identity as an American Jeremiah. His comments in the closing lines are an ultimatum from the Almighty ("By God!"): either destroy the profane hordes that prevent the realization of America's democratic vision or suffer Doomsday.

The recovery of America's democratic ideal is an important social goal that can indeed bring cultural renewal, but that ideal is enshrined in mythic self-perception, and cultural myth always creates a dichotomy. A "chosen people" (or "great race") always defines itself against the unchosen, the profane, who do not share the sacred vision of the culture. And through that process, differences in human culture are transmuted into differences in human nature: the chosen become the good, and others become the evil—or "vermin," as English Thornton says. In a culturally complex nation that can have tragic consequences—as Indians, Mormons, blacks, socialists, and others have discovered.

In other words, the American thrust toward the creation of a new social order contains within it the threat of repression and violent disorder, as the *Anthology* reveals. America's mythic self-perception can give rise to idealistic, culture-building heroes like the Wassons—and to jingoistic superpatriots like Many Soldiers, who crave "The thrill of carrying a gun" and want to destroy foes to fulfill "A dream of duty to country or to God." Cherishing a national ideal can bring purpose and meaning to the lives of everyday people, as "Anne Rutledge" so clearly reveals, but it can also bring disillusionment and psychological trauma, as it does to the innocent strugglers for "the dream" in "Godwin James," who end up "Sick, broken, crying, shorn of faith." A mythic national consciousness can even turn a horribly bloody civil war into "a dithyramb of recreative song" that expresses "The epic hopes of a people," as William H. Herndon points out, but it can also foster self-delusion and imperialism that brings hellish degradation and pointless death, as Harry Wilmans shows in his shockingly effective account of the Spanish-American War. Such insights reveal that *Spoon River Anthology* is a remarkably probing critique of American civic belief.

As Masters's convictions about cultural degeneracy and his quest for a restorative poetic vision demonstrate, a cultural myth may provide a simplistic explanation for complex historical developments, but it can also bring a meaningful new identity to those who embrace it. Certainly it did both for Masters. *Spoon River Anthology* was the great turning point in his career. By viewing American society as a degeneration from primal innocence, he placed himself in historical relationship to our greatest mythic poet, Whitman, whose vision of the great republic had "enthralled" him at Lewistown, and whom he regarded as a "child of Jefferson" and a "prophet of democracy."[82] He recognized that Whitman wrote for "the American tribe and the American idea," which is what Masters strove to do—and did, starting with the *Anthology*.[83] Even the word "leaves" suggests the connection to Whitman by recalling *Leaves of Grass*. As Webster Ford says, "O leaves of me / . . . themes / For hearts heroic, fearless singers and livers." And like Whitman, Masters became moralistic about literature: it had to serve the republic by helping to forge a democratically infused cultural consciousness. As Masters said in a 1926 interview, "I regard Whitman as the poet who made the commencement in the direction of a new authenticity in poetry. His chant is of the republic, always of the republic. . . . Poetry can do much for this republic. . . . It can unify and strengthen, as well as multiply the enlightened souls so that they shall be the governing force, supplanting those materialists who would continue to make of men a commercial commodity."[84] In his 1937 biographical study of the great poet, Masters says, "Whitman tried to sing America, thereby to create it." Surely in the *Anthology* Whitman's most devoted disciple also tried to sing America, thereby to restore it.[85]

Spoon River Anthology is Masters's finest work because it records the inner struggle that led to the achievement of his poetic vision and the assumption of his bardic role. The many books and poems that followed it—including *The New Spoon River*—

tended to be merely assertive and simplistic because they were not forged in the fire of self-examination. But the *Anthology* dramatized his struggle to become a version of the archetypal self-created American — the poet as Adamic cultural hero, containing within himself the vision of an uncorrupted America and coming from the spiritually infused Lincoln country to bring again that "nation / Shining with justice and truth."

This new understanding of *Spoon River Anthology* will hopefully provoke a reconsideration of its place in American literature. Despite the well-known assertion, repeated for seventy-five years, it is not simply an exposé of small-town life, akin to *Main Street* (1920) by Sinclair Lewis. It is a far more personal, experimental, and probing work. In many respects it more closely resembles the novels of John Dos Passos. Both *Spoon River Anthology* and *Manhattan Transfer* (1925) portray a huge gallery of characters struggling for self-realization within a single community, and both depict a spiritually impoverished, discordant world in which many individuals fail. Likewise, the *U.S.A.* trilogy (1930, 1932, 1936) is concerned with the historical decline of American culture and reveals the materialistic, frustrated, aimless lives of many individuals who have no commitment to the democratic ideal — just like the majority of those who inhabit Spoon River.

Viewed in this way, the most remarkable thing about *Spoon River Anthology* is that it began appearing in *Reedy's Mirror* before World War I, which was the cause of disillusionment — that central facet of the modern consciousness — for Dos Passos and so many other American writers of his generation. For Masters the disillusionment had already come, with the defeat of the Democratic cause in Bryan's presidential campaigns and the betrayal of America's national mission in the Spanish-American War, but the result was the same — a strong sense that America had gotten off the track, that the forces of commercialism and militarism had triumphed, and that social breakdown was taking place. Fifteen years before Dos Passos started publishing *U.S.A.*, Masters portrayed most Americans as frustrated, alienated citizens of a degenerated republic. But unlike the novelist, he viewed them from the inside. It is this multifaceted portrayal of the American consciousness that makes the *Anthology* one of the seminal works of twentieth-century American literature—and, perhaps, one of our most significant books of poetry.

Unlike Mark Twain, William Dean Howells, Sherwood Anderson, and others who lamented the great change wrought by industrialization and urbanization, and who yearned for an idealized past associated with their childhood, Masters asserted that a return to the Old Republic was still possible. He was, in a sense, the Jay Gatsby of American literature. He committed himself to a romantic illusion that transcended all limits, pursuing the lost Arcadia in a society that no longer resembled it—and, in fact, never had. Confronted with the massive cultural degeneration that he believed had taken place, he responded like Gatsby to Nick Carraway: "Can't repeat the past? . . . Why of course you can!"[86]

In a sense, the tragedy of Masters's life was that his poetic quest to resolve his inner conflicts and recover the American democratic ideal was successful. By viewing his past in mythic terms and returning through memory to the world of his childhood, he "authenticated" the American pastoral, which only increased his pathetic longing for "the Petersburg environment" that was gone. As *The Sangamon* and his nostalgic later lyrics so clearly show, he spent the rest of his life feeling dispossessed of the Garden. He was an Adamic poet-hero living in a ruined Eden.

As that unhappy situation suggests, Masters was both a traditionalist and a modernist. Like Edwin Arlington Robinson and Robert Frost, his subject was the American experience, and he often wrote in meter and rhyme. His native culture provided him with a meaningful place to stand, a perspective that had its roots in Whitman and Emerson and Jefferson, and his deepest desire was to express America's communal consciousness—to be the Homer of his country. But his sense of alienation from modern society and his convictions about cultural degeneracy, which prompted *Spoon River Anthology*, made him akin to T. S. Eliot, Ezra Pound, and the other modernists. Like Eliot's *The Waste Land* (1922), the *Anthology* is a kind of literary psychomachy based on the author's inner discord that reveals the spiritual disorder of the modern self and portrays a quest for regeneration. Like Pound's *Cantos* (1921-69), the *Anthology* is a kind of discontinuous epic, a quest for spiritual wholeness that provides models of exemplary conduct, good and bad, through which readers can adjust their lives. It is a tale of the tribe.[87] The poet's reflection of a mythic pattern, the return to a lost paradise, also relates his book to those more allusive and finely crafted works—and reminds us that the American myth of a New World Eden is, after all, a variation of the ancient Western myth of return to a Golden Age.

Like Eliot and Pound, Masters also created symbolic figures who represent aspects of his own consciousness. As this discussion has shown, the Spoon River villagers are not simply fictional and historical figures who speak for themselves: most of them also speak for the poet, dramatizing his views, frustrations, and conflicts. They are masks for Edgar Lee Masters, who employed them—as Eliot and Pound used their personae—to provide, not a jumble of perspectives, but an aesthetically controlled, highly personalized critique of modern culture. And the epitaph-poems are not just monologues, but dramatic monologues, like the poems of Eliot and Pound. The villagers (or most of them) are speaking to the community of Spoon River. That provides the dramatic context for their self-revelations: they are confessing their secrets to those who misunderstood, disregarded, or opposed them. The reader understands each monologue as a response to the community—a response that might have contributed to the restoration of that good, Whitmanesque, comrade-oriented America marked by interpersonal sympathy (as seen in "Aaron Hatfield"). But the responses to the community are made too late. The dead cannot change—only the reader, who is occasionally addressed as "Passer-by," a reminder of human transience. The enlarged sympathy and rekindled idealism of the reader hopefully make him or her one of the "hearts heroic" that Webster Ford anticipates. Cultural restoration must begin with the repair of alienation, with the renewal of meaning and purpose and community in American lives. In short, just like Eliot and Pound, Masters employed his symbolic, dramatic monologue technique not only to reflect, but to influence, the modern consciousness.

Of course, Masters suffers by comparison to such literary giants, for even in the *Anthology* his poetry is sometimes shallow and imprecise. Unlike most modern poets, he wrote very rapidly and seldom revised, so his poems commonly have a rough-hewn, unfinished quality. Also, he was a poor critic of his own work and never knew when he was writing badly. His language is frequently very effective, but it is also often prosaic or stilted. And he failed to see some of the deeper implications of *Spoon River Anthology*, as the two additional, inappropriate conclusions, "The Spooniad" and the "Epilogue," reveal. But his achievement is far greater than three generations of readers have recognized. He not only helped to initiate twentieth-century poetry, he created the most original poetic book since *Leaves of Grass*, forged his experience into a complex mythic image of cultural decline, struggled to resolve his inner discord and restore the American democratic ideal, and conveyed more effectively than any other American poet that the meaning of the past resides in the self.

NOTES

1. May Swenson, "Introduction," *Spoon River Anthology* (New York: Collier Books, 1962), p. 12.

2. William Marion Reedy, "The Writer of Spoon River," *Reedy's Mirror*, November 20, 1914, p. 1. (Because this article is printed on a single page, notes will not be provided for subsequent references to it.)

3. See Jensen's chapter on "Pioneer Traditionalism, 1800-40" in *Illinois: A Bicentennial History* (New York: W. W. Norton, 1978), pp. 3-31.

4. See "The Modernizers Arrive, 1830-60," in Jensen, *Illinois*, pp. 32-60.

5. Masters, *Across Spoon River: An Autobiography* (New York: Farrar and Rinehart, 1936), p. 10. (Hereafter page references to the autobiography in the text will be parenthetical and, when necessary, preceded by the abbreviation *ASR*.) The discussion of Masters's life is generally indebted to this revealing book. There is no biography of the poet, but several studies of his family background are available: Kimball Flaccus, *The Vermont Background of Edgar Lee Masters* (New York: The Author, 1954, 1955; reprinted from *Vermont History* 22-23 [January, April, July, October, 1954; January 1955]); Charles E. Burgess, "Maryland-Carolina Ancestry of Edgar Lee Masters," *Great Lakes Review: Special Double Issue* 8 (Fall 1982) and 9 (Spring 1983): 51-80; Burgess, "Edgar Lee Masters' Paternal Ancestry: A Pioneer Heritage and Influence," *Western Illinois Regional Studies* 7 (1984):

32-60; and Burgess, "Ancestral Lore in *Spoon River Anthology:* Fact and Fancy," *Papers on Language and Literature* 20 (1984): 185-204.

6. *The History of Menard and Mason Counties* (Chicago: O. L. Baskin, 1879), p. 298. Although no authors are listed on the title page, the Menard County section was written by Rev. R. D. Miller. There are various other sources of information on early Petersburg, including the *Illinois State Gazetteer and Business Directory for the Years 1864-65* (Chicago: J. C. W. Bailey, 1864), p. 514, and the *Illustrated Atlas Map of Menard County, Illinois* (Edwardsville: W. R. Brink, 1874), pp. 11, 14, 18, 23, 28, 117.

7. Masters, *The Sangamon* (New York: Farrar and Rinehart, 1942), pp. 30-31. (Hereafter page references to this book in the text will be parenthetical.) Another work in which the author views the Petersburg area as his spiritual home is "Days in the Lincoln Country," *Journal of the Illinois State Historical Society* 18 (1925-26): 779-92.

8. Masters to Edwin P. Reese, November 9, 1926, Edgar Lee Masters Papers, Illinois State Historical Library, Springfield.

9. Among the most useful sources of information on nineteenth-century Lewistown are the *Atlas Map of Fulton County, Illinois* (Davenport, Ia.: Andreas, Lyter, 1871), pp. 7, 11, 14, 98, 100; *History of Fulton County, Illinois* (Peoria: Charles C. Chapman, 1879), pp. 769-83; *Illinois State Gazetteer,* pp. 33-34; and *History of Fulton County,* ed. Jesse Heylin, bound together with *Historical Encyclopedia of Illinois,* ed. Newton Bateman and Paul Selby (Chicago: Munsell, 1908), pp. 650-55, 670-83, 688, 699-702.

10. Masters, "Father Malloy," *The Commonweal,* December 14, 1927, pp. 811-12.

11. Kimball Flaccus reprinted the 1884 poem, "The Minotaur, Bill Davidson," in "Edgar Lee Masters: A Biographical and Critical Study" (Ph.D. diss., New York University, 1952), pp. 126-28.

12. For an account of the response to Masters's depiction of the small town, see John T. Flanagan, *Edgar Lee Masters: The Spoon River Poet and His Critics* (Metuchen, N.J.: The Scarecrow Press, 1974), pp. 24-29.

13. Masters to H. L. Mencken, January 4, 1915 (misdated 1914), Folder 23, Box 3, Flaccus-Masters Archive, Special Collections Division, Georgetown University Library.

14. James Hurt, "The Sources of the Spoon: Edgar Lee Masters and the *Spoon River Anthology,*" *The Centennial Review* 24 (1980): 406.

15. Ibid., p. 420.

16. Masters, "In Memory of Alexander Dexter Masters," in *The*

Harmony of Deeper Music: Posthumous Poems of Edgar Lee Masters, ed. Frank K. Robinson (Austin: Humanities Research Center, University of Texas, 1976), p. 32.

17. Flaccus, "Edgar Lee Masters," pp. 267, 138. Also, Masters remarks in *Across Spoon River,* "It was Poe's stories which had led me to metaphysics" (p. 90).

18. Flaccus includes a document by Masters entitled "Books Read at Seventeen to Twenty-One," pp. 264-67, and Edwin P. Reese refers to the poet's early reading in an untitled typescript, Folder 2, Edgar Lee Masters Papers, Illinois State Historical Library. See also Masters, *Across Spoon River,* pp. 77, 84-85, 100, 109-20.

19. Masters's philosophical naturalism is evident in a number of poems, such as "Hymn to the Dead" and "Epitaph for Us" in *Starved Rock* (New York: Macmillan, 1919), pp. 5-9, 111-13, and "Nature" in *The Open Sea* (New York: Macmillan, 1921), pp. 299-302. Later in his career he sometimes referred to the presence of "Mind" in nature. That vitalism was probably the result of reading Henri Bergson's *Creative Evolution* (1907), which asserts that an *élan vital,* or life-drive, permeates the natural world and guides the evolutionary process. See "Hymn to the Earth," "Hymn to Nature," and "Ultimate Selection" in *Invisible Landscapes* (New York: Macmillan, 1935), pp. 8-18, 46-51, 52-59.

20. "The Origin of 'Spoon River,'" *St. Louis Post-Dispatch,* March 29, 1918, p. 21. (Because this article appears on a single page, notes will not be provided for subsequent references to it.)

21. Letters from the Lewistown correspondent to the *Fulton County Ledger* in 1889 often refer to members of the Masters family, and they mention such people as Lute Breeden, Margaret George, and William S. Strode, so they were almost certainly written by the poet.

22. Hurt, "The Sources of the Spoon," pp. 412, 415-17.

23. Masters, typescript of "The Genesis of Spoon River," p. 16, Edgar Lee Masters Collection, Clifton Waller Barrett Library, Manuscripts Division, Special Collections Department, University of Virginia Library.

24. Masters, "Worlds," *Poetry* 21 (October 1922): 31.

25. The most helpful brief commentary on Spinoza's thought is John Wild's introduction to *Spinoza: Selections* (1930; New York: Charles Scribner's Sons, 1958), pp. xi-lix, and that volume also contains Spinoza's *Ethics* (c. 1678), his most important work, as well as selected shorter writings. A very helpful volume of studies is *Spinoza: New Perspectives,* ed. Robert W. Shahan and J. I. Biro (Norman:

University of Oklahoma Press, 1978), and perhaps the most useful of those articles for students of Masters are William Sacksteder, "Spinoza on Part and Whole: The Worm's Eye View," pp. 139-59, and Douglas Lewis, "On the Aims and Methods of Spinoza's Philosophy," pp. 217-34. For a more thorough, technical study of Spinoza's thought, see R. J. Delahunty, *Spinoza* (London: Routledge & Kegan Paul, 1985).

26. Masters, as quoted in David Karsner, "Sifting Out the Hearts of Men," *New York Herald Tribune,* December 12, 1926, p. 28. This important interview was later included in a collection of interviews by Karsner: "Edgar Lee Masters," *Sixteen Authors to One* (New York: Lewis Copeland, 1928), pp. 125-42.

27. The important influences of Goethe and Shelley are discussed in Ronald Primeau, *Beyond Spoon River* (Austin: University of Texas Press, 1981), pp. 46-52, 116-38. However, Primeau does not point out the influence of Goethe on *Spoon River Anthology.*

28. Masters, "Nature," *The Open Sea,* p. 301.

29. Wild, "Introduction," *Spinoza,* p. lviii.

30. Goethe, "One and All," in *The Permanent Goethe,* ed. Thomas Mann (New York: The Dial Press, 1948), p. 644.

31. The discussion of Dreiser's influence is indebted to Robert D. Narveson, "Edgar Lee Masters' *Spoon River Anthology:* Background, Composition and Reputation" (Ph.D. diss., University of Chicago, 1962), pp. 75-81.

32. Masters to Theodore Dreiser, November 27, 1912, Theodore Dreiser Collection, Special Collections, Van Pelt Library, University of Pennsylvania.

33. Masters to Theodore Dreiser, December 3, 1912, Theodore Dreiser Collection.

34. Narveson, "Masters' *Anthology,*" pp. 78-79. The typescript of "The Oakford Derby" is in the Theodore Dreiser Collection.

35. Masters to Theodore Dreiser, August 20, 1914, Theodore Dreiser Collection.

36. For brief discussions of the Sandburg influence, see Narveson, "Masters' *Anthology,*" pp. 85-87; Lois Hartley, *Spoon River Revisited,* Ball State Monograph Number 1 (Muncie, Ind.: Ball State Teachers College, 1963), pp. 15-16; and John H. Wrenn and Margaret M. Wrenn, *Edgar Lee Masters* (Boston: Twayne, 1983), pp. 37-40.

37. Masters, "To William Marion Reedy," *Toward the Gulf* (New York: Macmillan, 1918), p. xi. The most helpful discussion of the influence of *The Greek Anthology* on Masters is in Willis Barnstone's

introduction to the modern edition of *The New Spoon River* (1924; New York: Macmillan, 1968), pp. xix-xxi.

38. Goethe, "The Dance of Death," in *The Permanent Goethe,* p. 344.

39. William Cullen Bryant, "Earth," in *Poetical Works of William Cullen Bryant* (New York: D. Appleton, 1909), pp. 161-62.

40. R. D. Miller, *Past and Present of Menard County, Illinois* (Chicago: S. J. Clarke, 1905), p. 92. Charles E. Burgess asserts that Masters was influenced by Miller in "Masters and Some Mentors," *Papers on Language and Literature* 10 (1974): 183-85.

41. William T. Davidson, "Major Newton Walker," Lewistown *Fulton Democrat,* September 20, 1899, p. 1.

42. Although he does not explore the connection, Joseph Allen Tetlow suggests that "Paracelsus" and "Sordello" influenced "Elijah Browning." See "The Intellectual Odyssey of Edgar Lee Masters, 1868-1950" (Ph.D. diss., Brown University, 1969), p. 111. Tetlow also discusses Masters's little-known essay "Browning as a Philosopher," pp. 101-8.

43. "Pauline," in *Robert Browning: The Poems,* vol. 1, ed. John Pettigrew and Thomas J. Collins (New Haven, Conn.: Yale University Press, 1981), p. 33.

44. "Paracelsus," ibid., p. 54.

45. "Sordello," ibid., p. 286.

46. Ibid., p. 191.

47. Ibid., pp. 234, 249.

48. Masters, as quoted in Karsner, "Sifting Out the Hearts of Men," p. 28.

49. Masters, "The Genesis of Spoon River," *The American Mercury* 28 (January 1933): 51.

50. See, for example, "The Story of Daphne" in the Myths and Legends Series volume by H. A. Guerber, *Greece and Rome* (London: Bracken Books, 1985), pp. 50-51.

51. There are many books and articles related to the myth of America as a New World Eden. These are some of the most helpful: Henry Nash Smith, *Virgin Land* (Cambridge, Mass.: Harvard University Press, 1950); R. W. B. Lewis, *The American Adam* (Chicago: University of Chicago Press, 1955); Leo Marx, *The Machine in the Garden* (New York: Oxford University Press, 1964); David W. Noble, *The Eternal Adam and the New World Garden* (New York: George Braziller, 1968); and David Mogen, "The Frontier Archetype and the Myth of America: Patterns That Shape the American Dream," in *The Frontier Experience and the American Dream,* ed. David

Mogen et al. (College Station: Texas A and M University, 1989), pp. 15-30.

52. Masters, "The Genesis of Spoon River," p. 53.

53. Masters, "Presenting Emerson," in *The Living Thoughts of Emerson* (New York: Longmans, Green, 1940), p. 17.

54. Masters, "A Democrat Looks at His Party," *The American Mercury* 27 (January 1932): 90.

55. Masters, *The Tale of Chicago* (New York: G. P. Putnam's, 1933), p. 66.

56. Masters, "I am America," *The Independent,* November 23, 1918, p. 264.

57. Masters, "The Great Race Passes," *Reedy's Mirror,* January 8, 1920, p. 22.

58. Masters, *Domesday Book* (New York: Macmillan, 1920), dedication page.

59. Robert van Gelder, "An Interview with Mr. Edgar Lee Masters," *New York Times Book Review,* February 15, 1942, p. 2.

60. Masters, "Give Us Back Our Country," *Invisible Landscapes,* p. 151.

61. Masters, "The Genesis of Spoon River," p. 55.

62. Northrop Frye, *The Stubborn Structure* (Ithaca, N.Y.: Cornell University Press, 1970), p. 301.

63. See the discussion of Bancroft's influence on the myth of America in Noble, *The Eternal Adam,* pp. 6-8.

64. Masters, "The Genesis of Spoon River," p. 52. See William H. Herndon and Jesse W. Weik, *Abraham Lincoln* (New York: D. Appleton, 1928), 1:120-22.

65. Masters, "The Genesis of Spoon River," p. 40.

66. Masters, typescript of "The Genesis of Spoon River," p. 40.

67. Marx, *The Machine in the Garden,* p. 141.

68. Masters, *Whitman* (New York: Charles Scribner's Sons, 1937), p. 295.

69. Jefferson, *Notes on the State of Virginia,* ed. William Peden (Chapel Hill: University of North Carolina Press, 1955), p. 165.

70. Walt Whitman, "Preface 1855 — Leaves of Grass," in *Leaves of Grass,* ed. Sculley Bradley and Harold W. Blodgett (New York: W. W. Norton, 1973), pp. 713-14.

71. Ibid., p. 722.

72. Ibid., p. 718.

73. Masters later strove to deal with his sexual conflict by creating two alter egos who were in continual opposition to one another. He called them "Dr. Lucius Atherton" and "Elmer Chubb, L.L.D,

Ph.D." Atherton was a rake whose interest in women was purely sexual, and Chubb was a religiously inspired smut-hound who strove to eliminate all reference to sexuality. Masters had business cards printed for Atherton and Chubb, which he handed out to friends, and he even had flyers printed, announcing lectures by them, which he also distributed. Moreover, when he wanted to play the role of Atherton, he wrote sexually explicit letters to his old friend Edwin P. Reese of Lewistown, which he often signed "Lewd" (his comic abbreviation for "Lucius"), and when he wanted to play the role of Chubb, he wrote letters to newspapers and magazines, promoting outrageously repressive views. When his Lucius Atherton alter ego turned to writing poetry, Masters often called him "Lute Puckett." Under those two names the poet wrote limericks and other obscene poems, which he sometimes read to friends. Atherton, Puckett, and Chubb materials can be found in folders 1-4 of the Edgar Lee Masters Papers at the Illinois State Historical Library and in the Dorothy Dow Scrapbook, Edgar Lee Masters Collection, Western Illinois University Library. For an account of this aspect of Masters's personality by a friend, see Eunice Tietjens, The World at My Shoulder (New York: Macmillan, 1938), pp. 46-47. See also Hartley, Spoon River Revisited, p. 18, n.57.

74. Sacvan Bercovitch, The American Jeremiad (Madison: University of Wisconsin Press, 1978), p. 72.

75. Whitman, "Preface 1855 — Leaves of Grass," pp. 713, 715, 722, 729.

76. Goethe, Faust: Part Two, tr. Philip Wayne (Harmondsworth, Eng.: Penguin Books, 1959), p. 269.

77. Masters, as quoted in van Gelder, "An Interview with Masters," p. 2.

78. Masters, "Presenting Emerson," p. 30.

79. Masters, Skeeters Kirby (New York: Macmillan, 1923), p. 328. The quotation from Faust appears on p. 390.

80. William T. Davidson, "Lewistown's Fourth," Lewistown Fulton Democrat, July 9, 1891, p. 4.

81. The following studies have influenced the present analysis of the myth of America, although none of them mentions Spoon River Anthology: Bercovitch, The American Jeremiad; Northrop Frye, The Critical Path (Bloomington: Indiana University Press, 1971), chap. 5; Richard Slotkin, Regeneration through Violence (Middleton, Conn.: Wesleyan University Press, 1973), and Slotkin, The Fatal Environment (New York: Atheneum, 1985).

82. Masters, Whitman, pp. 114, 326.

83. Ibid., p. 306.

84. Karsner, "Sifting Out the Hearts of Men," p. 28.

85. Masters, *Whitman*, p. 106.

86. F. Scott Fitzgerald, *The Great Gatsby* (New York: Charles Scribner's Sons, 1925), p. 111.

87. This view of the modern American verse epic was influenced by Michael André Bernstein, *The Tale of the Tribe: Ezra Pound and the Modern Verse Epic* (Princeton, N.J.: Princeton University Press, 1980), pp. 3-25.

SELECT BIBLIOGRAPHY

Burgess, Charles E. "Masters and Some Mentors." *Papers on Language and Literature* 10 (1974): 175-201.

——. "*Spoon River*: Politics and Poetry." *Papers on Language and Literature* 23 (1987): 347-63.

——. "The Use of Local Lore in *Spoon River Anthology*." Masters thesis, Southern Illinois University, Edwardsville, 1969.

Childs, Herbert E. "Agrarianism and Sex: Edgar Lee Masters and the Modern Spirit." *Sewanee Review* 41 (1933): 331-43.

Chandler, Josephine Craven. "The Spoon River Country." *Journal of the Illinois State Historical Society* 14 (1921-22): 252-39.

Duffey, Bernard. *The Chicago Renaissance in American Letters.* East Lansing: Michigan State College Press, 1954.

Flaccus, Kimball. "Edgar Lee Masters: A Biographical and Critical Study." Ph.D. diss., New York University, 1952.

Flanagan, John T. *Edgar Lee Masters: The Spoon River Poet and His Critics.* Metuchen, N.J.: Scarecrow Press, 1974.

Hallwas, John E., and Dennis J. Reader, eds. *The Vision of This Land: Studies of Vachel Lindsay, Edgar Lee Masters, and Carl Sandburg.* Macomb: Western Illinois University, 1976.

Hartley, Lois. *Spoon River Revisited.* Ball State Monograph Number 1. Muncie, Ind.: Ball State Teachers College, 1963.

Hilfer, Anthony Channell. *The Revolt from the Village, 1915-30.* Chapel Hill: University of North Carolina Press, 1969.

Hurt, James. "The Sources of the Spoon: Edgar Lee Masters and the *Spoon River Anthology*." *The Centennial Review* 24 (1980): 403-31.

Kramer, Dale. *Chicago Renaissance: The Literary Life of the Midwest, 1900-1930.* New York: Appleton-Century, 1966.

Masters, Edgar Lee. *Across Spoon River: An Autobiography.* With an introduction by Ronald Primeau. Urbana: University of Illinois Press, 1991.

————. "The Genesis of Spoon River," *The American Mercury* 28 (January 1933): 38-55.

————. *The Sangamon.* With an introduction by Charles E. Burgess. Urbana: University of Illinois Press, 1988.

Narveson, Robert D. "Edgar Lee Masters' *Spoon River Anthology*: Background, Composition and Reputation." Ph.D. diss., University of Chicago, 1962.

————. "*Spoon River Anthology*: An Introduction." *MidAmerica VII* (1980): 52-72.

Primeau, Ronald. *Beyond* Spoon River: *The Legacy of Edgar Lee Masters.* Austin: University of Texas Press, 1981.

Russell, Herbert K. "Edgar Lee Masters." In *Dictionary of Literary Biography: American Poets, 1880-1945.* Third Series, Part 1, edited by Peter Quartermain, pp. 293-312. Detroit: Gale Research, 1987.

————. "Edgar Lee Masters: A Selective Guide to Secondary Materials, 1914-50." *Bulletin of Bibliography and Magazine Notes* 37 (June 1980): 80-89.

Tetlow, Joseph Allen. "The Intellectual and Spiritual Odyssey of Edgar Lee Masters, 1868-1950." Ph.D. diss., Brown University, 1969.

Wagner, Linda W. "Edgar Lee Masters 1868-1950." In *American Writers: A Collection of Literary Biographies.* Supplement 1, Part 2, edited by Leonard Unger. New York: Charles Scribner's Sons, 1979, pp. 454-78.

Weeg, Mary Margaret. "The Prose of Edgar Lee Masters: Its Relation to His Views and Its Significance in His Canon." Ph.D. diss., Indiana University, 1964.

Wrenn, John H., and Margaret M. Wrenn. *Edgar Lee Masters.* Boston: Twayne, 1983.

Yatron, Michael. *America's Literary Revolt.* New York: Philosophical Library, 1959.

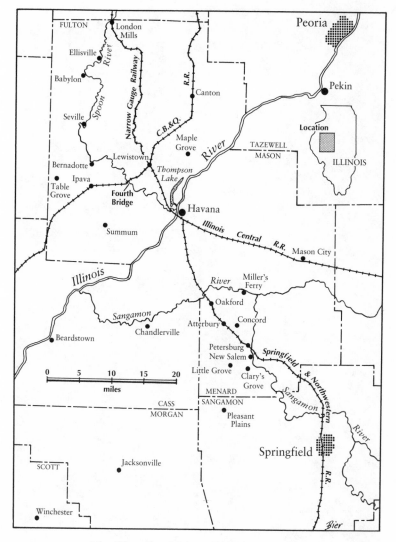

The Edgar Lee Masters Country, c. 1900.

Edgar Lee Masters at about the time *Spoon River Anthology* appeared
(courtesy of the Illinois State Historical Library).

The Masters family c. 1883. *From the left:* Madeline and Thomas (with the slate), Emma and Hardin, and the poet—then known as Lee (courtesy of Dartmouth College Library).

The poet's early home town, Petersburg, in 1890, as viewed from the east, looking across the Sangamon River (from the *Menard-Salem-Lincoln Souvenir Album*, 1893).

The muddy main street of Petersburg in 1890, showing local boys watching a team of surveyors. In the background is the dome of the Menard County Courthouse (from the *Menard-Salem-Lincoln Souvenir Album*).

Above: The poet's beloved grandparents, Lucinda and Squire Davis Masters, who inspired "Lucinda Matlock" and "Aaron Hatfield" (from Chandler, "The Spoon River Country," courtesy of the *Illinois Historical Journal,* published by the Illinois Historic Preservation Agency). *Below:* Their farmhouse at Sand Ridge, near Petersburg, where the grandparents are standing with other relatives (courtesy of the Edgar Lee Masters Memorial Museum).

Three Petersburg-area pioneers who are characterized in the *Anthology:* Lincoln's law partner William H. Herndon and Lincoln's old friend Hannah Armstrong (courtesy of the Illinois State Historical Library), and in the lower right, John ("Fiddler") Jones (from Chandler, courtesy of the *Illinois Historical Journal*). The photographs are c. 1880s.

The photographs on these pages tell the story of the famous Ann Rutledge grave, which has been a historic shrine since William H. Herndon publicized the Lincoln-Rutledge love story in the late 1860s. The top photograph on the facing page shows the Old Concord Cemetery, a few miles from the Masters farm, where the poet saw the grave as a boy and local residents erected a sign c. 1880 (courtesy of the Illinois State Historical Library). The grave was moved to Petersburg's Oakland Cemetery in 1890, when the photograph on this page was taken (from the *Menard-Salem-Lincoln Souvenir Album*). The chair invites the onlooker to reflect on the life of the famous pioneer woman. By the 1920s Masters's "Anne Rutledge" had become a famous poem, so it was carved on a new granite headstone, shown here (courtesy of the Edgar Lee Masters Memorial Museum).

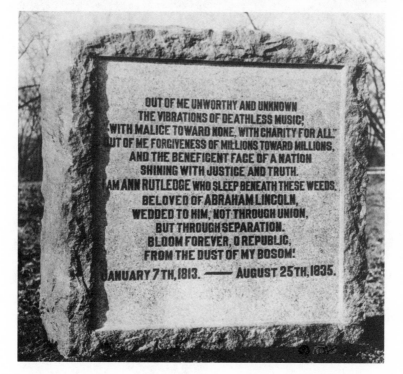

The Spoon River, flowing past the old mill at Bernadotte in the late nine-
teenth century. Masters often visited this picturesque area, located ten miles
west of Lewistown. The speaker in "Isaiah Beethoven" refers to this scene
(courtesy of Dartmouth College Library).

Above: The Lewis W. Ross mansion in Lewistown, which was the basis for "the great mansion-house" mentioned in "Washington McNeely" (courtesy of the Edgar Lee Masters Memorial Museum). The "cedar tree on the lawn" is at the left. *Below:* The Fulton County Courthouse in Lewistown, c. 1880s (from the *Standard Atlas of Fulton County,* 1912). It was burned by an incendiary in 1894, an event depicted in the poem "Silas Dement."

William T. Davidson was a Lewistown newspaper editor whom Masters hated, and he inspired the characterizations in "Editor Whedon," "Deacon Taylor," and "Robert Davidson" (from Jesse Heylin, ed., *History of Fulton County,* 1908). He eventually married Margaret George, shown below.

Margaret George, the brilliant young woman whom Masters loved as a teenager in Lewistown (courtesy of the Edgar Lee Masters Memorial Museum). She inspired the characterizations in "Caroline Branson," "Amelia Garrick," "Julia Miller," and "Louise Smith."

Julia Brown, a teacher and friend of the poet in Lewistown (courtesy of the Flaccus-Masters Archive, Special Collections Division, Georgetown University Library). She inspired the characterizations in "Margaret Fuller Slack" and "Tennessee Claflin Shope."

William S. Strode, the physician and naturalist of Bernadotte and, later, Lewistown, whose second wife was Julia Brown. He invited Masters to join the Fulton County Scientific Association and was later the inspiration for "William Jones" (from Chandler, courtesy of the *Illinois Historical Journal*).

The gravestone of William Cullen Bryant in Lewistown's Oak Hill Cemetery. He inspired "Percey Bysshe Shelley," which refers to this shaft topped by the statue of a woman (photograph by Ray Bial).

Above: The gravestone of Nathan Beadles in Lewistown's Oak Hill Cemetery. His life is reflected in "Nicholas Bindle" (photograph by Ray Bial). *Below:* The grave marker of Henry Willis Phelps and Elizabeth Turner Phelps in Lewistown's Oak Hill Cemetery. Their lives are reflected in "Ralph Rhodes" and "Amanda Barker" (photograph by Ray Bial).

The poet's gravestone at Oakland Cemetery in Petersburg. It is next to the graves of his beloved grandparents (courtesy of the Flaccus-Masters Archive, Special Collections Division, Georgetown University Library, and Herbert Georg Studio, Springfield, Illinois). The lines on the bronze plate are from "To-morrow is My Birthday," a favorite poem that first appeared in *Toward the Gulf*:

> Good friends, let's to the fields . . .
> After a little walk, and by your pardon
> I think I'll sleep. There is no sweeter thing
> Nor fate more blessed than to sleep.

SPOON RIVER ANTHOLOGY

CONTENTS

The Hill

Where are Elmer, Herman, Bert, Tom and Charley,
The weak of will, the strong of arm, the clown, the boozer, the
   fighter?
All, all are sleeping on the hill.

One passed in a fever,
One was burned in a mine,
One was killed in a brawl,
One died in a jail,
One fell from a bridge toiling for children and wife—
All, all are sleeping, sleeping, sleeping on the hill.

Where are Ella, Kate, Mag, Lizzie and Edith,
The tender heart, the simple soul, the loud, the proud, the happy
   one?—
All, all are sleeping on the hill.

One died in shameful child-birth,
One of a thwarted love,
One at the hands of a brute in a brothel,
One of a broken pride, in the search for heart's desire;
One after life in far-away London and Paris
Was brought to her little space by Ella and Kate and Mag—
All, all are sleeping, sleeping, sleeping on the hill.

Where are Uncle Isaac and Aunt Emily,
And old Towny Kincaid and Sevigne Houghton,
And Major Walker who had talked
With venerable men of the revolution?—
All, all are sleeping on the hill.

They brought them dead sons from the war,
And daughters whom life had crushed,
And their children fatherless, crying—
All, all are sleeping, sleeping, sleeping on the hill.

Where is Old Fiddler Jones
Who played with life all his ninety years,
Braving the sleet with bared breast,
Drinking, rioting, thinking neither of wife nor kin,
Nor gold, nor love, nor heaven?
Lo! he babbles of the fish-frys of long ago,
Of the horse-races of long ago at Clary's Grove,
Of what Abe Lincoln said
One time at Springfield.

Hod Putt

Here I lie close to the grave
Of Old Bill Piersol,
Who grew rich trading with the Indians, and who
Afterwards took the bankrupt law
And emerged from it richer than ever.
Myself grown tired of toil and poverty
And beholding how Old Bill and others grew in wealth,
Robbed a traveler one night near Proctor's Grove,
Killing him unwittingly while doing so,
For the which I was tried and hanged.
That was my way of going into bankruptcy.
Now we who took the bankrupt law in our respective ways
Sleep peacefully side by side.

Ollie McGee

Have you seen walking through the village
A man with downcast eyes and haggard face?
That is my husband who, by secret cruelty
Never to be told, robbed me of my youth and my beauty;
Till at last, wrinkled and with yellow teeth,
And with broken pride and shameful humility,
I sank into the grave.
But what think you gnaws at my husband's heart?
The face of what I was, the face of what he made me!
These are driving him to the place where I lie.
In death, therefore, I am avenged.

Fletcher McGee

She took my strength by minutes,
She took my life by hours,
She drained me like a fevered moon
That saps the spinning world.
The days went by like shadows,
The minutes wheeled like stars.
She took the pity from my heart
And made it into smiles.
She was a hunk of sculptor's clay,
My secret thoughts were fingers:
They flew behind her pensive brow
And lined it deep with pain.
They set the lips, and sagged the cheeks,
And drooped the eyes with sorrow.
My soul had entered in the clay,
Fighting like seven devils.
It was not mine, it was not hers;
She held it, but its struggles
Modeled a face she hated,
And a face I feared to see.
I beat the windows, shook the bolts.
I hid me in a corner—
And then she died and haunted me,
And hunted me for life.

Robert Fulton Tanner

If a man could bite the giant hand
That catches and destroys him,
As I was bitten by a rat
While demonstrating my patent trap,
In my hardware store that day.
But a man can never avenge himself
On the monstrous ogre Life.
You enter the room—that's being born;
And then you must live—work out your soul.
Aha! the bait that you crave is in view:
A woman with money you want to marry,
Prestige, place, or power in the world.
But there's work to do and things to conquer—
Oh, yes! the wires that screen the bait.
At last you get in—but you hear a step:
The ogre, Life, comes into the room,
(He was waiting and heard the clang of the spring)
To watch you nibble the wondrous cheese,
And stare with his burning eyes at you,
And scowl and laugh, and mock and curse you,
Running up and down in the trap,
Until your misery bores him.

Cassius Hueffer

They have chiseled on my stone the words:
"His life was gentle, and the elements so mixed in him
That nature might stand up and say to all the world,
This was a man."
Those who knew me smile
As they read this empty rhetoric.

My epitaph should have been:
"Life was not gentle to him,
And the elements so mixed in him
That he made warfare on life,
In the which he was slain."
While I lived I could not cope with slanderous tongues;
Now that I am dead I must submit to an epitaph
Graven by a fool!

Serepta Mason

My life's blossom might have bloomed on all sides
Save for a bitter wind which stunted my petals
On the side of me which you in the village could see.
From the dust I lift a voice of protest:
My flowering side you never saw!
Ye living ones, ye are fools indeed
Who do not know the ways of the wind
And the unseen forces
That govern the processes of life.

Amanda Barker

Henry got me with child,
Knowing that I could not bring forth life
Without losing my own.
In my youth therefore I entered the portals of dust.
Traveler, it is believed in the village where I lived
That Henry loved me with a husband's love,
But I proclaim from the dust
That he slew me to gratify his hatred.

Constance Hately

You praise my self-sacrifice, Spoon River,
In rearing Irene and Mary,
Orphans of my older sister!
And you censure Irene and Mary
For their contempt for me!
But praise not my self-sacrifice,
And censure not their contempt;
I reared them, I cared for them, true enough!—
But I poisoned my benefactions
With constant reminders of their dependence.

Chase Henry

In life I was the town drunkard;
When I died the priest denied me burial
In holy ground,
The which redounded to my good fortune.
For the Protestants bought this lot,
And buried my body here,
Close to the grave of the banker Nicholas,
And of his wife Priscilla.
Take note, ye prudent and pious souls,
Of the cross-currents in life
Which bring honor to the dead, who lived in shame.

Harry Carey Goodhue

You never marveled, dullards of Spoon River,
When Chase Henry voted against the saloons
To revenge himself for being shut off.
But none of you was keen enough
To follow my steps, or trace me home
As Chase's spiritual brother.
Do you remember when I fought
The bank and the courthouse ring,
For pocketing the interest on public funds?
And when I fought our leading citizens
For making the poor the pack-horses of the taxes?
And when I fought the water works
For stealing streets and raising rates?
And when I fought the businessmen
Who fought me in these fights?
Then do you remember:
That staggering up from the wreck of defeat,
And the wreck of a ruined career,
I slipped from my cloak my last ideal,
Hidden from all eyes until then,
Like the cherished jawbone of an ass,
And smote the bank and the water works,
And the businessmen with prohibition,
And made Spoon River pay the cost
Of the fights that I had lost?

Judge Somers

How does it happen, tell me,
That I who was most erudite of lawyers,
Who knew Blackstone and Coke
Almost by heart, who made the greatest speech
The court-house ever heard, and wrote
A brief that won the praise of Justice Breese—
How does it happen, tell me,
That I lie here unmarked, forgotten,
While Chase Henry, the town drunkard,
Has a marble block, topped by an urn,
Wherein Nature, in a mood ironical,
Has sown a flowering weed?

Kinsey Keene

Your attention, Thomas Rhodes, president of the bank;
Coolbaugh Whedon, editor of the *Argus;*
Rev. Peet, pastor of the leading church;
A. D. Blood, several times Mayor of Spoon River;
And finally all of you, members of the Social Purity Club—
Your attention to Cambronne's dying words,
Standing with the heroic remnant
Of Napoleon's guard on Mount Saint Jean
At the battlefield of Waterloo,
When Maitland, the Englishman, called to them:
"Surrender, brave Frenchmen!"—
There at close of day with the battle hopelessly lost,
And hordes of men no longer the army
Of the great Napoleon
Streamed from the field like ragged strips
Of thunder clouds in the storm.
Well, what Cambronne said to Maitland
Ere the English fire made smooth the brow of the hill
Against the sinking light of day
Say I to you, and all of you,
And to you, O world.
And I charge you to carve it
Upon my stone.

Benjamin Pantier

Together in this grave lie Benjamin Pantier, attorney at law,
And Nig, his dog, constant companion, solace and friend.
Down the gray road, friends, children, men and women,
Passing one by one out of life, left me till I was alone
With Nig for partner, bed-fellow, comrade in drink.
In the morning of life I knew aspiration and saw glory.
Then she, who survives me, snared my soul
With a snare which bled me to death,
Till I, once strong of will, lay broken, indifferent,
Living with Nig in a room back of a dingy office.
Under my jaw-bone is snuggled the bony nose of Nig—
Our story is lost in silence. Go by, mad world!

Mrs. Benjamin Pantier

I know that he told that I snared his soul
With a snare which bled him to death.
And all the men loved him,
And most of the women pitied him.
But suppose you are really a lady, and have delicate tastes,
And loathe the smell of whiskey and onions.
And the rhythm of Wordsworth's "Ode" runs in your ears,
While he goes about from morning till night
Repeating bits of that common thing,
"Oh, why should the spirit of mortal be proud?"
And then, suppose:
You are a woman well endowed,
And the only man with whom the law and morality
Permit you to have the marital relation
Is the very man that fills you with disgust
Every time you think of it—while you think of it
Every time you see him?
That's why I drove him away from home
To live with his dog in a dingy room
Back of his office.

Reuben Pantier

Well, Emily Sparks, your prayers were not wasted,
Your love was not all in vain.
I owe whatever I was in life
To your hope that would not give me up,
To your love that saw me still as good.
Dear Emily Sparks, let me tell you the story.
I pass the effect of my father and mother;
The milliner's daughter made me trouble
And out I went in the world,
Where I passed through every peril known
Of wine and women and joy of life.
One night, in a room in the Rue de Rivoli,
I was drinking wine with a black-eyed cocotte,
And the tears swam into my eyes.
She thought they were amorous tears and smiled
For thought of her conquest over me.
But my soul was three thousand miles away,
In the days when you taught me in Spoon River.
And just because you no more could love me,
Nor pray for me, nor write me letters,
The eternal silence of you spoke instead.
And the black-eyed cocotte took the tears for hers,
As well as the deceiving kisses I gave her.
Somehow, from that hour, I had a new vision—
Dear Emily Sparks!

Emily Sparks

Where is my boy, my boy—
In what far part of the world?
The boy I loved best of all in the school?—
I, the teacher, the old maid, the virgin heart,
Who made them all my children.
Did I know my boy aright,
Thinking of him as spirit aflame,
Active, ever aspiring?
Oh, boy, boy, for whom I prayed and prayed
In many a watchful hour at night,
Do you remember the letter I wrote you
Of the beautiful love of Christ?
And whether you ever took it or not,
My boy, wherever you are,
Work for your soul's sake,
That all the clay of you, all the dross of you,
May yield to the fire of you,
Till the fire is nothing but light!...
Nothing but light!

Trainor, the Druggist

Only the chemist can tell, and not always the chemist,
What will result from compounding
Fluids or solids.
And who can tell
How men and women will interact
On each other, or what children will result?
There were Benjamin Pantier and his wife,
Good in themselves, but evil toward each other:
He oxygen, she hydrogen,
Their son, a devastating fire.
I Trainor, the druggist, a mixer of chemicals,
Killed while making an experiment,
Lived unwedded.

Daisy Fraser

Did you ever hear of Editor Whedon
Giving to the public treasury any of the money he received
For supporting candidates for office?
Or for writing up the canning factory
To get people to invest?
Or for suppressing the facts about the bank,
When it was rotten and ready to break?
Did you ever hear of the Circuit Judge
Helping anyone except the "Q" railroad,
Or the bankers? Or did Rev. Peet or Rev. Sibley
Give any part of their salary, earned by keeping still,
Or speaking out as the leaders wished them to do,
To the building of the water works?
But I, Daisy Fraser, who always passed
Along the streets through rows of nods and smiles,
And coughs and words such as "there she goes,"
Never was taken before Justice Arnett
Without contributing ten dollars and costs
To the school fund of Spoon River!

Benjamin Fraser

Their spirits beat upon mine
Like the wings of a thousand butterflies.
I closed my eyes and felt their spirits vibrating.
I closed my eyes, yet I knew when their lashes
Fringed their cheeks from downcast eyes,
And when they turned their heads,
And when their garments clung to them,
Or fell from them, in exquisite draperies.
Their spirits watched my ecstasy
With wide looks of starry unconcern.
Their spirits looked upon my torture;
They drank it as it were the water of life,
With reddened cheeks, brightened eyes.
The rising flame of my soul made their spirits gilt,
Like the wings of a butterfly drifting suddenly into sunlight.
And they cried to me for life, life, life.
But in taking life for myself,
In seizing and crushing their souls,
As a child crushes grapes and drinks
From its palms the purple juice,
I came to this wingless void,
Where neither red, nor gold, nor wine,
Nor the rhythm of life is known.

Minerva Jones

I am Minerva, the village poetess,
Hooted at, jeered at by the Yahoos of the street
For my heavy body, cock-eye, and rolling walk,
And all the more when "Butch" Weldy
Captured me after a brutal hunt.
He left me to my fate with Doctor Meyers;
And I sank into death, growing numb from the feet up,
Like one stepping deeper and deeper into a stream of ice.
Will someone go to the village newspaper
And gather into a book the verses I wrote?—
I thirsted so for love!
I hungered so for life!

"Indignation" Jones

You would not believe, would you,
That I came from good Welsh stock?
That I was purer blooded than the white trash here?
And of more direct lineage than the New Englanders
And Virginians of Spoon River?
You would not believe that I had been to school
And read some books.
You saw me only as a run-down man,
With matted hair and beard
And ragged clothes.
Sometimes a man's life turns into a cancer
From being bruised and continually bruised,
And swells into a purplish mass,
Like growths on stalks of corn.
Here was I, a carpenter, mired in a bog of life
Into which I walked, thinking it was a meadow,
With a slattern for a wife, and poor Minerva, my daughter
Whom you tormented and drove to death.
So I crept, crept, like a snail through the days
Of my life.
No more you hear my footsteps in the morning,
Resounding on the hollow sidewalk,
Going to the grocery store for a little corn meal
And a nickel's worth of bacon.

Doctor Meyers

No other man, unless it was Doc Hill,
Did more for people in this town than I.
And all the weak, the halt, the improvident
And those who could not pay flocked to me.
I was good-hearted, easy Doctor Meyers.
I was healthy, happy, in comfortable fortune,
Blest with a congenial mate, my children raised,
All wedded, doing well in the world.
And then one night, Minerva, the poetess,
Came to me in her trouble, crying.
I tried to help her out—she died—
They indicted me, the newspapers disgraced me,
My wife perished of a broken heart,
And pneumonia finished me.

Mrs. Meyers

He protested all his life long
That newspapers lied about him villainously;
That he was not at fault for Minerva's fall,
But only tried to help her.
Poor soul so sunk in sin he could not see
That even trying to help her, as he called it,
He had broken the law human and divine.
Passers-by, an ancient admonition to you:
If your ways would be ways of pleasantness,
And all your pathways peace,
Love God and keep his commandments.

"Butch" Weldy

After I got religion and steadied down
They gave me a job in the canning works,
And every morning I had to fill
The tank in the yard with gasoline,
That fed the blow-fires in the sheds
To heat the soldering irons.
And I mounted a rickety ladder to do it,
Carrying buckets full of the stuff.
One morning, as I stood there pouring,
The air grew still and seemed to heave,
And I shot up as the tank exploded,
And down I came with both legs broken
And my eyes burned crisp as a couple of eggs,
For someone left a blow-fire going,
And something sucked the flame in the tank.
The Circuit Judge said whoever did it
Was a fellow-servant of mine, and so
Old Rhodes' son didn't have to pay me.
And I sat on the witness stand as blind
As Jack the Fiddler, saying over and over,
"I didn't know him at all."

Knowlt Hoheimer

I was the first fruits of the battle of Missionary Ridge.
When I felt the bullet enter my heart
I wished I had stayed at home and gone to jail
For stealing the hogs of Curl Trenary,
Instead of running away and joining the army.
Rather a thousand times the county jail
Than to lie under this marble figure with wings,
And this granite pedestal
Bearing the words, *"Pro Patria."*
What do they mean, anyway?

Lydia Puckett

Knowlt Hoheimer ran away to the war
The day before Curl Trenary
Swore out a warrant through Justice Arnett
For stealing hogs.
But that's not the reason he turned a soldier.
He caught me running with Lucius Atherton.
We quarreled and I told him never again
To cross my path.
Then he stole the hogs and went to the war—
Back of every soldier is a woman.

Frank Drummer

Out of a cell into this darkened space—
The end at twenty-five!
My tongue could not speak what stirred within me,
And the village thought me a fool.
Yet at the start there was a clear vision,
A high and urgent purpose in my soul
Which drove me on trying to memorize
The Encyclopedia Britannica!

Hare Drummer

Do the boys and girls still go to Siever's
For cider, after school, in late September?
Or gather hazel nuts among the thickets
On Aaron Hatfield's farm when the frosts begin?
For many times with the laughing girls and boys
Played I along the road and over the hills
When the sun was low and the air was cool,
Stopping to club the walnut tree
Standing leafless against a flaming west.
Now, the smell of the autumn smoke,
And the dropping acorns,
And the echoes about the vales
Bring dreams of life. They hover over me.
They question me:
Where are those laughing comrades?
How many are with me, how many
In the old orchards along the way to Siever's,
And in the woods that overlook
The quiet water?

Conrad Siever

Not in that wasted garden
Where bodies are drawn into grass
That feeds no flocks, and into evergreens
That bear no fruit—
There where along the shaded walks
Vain sighs are heard,
And vainer dreams are dreamed
Of close communion with departed souls—
But here under the apple tree
I loved and watched and pruned
With gnarled hands
In the long, long years;
Here under the roots of this northern-spy
To move in the chemic change and circle of life,
Into the soil and into the flesh of the tree,
And into the living epitaphs
Of redder apples!

Doc Hill

I went up and down the streets
Here and there by day and night,
Through all hours of the night caring for the poor who were
    sick.
Do you know why?
My wife hated me, my son went to the dogs.
And I turned to the people and poured out my love to them.
Sweet it was to see the crowds about the lawns on the day of
    my funeral,
And hear them murmur their love and sorrow.
But oh, dear God, my soul trembled, scarcely able
To hold to the railing of the new life,
When I saw Em Stanton behind the oak tree
At the grave,
Hiding herself, and her grief!

Andy the Night-Watch

In my Spanish cloak,
And old slouch hat,
And overshoes of felt,
And Tyke, my faithful dog,
And my knotted hickory cane,
I slipped about with a bull's-eye lantern
From door to door on the square,
As the midnight stars wheeled round,
And the bell in the steeple murmured
From the blowing of the wind;
And the weary steps of old Doc Hill
Sounded like one who walks in sleep,
And a far-off rooster crew.
And now another is watching Spoon River
As others watched before me.
And here we lie, Doc Hill and I,
Where none breaks through and steals,
And no eye needs to guard.

Sarah Brown

Maurice, weep not, I am not here under this pine tree.
The balmy air of spring whispers through the sweet grass,
The stars sparkle, the whippoorwill calls,
But thou grievest, while my soul lies rapturous
In the blest Nirvana of eternal light!
Go to the good heart that is my husband,
Who broods upon what he calls our guilty love:
Tell him that my love for you, no less than my love for him,
Wrought out my destiny—that through the flesh
I won spirit, and through spirit, peace.
There is no marriage in heaven,
But there is love.

Percy Bysshe Shelley

My father who owned the wagon-shop
And grew rich shoeing horses
Sent me to the University of Montreal.
I learned nothing and returned home,
Roaming the fields with Bert Kessler,
Hunting quail and snipe.
At Thompson's Lake the trigger of my gun
Caught in the side of the boat
And a great hole was shot through my heart.
Over me a fond father erected this marble shaft,
On which stands the figure of a woman
Carved by an Italian artist.
They say the ashes of my namesake
Were scattered near the pyramid of Caius Cestius
Somewhere near Rome.

Flossie Cabanis

From Bindle's opera house in the village
To Broadway is a great step.
But I tried to take it, my ambition fired
When sixteen years of age,
Seeing *East Lynne* played here in the village
By Ralph Barrett, the coming
Romantic actor, who enthralled my soul.
True, I trailed back home, a broken failure,
When Ralph disappeared in New York,
Leaving me alone in the city—
But life broke him also.
In all this place of silence
There are no kindred spirits.
How I wish Duse could stand amid the pathos
Of these quiet fields
And read these words.

Julia Miller

We quarreled that morning,
For he was sixty-five, and I was thirty,
And I was nervous and heavy with the child
Whose birth I dreaded.
I thought over the last letter written me
By that estranged young soul
Whose betrayal of me I had concealed
By marrying the old man.
Then I took morphine and sat down to read.
Across the blackness that came over my eyes
I see the flickering light of these words even now:
"And Jesus said unto him, Verily
I say unto thee, To-day thou shalt
Be with me in paradise."

Johnnie Sayre

Father, thou canst never know
The anguish that smote my heart
For my disobedience, the moment I felt
The remorseless wheel of the engine
Sink into the crying flesh of my leg.
As they carried me to the home of widow Morris
I could see the school-house in the valley
To which I played truant to steal rides upon the trains.
I prayed to live until I could ask your forgiveness—
And then your tears, your broken words of comfort!
From the solace of that hour I have gained infinite happiness.
Thou wert wise to chisel for me:
"Taken from the evil to come."

Charlie French

Did you ever find out
Which one of the O'Brien boys it was
Who snapped the toy pistol against my hand?
There when the flags were red and white
In the breeze and "Bucky" Estil
Was firing the cannon brought to Spoon River
From Vicksburg by Captain Harris;
And the lemonade stands were running
And the band was playing,
To have it all spoiled
By a piece of a cap shot under the skin of my hand,
And the boys all crowding about me saying:
"You'll die of lock-jaw, Charlie, sure."
Oh, dear! oh, dear!
What chum of mine could have done it?

Zenas Witt

I was sixteen, and I had the most terrible dreams,
And specks before my eyes, and nervous weakness.
And I couldn't remember the books I read,
Like Frank Drummer who memorized page after page.
And my back was weak, and I worried and worried,
And I was embarrassed and stammered my lessons,
And when I stood up to recite I'd forget
Everything that I had studied.
Well, I saw Dr. Weese's advertisement,
And there I read everything in print,
Just as if he had known me,
And about the dreams which I couldn't help.
So I know I was marked for an early grave.
And I worried until I had a cough,
And then the dreams stopped.
And then I slept the sleep without dreams
Here on the hill by the river.

Theodore the Poet

As a boy, Theodore, you sat for long hours
On the shore of the turbid Spoon
With deep-set eye staring at the door of the craw-fish's burrow,
Waiting for him to appear, pushing ahead,
First his waving antennae, like straws of hay,
And soon his body, colored like soap-stone,
Gemmed with eyes of jet.
And you wondered in a trance of thought
What he knew, what he desired, and why he lived at all.
But later your vision watched for men and women
Hiding in burrows of fate amid great cities,
Looking for the souls of them to come out,
So that you could see
How they lived, and for what,
And why they kept crawling so busily
Along the sandy way where water fails
As the summer wanes.

The Town Marshal

The Prohibitionists made me Town Marshal
When the saloons were voted out,
Because when I was a drinking man,
Before I joined the church, I killed a Swede
At the saw-mill near Maple Grove.
And they wanted a terrible man,
Grim, righteous, strong, courageous,
And a hater of saloons and drinkers,
To keep law and order in the village.
And they presented me with a loaded cane
With which I struck Jack McGuire
Before he drew the gun with which he killed me.
The Prohibitionists spent their money in vain
To hang him, for in a dream
I appeared to one of the twelve jurymen
And told him the whole secret story.
Fourteen years were enough for killing me.

Jack McGuire

They would have lynched me
Had I not been secretly hurried away
To the jail at Peoria.
And yet I was going peacefully home,
Carrying my jug, a little drunk,
When Logan, the marshal, halted me,
Called me a drunken hound and shook me,
And, when I cursed him for it, struck me
With that Prohibition loaded cane—
All this before I shot him.
They would have hanged me except for this:
My lawyer, Kinsey Keene, was helping to land
Old Thomas Rhodes for wrecking the bank,
And the judge was a friend of Rhodes
And wanted him to escape,
And Kinsey offered to quit on Rhodes
For fourteen years for me.
And the bargain was made. I served my time
And learned to read and write.

Dorcas Gustine

I was not beloved of the villagers,
But all because I spoke my mind,
And met those who transgressed against me
With plain remonstrance, hiding nor nurturing
Nor secret griefs nor grudges.
That act of the Spartan boy is greatly praised,
Who hid the wolf under his cloak,
Letting it devour him, uncomplainingly.
It is braver, I think, to snatch the wolf forth
And fight him openly, even in the street,
Amid dust and howls of pain.
The tongue may be an unruly member—
But silence poisons the soul.
Berate me who will—I am content.

Nicholas Bindle

Were you not ashamed, fellow citizens,
When my estate was probated and everyone knew
How small a fortune I left?—
You who hounded me in life,
To give, give, give to the churches, to the poor,
To the village!—me who had already given much.
And think you not I did not know
That the pipe-organ, which I gave to the church,
Played its christening songs when Deacon Rhodes,
Who broke and all but ruined me,
Worshipped for the first time after his acquittal?

Jacob Goodpasture

When Fort Sumter fell and the war came
I cried out in bitterness of soul:
"O glorious republic now no more!"
When they buried my soldier son
To the call of trumpets and the sound of drums
My heart broke beneath the weight
Of eighty years, and I cried:
"Oh, son who died in a cause unjust!
In the strife of Freedom slain!"
And I crept here under the grass.
And now from the battlements of time, behold:
Thrice thirty million souls being bound together
In the love of larger truth,
Rapt in the expectation of the birth
Of a new Beauty,
Sprung from Brotherhood and Wisdom.
I with eyes of spirit see the Transfiguration
Before you see it.
But ye infinite brood of golden eagles nesting ever higher,
Wheeling ever higher, the sun-light wooing
Of lofty places of Thought,
Forgive the blindness of the departed owl.

Harold Arnett

I leaned against the mantel, sick, sick,
Thinking of my failure, looking into the abysm,
Weak from the noon-day heat.
A church bell sounded mournfully far away.
I heard the cry of a baby,
And the coughing of John Yarnell,
Bed-ridden, feverish, feverish, dying,
Then the violent voice of my wife:
"Watch out, the potatoes are burning!"
I smelled them ... then there was irresistible disgust.
I pulled the trigger ... blackness ... light ...
Unspeakable regret ... fumbling for the world again.
Too late! Thus I came here,
With lungs for breathing ... one cannot breathe here with lungs,
Though one must breathe. ... Of what use is it
To rid one's self of the world,
When no soul may ever escape the eternal destiny of life?

Margaret Fuller Slack

I would have been as great as George Eliot
But for an untoward fate.
For look at the photograph of me made by Penniwit,
Chin resting on hand, and deep-set eyes—
Gray, too, and far-searching.
But there was the old, old problem:
Should it be celibacy, matrimony or unchastity?
Then John Slack, the rich druggist, wooed me,
Luring me with the promise of leisure for my novel,
And I married him, giving birth to eight children,
And had no time to write.
It was all over with me, anyway,
When I ran the needle in my hand
While washing the baby's things,
And died from lock-jaw, an ironical death.
Hear me, ambitious souls,
Sex is the curse of life!

George Trimble

Do you remember when I stood on the steps
Of the court-house and talked free-silver,
And the single-tax of Henry George?
Then do you remember that, when the Peerless Leader
Lost the first battle, I began to talk prohibition,
And became active in the church?
That was due to my wife,
Who pictured to me my destruction
If I did not prove my morality to the people.
Well, she ruined me:
For the radicals grew suspicious of me,
And the conservatives were never sure of me—
And here I lie, unwept of all.

Dr. Siegfried Iseman

I said when they handed me my diploma,
I said to myself I will be good
And wise and brave and helpful to others;
I said I will carry the Christian creed
Into the practice of medicine!
Somehow the world and the other doctors
Know what's in your heart as soon as you make
This high-souled resolution.
And the way of it is they starve you out.
And no one comes to you but the poor.
And you find too late that being a doctor
Is just a way of making a living.
And when you are poor and have to carry
The Christian creed and wife and children
All on your back, it is too much!
That's why I made the Elixir of Youth,
Which landed me in the jail at Peoria,
Branded a swindler and a crook
By the upright Federal Judge!

"Ace" Shaw

I never saw any difference
Between playing cards for money
And selling real estate,
Practicing law, banking, or anything else.
For everything is chance.
Nevertheless,
Seest thou a man diligent in business?
He shall stand before Kings!

Lois Spears

Here lies the body of Lois Spears,
Born Lois Fluke, daughter of Willard Fluke,
Wife of Cyrus Spears,
Mother of Myrtle and Virgil Spears,
Children with clear eyes and sound limbs—
(I was born blind).
I was the happiest of women
As wife, mother and housekeeper,
Caring for my loved ones,
And making my home
A place of order and bounteous hospitality;
For I went about the rooms,
And about the garden
With an instinct as sure as sight,
As though there were eyes in my finger tips—
Glory to God in the highest.

Justice Arnett

It is true, fellow citizens,
That my old docket lying there for years
On a shelf above my head and over
The seat of justice, I say it is true
That docket had an iron rim
Which gashed my baldness when it fell—
(Somehow I think it was shaken loose
By the heave of the air all over town
When the gasoline tank at the canning works
Blew up and burned Butch Weldy)—
But let us argue points in order,
And reason the whole case carefully:
First I concede my head was cut,
But second the frightful thing was this:
The leaves of the docket shot and showered
Around me like a deck of cards
In the hands of a sleight of hand performer.
And up to the end I saw those leaves
Till I said at last, "Those are not leaves.
Why, can't you see they are days and days
And the days and days of seventy years?
And why do you torture me with leaves
And the little entries on them?"

Willard Fluke

My wife lost her health,
And dwindled until she weighed scarce ninety pounds.
Then that woman, whom the men
Styled Cleopatra, came along.
And we — we married ones —
All broke our vows, myself among the rest.
Years passed and one by one
Death claimed them all in some hideous form,
And I was borne along by dreams
Of God's particular grace for me,
And I began to write, write, write, reams on reams
Of the second coming of Christ.
Then Christ came to me and said,
"Go into the church and stand before the congregation
And confess your sin."
But just as I stood up and began to speak
I saw my little girl, who was sitting in the front seat —
My little girl who was born blind!
After that, all is blackness!

Aner Clute

Over and over they used to ask me,
While buying the wine or the beer,
In Peoria first, and later in Chicago,
Denver, Frisco, New York, wherever I lived,
How I happened to lead the life,
And what was the start of it.
Well, I told them a silk dress,
And a promise of marriage from a rich man—
(It was Lucius Atherton).
But that was not really it at all.
Suppose a boy steals an apple
From the tray at the grocery store,
And they all begin to call him a thief,
The editor, minister, judge, and all the people—
"A thief," "a thief," "a thief," wherever he goes.
And he can't get work, and he can't get bread
Without stealing it, why the boy will steal.
It's the way the people regard the theft of the apple
That makes the boy what he is.

Lucius Atherton

When my moustache curled,
And my hair was black,
And I wore tight trousers
And a diamond stud,
I was an excellent knave of hearts and took many a trick.
But when the gray hairs began to appear—
Lo! a new generation of girls
Laughed at me, not fearing me,
And I had no more exciting adventures
Wherein I was all but shot for a heartless devil,
But only drabby affairs, warmed-over affairs
Of other days and other men.
And time went on until I lived at Mayer's restaurant,
Partaking of short-orders, a gray, untidy,
Toothless, discarded, rural Don Juan. . . .
There is a mighty shade here who sings
Of one named Beatrice;
And I see now that the force that made him great
Drove me to the dregs of life.

Homer Clapp

Often Aner Clute at the gate
Refused me the parting kiss,
Saying we should be engaged before that;
And just with a distant clasp of the hand
She bade me good-night, as I brought her home
From the skating rink or the revival.
No sooner did my departing footsteps die away
Than Lucius Atherton,
(So I learned when Aner went to Peoria)
Stole in at her widow, or took her riding
Behind his spanking team of bays
Into the country.
The shock of it made me settle down,
And I put all the money I got from my father's estate
Into the canning factory, to get the job
Of head accountant, and lost it all.
And then I knew I was one of Life's fools,
Whom only death would treat as the equal
Of other men, making me feel like a man.

Deacon Taylor

I belonged to the church,
And to the party of prohibition;
And the villagers thought I died of eating watermelon.
In truth I had cirrhosis of the liver,
For every noon for thirty years
I slipped behind the prescription partition
In Trainor's drug store
And poured a generous drink
From the bottle marked
"Spiritus frumenti."

Sam Hookey

I ran away from home with the circus,
Having fallen in love with Mademoiselle Estralada,
The lion tamer.
One time, having starved the lions
For more than a day,
I entered the cage and began to beat Brutus
And Leo and Gypsy.
Whereupon Brutus sprang upon me,
And killed me.
On entering these regions
I met a shadow who cursed me,
And said it served me right. . . .
It was Robespierre!

Cooney Potter

I inherited forty acres from my Father
And, by working my wife, my two sons and two daughters
From dawn to dusk, I acquired
A thousand acres. But not content,
Wishing to own two thousand acres,
I bustled through the years with axe and plow,
Toiling, denying myself, my wife, my sons, my daughters.
Squire Higbee wrongs me to say
That I died from smoking Red Eagle cigars.
Eating hot pie and gulping coffee
During the scorching hours of harvest time
Brought me here ere I had reached my sixtieth year.

Fiddler Jones

The earth keeps some vibration going
There in your heart, and that is you.
And if the people find you can fiddle,
Why, fiddle you must, for all your life.
What do you see, a harvest of clover?
Or a meadow to walk through to the river?
The wind's in the corn; you rub your hands
For beeves hereafter ready for market;
Or else you hear the rustle of skirts
Like the girls when dancing at Little Grove.
To Cooney Potter a pillar of dust
Or whirling leaves meant ruinous drouth;
They looked to me like Red-Head Sammy
Stepping it off, to "Toor-a-Loor."
How could I till my forty acres
Not to speak of getting more,
With a medley of horns, bassoons and piccolos
Stirred in my brain by crows and robins
And the creak of a wind-mill—only these?
And I never started to plow in my life
That someone did not stop in the road
And take me away to a dance or picnic.
I ended up with forty acres;
I ended up with a broken fiddle—
And a broken laugh, and a thousand memories,
And not a single regret.

Nellie Clark

I was only eight years old;
And before I grew up and knew what it meant
I had no words for it, except
That I was frightened and told my mother;
And that my father got a pistol
And would have killed Charlie, who was a big boy,
Fifteen years old, except for his mother.
Nevertheless the story clung to me.
But the man who married me, a widower of thirty-five,
Was a newcomer and never heard it
Till two years after we were married.
Then he considered himself cheated,
And the village agreed that I was not really a virgin.
Well, he deserted me, and I died
The following winter.

Louise Smith

Herbert broke our engagement of eight years
When Annabelle returned to the village
From the Seminary. Ah me!
If I had let my love for him alone
It might have grown into a beautiful sorrow—
Who knows?—filling my life with healing fragrance.
But I tortured it, I poisoned it,
I blinded its eyes, and it became hatred—
Deadly ivy instead of clematis.
And my soul fell from its support,
Its tendrils tangled in decay.
Do not let the will play gardener to your soul
Unless you are sure
It is wiser than your soul's nature.

Herbert Marshall

All your sorrow, Louise, and hatred of me
Sprang from your delusion that it was wantonness
Of spirit and contempt of your soul's rights
Which made me turn to Annabelle and forsake you.
You really grew to hate me for love of me,
Because I was your soul's happiness,
Formed and tempered
To solve your life for you, and would not.
But you were my misery. If you had been
My happiness would I not have clung to you?
This is life's sorrow:
That one can be happy only where two are;
And that our hearts are drawn to stars
Which want us not.

George Gray

I have studied many times
The marble which was chiseled for me—
A boat with a furled sail at rest in a harbor.
In truth it pictures not my destination
But my life.
For love was offered me and I shrank from its disillusionment;
Sorrow knocked at my door, but I was afraid;
Ambition called to me, but I dreaded the chances.
Yet all the while I hungered for meaning in my life.
And now I know that we must lift the sail
And catch the winds of destiny
Wherever they drive the boat.
To put meaning in one's life may end in madness,
But life without meaning is the torture
Of restlessness and vague desire—
It is a boat longing for the sea and yet afraid.

Hon. Henry Bennett

It never came into my mind
Until I was ready to die
That Jenny had loved me to death, with malice of heart.
For I was seventy, she was thirty-five,
And I wore myself to a shadow trying to husband
Jenny, rosy Jenny full of the ardor of life.
For all my wisdom and grace of mind
Gave her no delight at all, in very truth,
But ever and anon she spoke of the giant strength
Of Willard Shafer, and of his wonderful feat
Of lifting a traction engine out of the ditch
One time at Georgie Kirby's.
So Jenny inherited my fortune and married Willard—
That mount of brawn! That clownish soul!

Griffy the Cooper

The cooper should know about tubs.
But I learned about life as well,
And you who loiter around these graves
Think you know life.
You think your eye sweeps about a wide horizon, perhaps;
In truth you are only looking around the interior of your tub.
You cannot lift yourself to its rim
And see the outer world of things,
And at the same time see yourself.
You are submerged in the tub of yourself—
Taboos and rules and appearances
Are the staves of your tub.
Break them and dispel the witchcraft
Of thinking your tub is life!
And that you know life!

Sexsmith the Dentist

Do you think that odes and sermons,
And the ringing of church bells,
And the blood of old men and young men,
Martyred for the truth they saw
With eyes made bright by faith in God,
Accomplished the world's great reformations?
Do you think that the "Battle Hymn of the Republic"
Would have been heard if the chattel slave
Had crowned the dominant dollar,
In spite of Whitney's cotton gin,
And steam and rolling mills and iron
And telegraphs and white free labor?
Do you think that Daisy Fraser
Had been put out and driven out
If the canning works had never needed
Her little house and lot?
Or do you think the poker room
Of Johnnie Taylor and Burchard's bar
Had been closed up if the money lost
And spent for beer had not been turned,
By closing them, to Thomas Rhodes
For larger sales of shoes and blankets,
And children's cloaks and gold-oak cradles?
Why, a moral truth is a hollow tooth
Which must be propped with gold.

A. D. Blood

If you in the village think that my work was a good one,
Who closed the saloons and stopped all playing at cards,
And haled old Daisy Fraser before Justice Arnett,
In many a crusade to purge the people of sin;
Why do you let the milliner's daughter, Dora,
And the worthless son of Benjamin Pantier
Nightly make my grave their unholy pillow?

Robert Southey Burke

I spent my money trying to elect you Mayor,
A. D. Blood.
I lavished my admiration upon you,
You were to my mind the almost perfect man.
You devoured my personality,
And the idealism of my youth,
And the strength of a high-souled fealty.
And all my hopes for the world,
And all my beliefs in Truth,
Were smelted up in the blinding heat
Of my devotion to you,
And molded into your image.
And then when I found what you were—
That your soul was small
And your words were false
As your blue-white porcelain teeth—
And your cuffs of celluloid—
I hated the love I had for you,
I hated myself, I hated you
For my wasted soul, and wasted youth.
And I say to all, beware of ideals,
Beware of giving your love away
To any man alive.

Dora Williams

When Reuben Pantier ran away and threw me
I went to Springfield. There I met a lush,
Whose father just deceased left him a fortune.
He married me when drunk. My life was wretched.
A year passed and one day they found him dead.
That made me rich. I moved on to Chicago.
After a time met Tyler Rountree, villain.
I moved on to New York. A gray-haired magnate
Went mad about me—so another fortune.
He died one night right in my arms, you know.
(I saw his purple face for years thereafter.)
There was almost a scandal. I moved on,
This time to Paris. I was now a woman,
Insidious, subtle, versed in the world and rich.
My sweet apartment near the Champs Élysées
Became a center for all sorts of people,
Musicians, poets, dandies, artists, nobles,
Where we spoke French and German, Italian, English.
I wed Count Navigato, native of Genoa.
We went to Rome. He poisoned me, I think.
Now in the Campo Santo overlooking
The sea where young Columbus dreamed new worlds,
See what they chiseled: "*Contessa Navigato*
Implora eterna quiete."

Mrs. Williams

I was the milliner,
Talked about, lied about,
Mother of Dora,
Whose strange disappearance
Was charged to her rearing.
My eye quick to beauty
Saw much beside ribbons
And buckles and feathers
And leghorns and felts,
To set off sweet faces,
And dark hair and gold.
One thing I will tell you
And one I will ask:
The stealers of husbands
Wear powder and trinkets,
And fashionable hats.
Wives, wear them yourselves.
Hats may make divorces—
They also prevent them.
Well now, let me ask you:
If all of the children born here in Spoon River
Had been reared by the county, somewhere on a farm;
And the fathers and mothers had been given their freedom
To live and enjoy, change mates if they wished,
Do you think that Spoon River
Had been any the worse?

William and Emily

There is something about Death
Like love itself!
If with someone with whom you have known passion,
And the glow of youthful love,
You also, after years of life
Together, feel the sinking of the fire,
And thus fade away together,
Gradually, faintly, delicately,
As it were in each other's arms,
Passing from the familiar room—
That is a power of unison between souls
Like love itself!

The Circuit Judge

Take note, passers-by, of the sharp erosions
Eaten in my head-stone by the wind and rain—
Almost as if an intangible Nemesis or hatred
Were marking scores against me,
But to destroy, and not preserve, my memory.
I in life was the Circuit Judge, a maker of notches,
Deciding cases on the points the lawyers scored,
Not on the right of the matter.
O wind and rain, leave my head-stone alone!
For worse than the anger of the wronged,
The curses of the poor,
Was to lie speechless, yet with vision clear,
Seeing that even Hod Putt, the murderer,
Hanged by my sentence,
Was innocent in soul compared with me.

Blind Jack

I had fiddled all day at the county fair.
But driving home "Butch" Weldy and Jack McGuire,
Who were roaring full, made me fiddle and fiddle
To the song of "Susie Skinner," while whipping the horses
Till they ran away.
Blind as I was, I tried to get out
As the carriage fell in the ditch,
And was caught in the wheels and killed.
There's a blind man here with a brow
As big and white as a cloud.
And all we fiddlers, from highest to lowest,
Writers of music and tellers of stories,
Sit at his feet,
And hear him sing of the fall of Troy.

John Horace Burleson

I won the prize essay at school
Here in the village,
And published a novel before I was twenty-five.
I went to the city for themes and to enrich my art;
There married the banker's daughter,
And later became president of the bank—
Always looking forward to some leisure
To write an epic novel of the war.
Meanwhile friend of the great, and lover of letters,
And host to Matthew Arnold and to Emerson.
An after dinner speaker, writing essays
For local clubs. At last brought here—
My boyhood home, you know—
Not even a little tablet in Chicago
To keep my name alive.
How great it is to write the single line:
"Roll on, thou deep and dark blue Ocean, roll!"

Nancy Knapp

Well, don't you see this was the way of it:
We bought the farm with what he inherited,
And his brothers and sisters accused him of poisoning
His father's mind against the rest of them.
And we never had any peace with our treasure.
The murrain took the cattle, and the crops failed.
And lightning struck the granary.
So we mortgaged the farm to keep going.
And he grew silent and was worried all the time.
Then some of the neighbors refused to speak to us,
And took sides with his brothers and sisters.
And I had no place to turn, as one may say to himself,
At an earlier time in life, "No matter,
So and so is my friend, or I can shake this off
With a little trip to Decatur."
Then the dreadfulest smells infested the rooms.
So I set fire to the beds and the old witch-house
Went up in a roar of flame,
As I danced in the yard with waving arms,
While he wept like a freezing steer.

Barry Holden

The very fall my sister Nancy Knapp
Set fire to the house
They were trying Dr. Duval
For the murder of Zora Clemens,
And I sat in the court two weeks
Listening to every witness.
It was clear he had got her in a family way;
And to let the child be born
Would not do.
Well, how about me with eight children,
And one coming, and the farm
Mortgaged to Thomas Rhodes?
And when I got home that night,
(After listening to the story of the buggy ride,
And the finding of Zora in the ditch,)
The first thing I saw, right there by the steps,
Where the boys had hacked for angle worms,
Was the hatchet!
And just as I entered there was my wife,
Standing before me, big with child.
She started the talk of the mortgaged farm,
And I killed her.

State's Attorney Fallas

I, the scourge-wielder, balance-wrecker,
Smiter with whips and swords;
I, hater of the breakers of the law;
I, legalist, inexorable and bitter,
Driving the jury to hang the madman, Barry Holden,
Was made as one dead by light too bright for eyes,
And woke to face a Truth with bloody brow:
Steel forceps fumbled by a doctor's hand
Against my boy's head as he entered life
Made him an idiot.
I turned to books of science
To care for him.
That's how the world of those whose minds are sick
Became my work in life, and all my world.
Poor ruined boy! You were, at last, the potter
And I and all my deeds of charity
The vessels of your hand.

Wendell P. Bloyd

They first charged me with disorderly conduct,
There being no statute on blasphemy.
Later they locked me up as insane
Where I was beaten to death by a Catholic guard.
My offense was this:
I said God lied to Adam, and destined him
To lead the life of a fool,
Ignorant that there is evil in the world as well as good.
And when Adam outwitted God by eating the apple
And saw through the lie,
God drove him out of Eden to keep him from taking
The fruit of immortal life.
For Christ's sake, you sensible people,
Here's what God Himself says about it in the book of Genesis:
"And the Lord God said, behold the man
Is become as one of us" (a little envy, you see),
"To know good and evil" (the all-is-good lie exposed):
"And now lest he put forth his hand and take
Also of the tree of life and eat, and live forever:
Therefore the Lord God sent Him forth from the garden of Eden."
(The reason I believe God crucified His Own Son
To get out of the wretched tangle is, because it
sounds just like Him.)

Francis Turner

I could not run or play
In boyhood.
In manhood I could only sip the cup,
Not drink—
For scarlet-fever left my heart diseased.
Yet I lie here
Soothed by a secret none but Mary knows:
There is a garden of acacia,
Catalpa trees, and arbors sweet with vines—
There on that afternoon in June
By Mary's side,
Kissing her with my soul upon my lips,
It suddenly took flight.

Franklin Jones

If I could have lived another year
I could have finished my flying machine,
And become rich and famous.
Hence it is fitting the workman
Who tried to chisel a dove for me
Made it look more like a chicken.
For what is it all but being hatched,
And running about the yard,
To the day of the block?
Save that a man has an angel's brain,
And sees the ax from the first!

John M. Church

I was attorney for the "Q"
And the Indemnity Company which insured
The owners of the mine.
I pulled the wires with judge and jury,
And the upper courts, to beat the claims
Of the crippled, the widow and orphan,
And made a fortune thereat.
The bar association sang my praises
In a high-flown resolution.
And the floral tributes were many—
But the rats devoured my heart
And a snake made a nest in my skull!

Russian Sonia

I, born in Weimar
Of a mother who was French
And German father, a most learned professor,
Orphaned at fourteen years,
Became a dancer, known as Russian Sonia,
All up and down the boulevards of Paris,
Mistress betimes of sundry dukes and counts,
And later of poor artists and of poets.
At forty years, *passée*, I sought New York
And met old Patrick Hummer on the boat,
Red-faced and hale, though turned his sixtieth year,
Returning after having sold a ship-load
Of cattle in the German city, Hamburg.
He brought me to Spoon River and we lived here
For twenty years—they thought that we were married!
This oak tree near me is the favorite haunt
Of blue jays chattering, chattering all the day.
And why not? for my very dust is laughing
For thinking of the humorous thing called life.

Isa Nutter

Doc Meyers said I had satyriasis,
And Doc Hill called it leucaemia—
But I know what brought me here:
I was sixty-four but strong as a man
Of thirty-five or forty.
And it wasn't writing a letter a day,
And it wasn't late hours seven nights a week,
And it wasn't the strain of thinking of Minnie,
And it wasn't fear or a jealous dread,
Or the endless task of trying to fathom
Her wonderful mind, or sympathy
For the wretched life she led
With her first and second husband—
It was none of these that laid me low—
But the clamor of daughters and threats of sons,
And the sneers and curses of all my kin
Right up to the day I sneaked to Peoria
And married Minnie in spite of them.
And why do you wonder my will was made
For the best and purest of women?

Barney Hainsfeather

If the excursion train to Peoria
Had just been wrecked, I might have escaped with my life—
Certainly I should have escaped this place.
But as it was burned as well, they mistook me
For John Allen who was sent to the Hebrew Cemetery
At Chicago,
And John for me, so I lie here.
It was bad enough to run a clothing store in this town,
But to be buried here—*ach!*

Petit, the Poet

Seeds in a dry pod, tick, tick, tick,
Tick, tick, tick, like mites in a quarrel —
Faint iambics that the full breeze wakens —
But the pine tree makes a symphony thereof.
Triolets, villanelles, rondels, rondeaus,
Ballades by the score with the same old thought:
The snows and the roses of yesterday are vanished;
And what is love but a rose that fades?
Life all around me here in the village:
Tragedy, comedy, valor and truth,
Courage, constancy, heroism, failure —
All in the loom, and oh what patterns!
Woodlands, meadows, streams and rivers —
Blind to all of it all my life long.
Triolets, villanelles, rondels, rondeaus,
Seeds in a dry pod, tick, tick, tick,
Tick, tick, tick, what little iambics,
While Homer and Whitman roared in the pines.

Pauline Barrett

Almost the shell of a woman after the surgeon's knife!
And almost a year to creep back into strength,
Till the dawn of our wedding decennial
Found me my seeming self again.
We walked the forest together,
By a path of soundless moss and turf.
But I could not look in your eyes,
And you could not look in my eyes,
For such sorrow was ours—the beginning of gray in your hair,
And I but a shell of myself.
And what did we talk of?—sky and water,
Anything, 'most, to hide our thoughts.
And then your gift of wild roses,
Set on the table to grace our dinner.
Poor heart, how bravely you struggled
To imagine and live a remembered rapture!
Then my spirit drooped as the night came on,
And you left me alone in my room for a while,
As you did when I was a bride, poor heart.
And I looked in the mirror and something said:
"One should be all dead when one is half-dead—
Nor ever mock life, nor ever cheat love."
And I did it looking there in the mirror—
Dear, have you ever understood?

Mrs. Charles Bliss

Reverend Wiley advised me not to divorce him
For the sake of the children,
And Judge Somers advised him the same.
So we stuck to the end of the path.
But two of the children thought he was right,
And two of the children thought I was right.
And the two who sided with him blamed me,
And the two who sided with me blamed him,
And they grieved for the one they sided with.
And all were torn with the guilt of judging,
And tortured in soul because they could not admire
Equally him and me.
Now every gardener knows that plants grown in cellars
Or under stones are twisted and yellow and weak.
And no mother would let her baby suck
Diseased milk from her breast.
Yet preachers and judges advise the raising of souls
Where there is no sunlight, but only twilight,
No warmth, but only dampness and cold—
Preachers and judges!

Mrs. George Reece

To this generation I would say:
Memorize some bit of verse of truth or beauty.
It may serve a turn in your life.
My husband had nothing to do
With the fall of the bank—he was only cashier.
The wreck was due to the president, Thomas Rhodes,
And his vain, unscrupulous son.
Yet my husband was sent to prison,
And I was left with the children,
To feed and clothe and school them.
And I did it, and sent them forth
Into the world all clean and strong,
And all through the wisdom of Pope, the poet:
"Act well your part, there all the honor lies."

Rev. Lemuel Wiley

I preached four thousand sermons,
I conducted forty revivals,
And baptized many converts.
Yet no deed of mine
Shines brighter in the memory of the world,
And none is treasured more by me:
Look how I saved the Blisses from divorce,
And kept the children free from that disgrace,
To grow up into moral men and women,
Happy themselves, a credit to the village.

Thomas Ross, Jr.

This I saw with my own eyes:
A cliff-swallow
Made her nest in a hole of the high clay-bank
There near Miller's Ford.
But no sooner were the young hatched
Than a snake crawled up to the nest
To devour the brood.
Then the mother swallow with swift flutterings
And shrill cries
Fought at the snake,
Blinding him with the beat of her wings,
Until he, wriggling and rearing his head,
Fell backward down the bank
Into Spoon River and was drowned.
Scarcely an hour passed
Until a shrike
Impaled the mother swallow on a thorn.
As for myself I overcame my lower nature
Only to be destroyed by my brother's ambition.

Rev. Abner Peet

I had no objection at all
To selling my household effects at auction
On the village square.
It gave my beloved flock the chance
To get something which had belonged to me
For a memorial.
But that trunk which was struck off
To Burchard, the grog-keeper!
Did you know it contained the manuscripts
Of a lifetime of sermons?
And he burned them as waste paper.

Jefferson Howard

My valiant fight! For I call it valiant,
With my father's beliefs from old Virginia:
Hating slavery, but no less war.
I, full of spirit, audacity, courage,
Thrown into life here in Spoon River,
With its dominant forces drawn from New England,
Republicans, Calvinists, merchants, bankers,
Hating me, yet fearing my arm.
With wife and children heavy to carry—
Yet fruits of my very zest of life.
Stealing odd pleasures that cost me prestige,
And reaping evils I had not sown;
Foe of the church with its charnel dankness,
Friend of the human touch of the tavern;
Tangled with fates all alien to me,
Deserted by hands I called my own.
Then just as I felt my giant strength
Short of breath, behold my children
Had wound their lives in stranger gardens—
And I stood alone, as I started alone!
My valiant life! I died on my feet,
Facing the silence—facing the prospect
That no one would know of the fight I made.

Judge Selah Lively

Suppose you stood just five feet two,
And had worked your way as a grocery clerk,
Studying law by candle light
Until you became an attorney at law?
And then suppose through your diligence,
And regular church attendance,
You became attorney for Thomas Rhodes,
Collecting notes and mortgages,
And representing all the widows
In the Probate Court? And through it all
They jeered at your size, and laughed at your clothes
And your polished boots? And then suppose
You became the County Judge?
And Jefferson Howard and Kinsey Keene,
And Harmon Whitney, and all the giants
Who had sneered at you, were forced to stand
Before the bar and say "Your Honor" —
Well, don't you think it was natural
That I made it hard for them?

Albert Schirding

Jonas Keene thought his lot a hard one
Because his children were all failures.
But I know of a fate more trying than that:
It is to be a failure while your children are successes.
For I raised a brood of eagles
Who flew away at last, leaving me
A crow on the abandoned bough.
Then, with the ambition to prefix Honorable to my name,
And thus to win my children's admiration,
I ran for County Superintendent of Schools,
Spending my accumulations to win—and lost.
That fall my daughter received first prize in Paris
For her picture, entitled "The Old Mill"—
(It was of the water mill before Henry Wilkin put in steam.)
The feeling that I was not worthy of her finished me.

Jonas Keene

Why did Albert Schirding kill himself
Trying to be County Superintendent of Schools,
Blest as he was with the means of life
And wonderful children, bringing him honor
Ere he was sixty?
If even one of my boys could have run a news-stand,
Or one of my girls could have married a decent man,
I should not have walked in the rain
And jumped into bed with clothes all wet,
Refusing medical aid.

Eugenia Todd

Have any of you, passers-by,
Had an old tooth that was an unceasing discomfort?
Or a pain in the side that never quite left you?
Or a malignant growth that grew with time?
So that even in profoundest slumber
There was shadowy consciousness or the phantom of thought
Of the tooth, the side, the growth?
Even so thwarted love, or defeated ambition,
Or a blunder in life which mixed your life
Hopelessly to the end,
Will, like a tooth, or a pain in the side,
Float through your dreams in the final sleep
Till perfect freedom from the earth-sphere
Comes to you as one who wakes
Healed and glad in the morning!

Yee Bow

They got me into the Sunday school
In Spoon River
And tried to get me to drop Confucius for Jesus.
I could have been no worse off
If I had tried to get them to drop Jesus for Confucius.
For, without any warning, as if it were a prank,
And sneaking up behind me, Harry Wiley,
The minister's son, caved my ribs into my lungs,
With a blow of his fist.
Now I shall never sleep with my ancestors in Pekin,
And no children shall worship at my grave.

Washington McNeely

Rich, honored by my fellow citizens,
The father of many children, born of a noble mother,
All raised there
In the great mansion-house, at the edge of town.
Note the cedar tree on the lawn!
I sent all the boys to Ann Arbor, all the girls to Rockford,
The while my life went on, getting more riches and honors—
Resting under my cedar tree at evening.
The years went on.
I sent the girls to Europe;
I dowered them when married.
I gave the boys money to start in business.
They were strong children, promising as apples
Before the bitten places show.
But John fled the country in disgrace.
Jenny died in child-birth—
I sat under my cedar tree.
Harry killed himself after a debauch,
Susan was divorced—
I sat under my cedar tree.
Paul was invalided from over-study,
Mary became a recluse at home for love of a man—
I sat under my cedar tree.
All were gone, or broken-winged or devoured by life—
I sat under my cedar tree.
My mate, the mother of them, was taken—
I sat under my cedar tree
Till ninety years were tolled.
O maternal Earth, which rocks the fallen leaf to sleep!

Paul McNeely

Dear Jane! dear winsome Jane!
How you stole in the room (where I lay so ill)
In your nurse's cap and linen cuffs,
And took my hand and said with a smile:
"You are not so ill—you'll soon be well."
And how the liquid thought of your eyes
Sank in my eyes like dew that slips
Into the heart of a flower.
Dear Jane! the whole McNeely fortune
Could not have bought your care of me,
By day and night, and night and day;
Nor paid for you smile, nor the warmth of your soul,
In your little hands laid on my brow.
Jane, till the flame of life went out
In the dark above the disk of night
I longed and hoped to be well again
To pillow my head on your little breasts,
And hold you fast in a clasp of love.
Did my father provide for you when he died,
Jane, dear Jane?

Mary McNeely

Passer-by,
To love is to find your own soul
Through the soul of the beloved one.
When the beloved one withdraws itself from your soul
Then you have lost your soul.
It is written: "I have a friend,
But my sorrow has no friend."
Hence my long years of solitude at the home of my father.
Trying to get myself back,
And to turn my sorrow into a supremer self.
But there was my father with his sorrows,
Sitting under the cedar tree,
A picture that sank into my heart at last
Bringing infinite repose.
Oh, ye souls who have made life
Fragrant and white as tube roses
From earth's dark soil,
Eternal peace!

Daniel M'Cumber

When I went to the city, Mary McNeely,
I meant to return for you, yes I did.
But Laura, my landlady's daughter,
Stole into my life somehow, and won me away.
Then after some years whom should I meet
But Georgine Miner from Niles—a sprout
Of the free love, Fourierist gardens that flourished
Before the war all over Ohio.
Her dilettante lover had tired of her,
And she turned to me for strength and solace.
She was some kind of a crying thing
One takes in one's arms, and all at once
It slimes your face with its running nose,
And voids its essence all over you,
Then bites your hand and springs away.
And there you stand bleeding and smelling to heaven!
Why, Mary McNeely, I was not worthy
To kiss the hem of your robe!

Georgine Sand Miner

A step-mother drove me from home, embittering me.
A squaw-man, a flaneur and dilettante, took my virtue.
For years I was his mistress—no one knew.
I learned from him the parasite cunning
With which I moved with the bluffs, like a flea on a dog.
All the time I was nothing but "very private" with different men.
Then Daniel, the radical, had me for years.
His sister called me his mistress;
And Daniel wrote me: "Shameful word, soiling our beautiful love!"
But my anger coiled, preparing its fangs.
My Lesbian friend next took a hand.
She hated Daniel's sister.
And Daniel despised her midget husband.
And she saw a chance for a poisonous thrust:
I must complain to the wife of Daniel's pursuit!
But before I did that I begged him to fly to London with me.
"Why not stay in the city just as we have?" he asked.
Then I turned submarine and revenged his repulse
In the arms of my dilettante friend. Then up to the surface,
Bearing the letter that Daniel wrote me,
To prove my honor was all intact, showing it to his wife,
My Lesbian friend and everyone.
If Daniel had only shot me dead!
Instead of stripping me naked of lies,
A harlot in body and soul!

Thomas Rhodes

Very well, you liberals,
And navigators into realms intellectual,
You sailors through heights imaginative,
Blown about by erratic currents, tumbling into air pockets,
You Margaret Fuller Slacks, Petits,
And Tennessee Claflin Shopes—
You found with all your boasted wisdom
How hard at the last it is
To keep the soul from splitting into cellular atoms.
While we, seekers of earth's treasures,
Getters and hoarders of gold,
Are self-contained, compact, harmonized,
Even to the end.

Ida Chicken

After I had attended lectures
At our Chautauqua, and studied French
For twenty years, committing the grammar
Almost by heart,
I thought I'd take a trip to Paris
To give my culture a final polish.
So I went to Peoria for a passport—
(Thomas Rhodes was on the train that morning.)
And there the clerk of the district Court
Made me swear to support and defend
The constitution—yes, even me—
Who couldn't defend or support it at all!
And what do you think? That very morning
The Federal Judge, in the very next room
To the room where I took the oath,
Decided the constitution
Exempted Rhodes from paying taxes
For the water works of Spoon River!

Penniwit, the Artist

I lost my patronage in Spoon River
From trying to put my mind in the camera
To catch the soul of the person.
The very best picture I ever took
Was of Judge Somers, attorney at law.
He sat upright and had me pause
Till he got his cross-eye straight.
Then when he was ready he said "all right."
And I yelled "overruled" and his eye turned up.
And I caught him just as he used to look
When saying "I except."

Jim Brown

While I was handling Dom Pedro
I got at the thing that divides the race between men who are
For singing "Turkey in the straw" or "There is a fountain filled
   with blood"—
(Like Rile Potter used to sing it over at Concord);
For cards, or for Rev. Peet's lecture on the holy land;
For skipping the light fantastic, or passing the plate;
For *Pinafore*, or a Sunday school cantata;
For men, or for money;
For the people or against them.
This was it:
Rev. Peet and the Social Purity Club,
Headed by Ben Pantier's wife,
Went to the village trustees,
And asked them to make me take Dom Pedro
From the barn of Wash McNeely, there at the edge of town,
To a barn outside of the corporation,
On the ground that it corrupted public morals.
Well, Ben Pantier and Fiddler Jones saved the day—
They thought it a slam on colts.

Robert Davidson

I grew spiritually fat living off the souls of men.
If I saw a soul that was strong
I wounded its pride and devoured its strength.
The shelters of friendship knew my cunning,
For where I could steal a friend I did so.
And wherever I could enlarge my power
By undermining ambition, I did so,
Thus to make smooth my own.
And to triumph over other souls,
Just to assert and prove my superior strength,
Was with me a delight,
The keen exhilaration of soul gymnastics.
Devouring souls, I should have lived forever.
But their undigested remains bred in me a deadly nephritis,
With fear, restlessness, sinking spirits,
Hatred, suspicion, vision disturbed.
I collapsed at last with a shriek.
Remember the acorn;
It does not devour other acorns.

Elsa Wertman

I was a peasant girl from Germany,
Blue-eyed, rosy, happy and strong.
And the first place I worked was at Thomas Greene's.
On a summer's day when she was away
He stole into the kitchen and took me
Right in his arms and kissed me on my throat,
I turning my head. Then neither of us
Seemed to know what happened.
And I cried for what would become of me.
And cried and cried as my secret began to show.
One day Mrs. Greene said she understood,
And would make no trouble for me,
And, being childless, would adopt it.
(He had given her a farm to be still.)
So she hid in the house and sent out rumors,
As if it were going to happen to her.
And all went well and the child was born—They were so kind
    to me.
Later I married Gus Wertman, and years passed.
But—at political rallies when sitters-by thought I was crying
At the eloquence of Hamilton Greene—
That was not it.
No! I wanted to say:
That's my son! That's my son!

Hamilton Greene

I was the only child of Frances Harris of Virginia
And Thomas Greene of Kentucky,
Of valiant and honorable blood both.
To them I owe all that I became,
Judge, member of Congress, leader in the State.
From my mother I inherited
Vivacity, fancy, language;
From my father will, judgment, logic.
All honor to them
For what service I was to the people!

Ernest Hyde

My mind was a mirror:
It saw what it saw, it knew what it knew.
In youth my mind was just a mirror
In a rapidly flying car,
Which catches and loses bits of the landscape.
Then in time
Great scratches were made on the mirror,
Letting the outside world come in,
And letting my inner self look out.
For this is the birth of the soul in sorrow,
A birth with gains and losses.
The mind sees the world as a thing apart,
And the soul makes the world at one with itself.
A mirror scratched reflects no image—
And this is the silence of wisdom.

Roger Heston

Oh, many times did Ernest Hyde and I
Argue about the freedom of the will.
My favorite metaphor was Prickett's cow
Roped out to grass, and free, you know, as far
As the length of the rope.
One day while arguing so, watching the cow
Pull at the rope to get beyond the circle
Which she had eaten bare,
Out came the stake, and tossing up her head,
She ran for us.
"What's that, free-will or what?" said Ernest, running.
I fell just as she gored me to my death.

Amos Sibley

Not character, not fortitude, not patience
Were mine, the which the village thought I had
In bearing with my wife, while preaching on,
Doing the work God chose for me.
I loathed her as a termagant, as a wanton.
I knew of her adulteries, every one.
But even so, if I divorced the woman
I must forsake the ministry.
Therefore to do God's work and have it crop,
I bore with her!
So lied I to myself!
So lied I to Spoon River!
Yet I tried lecturing, ran for the legislature,
Canvassed for books, with just the thought in mind:
If I make money thus, I will divorce her.

Mrs. Sibley

The secret of the stars,—gravitation.
The secret of the earth,—layers of rock.
The secret of the soil,—to receive seed.
The secret of the seed,—the germ.
The secret of man,—the sower.
The secret of woman,—the soil.
My secret: Under a mound that you shall never find.

Adam Weirauch

I was crushed between Altgeld and Armour.
I lost many friends, much time and money
Fighting for Altgeld whom Editor Whedon
Denounced as the candidate of gamblers and anarchists.
Then Armour started to ship dressed meat to Spoon River,
Forcing me to shut down my slaughter-house,
And my butcher shop went all to pieces.
The new forces of Altgeld and Armour caught me
At the same time.
I thought it due me, to recoup the money I lost
And to make good the friends that left me,
For the Governor to appoint me Canal Commissioner.
Instead he appointed Whedon of the Spoon River *Argus*,
So I ran for the legislature and was elected.
I said to hell with principle and sold my vote
On Charles T. Yerkes' street-car franchise.
Of course I was one of the fellows they caught.
Who was it, Armour, Altgeld or myself,
That ruined me?

Ezra Bartlett

A chaplain in the army,
A chaplain in the prisons,
An exhorter in Spoon River,
Drunk with divinity, Spoon River—
Yet bringing poor Eliza Johnson to shame,
And myself to scorn and wretchedness.
But why will you never see that love of women,
And even love of wine,
Are the stimulants by which the soul, hungering for divinity,
Reaches the ecstatic vision
And sees the celestial outposts?
Only after many trials for strength,
Only when all stimulants fail,
Does the aspiring soul
By its own sheer power
Find the divine
By resting upon itself.

Amelia Garrick

Yes, here I lie close to a stunted rose bush
In a forgotten place near the fence
Where the thickets from Siever's woods
Have crept over, growing sparsely.
And you, you are a leader in New York,
The wife of a noted millionaire,
A name in the society columns,
Beautiful, admired, magnified perhaps
By the mirage of distance.
You have succeeded, I have failed
In the eyes of the world.
You are alive, I am dead.
Yet I know that I vanquished your spirit;
And I know that lying here far from you,
Unheard of among your great friends
In the brilliant world where you move,
I am really the unconquerable power over your life
That robs it of complete triumph.

John Hancock Otis

As to democracy, fellow citizens,
Are you not prepared to admit
That I, who inherited riches and was to the manor born,
Was second to none in Spoon River
In my devotion to the cause of Liberty?
While my contemporary, Anthony Findlay,
Born in a shanty and beginning life
As a water carrier to the section hands,
Then becoming a section hand when he was grown,
Afterwards foreman of the gang, until he rose
To the superintendency of the railroad,
Living in Chicago,
Was a veritable slave driver,
Grinding the faces of labor,
And a bitter enemy of democracy.
And I say to you, Spoon River,
And to you, O republic,
Beware of the man who rises to power
From one suspender.

Anthony Findlay

Both for the country and for the man,
And for a country as well as a man,
'Tis better to be feared than loved.
And if this country would rather part
With the friendship of every nation
Than surrender its wealth,
I say of a man 'tis worse to lose
Money than friends.
And I rend the curtain that hides the soul
Of an ancient aspiration:
When the people clamor for freedom
They really seek for power o'er the strong.
I, Anthony Findlay, rising to greatness
From a humble water carrier,
Until I could say to thousands "Come,"
And say to thousands "Go,"
Affirm that a nation can never be good,
Or achieve the good,
Where the strong and the wise have not the rod
To use on the dull and weak.

John Cabanis

Neither spite, fellow citizens,
Nor forgetfulness of the shiftlessness,
And the lawlessness and waste
Under democracy's rule in Spoon River
Made me desert the party of law and order
And lead the liberal party.
Fellow citizens! I saw as one with second sight
That every man of the millions of men
Who give themselves to Freedom,
And fail while Freedom fails,
Enduring waste and lawlessness,
And the rule of the weak and the blind,
Dies in the hope of building earth,
Like the coral insect, for the temple
To stand on at the last.
And I swear that Freedom will wage to the end
The war for making every soul
Wise and strong and as fit to rule
As Plato's lofty guardians
In a world republic girdled!

The Unknown

Ye aspiring ones, listen to the story of the unknown
Who lies here with no stone to mark the place.
As a boy reckless and wanton,
Wandering with gun in hand through the forest
Near the mansion of Aaron Hatfield,
I shot a hawk perched on the top
Of a dead tree.
He fell with guttural cry
At my feet, his wing broken.
Then I put him in a cage
Where he lived many days cawing angrily at me
When I offered him food.
Daily I search the realms of Hades
For the soul of the hawk,
That I may offer him the friendship
Of one whom life wounded and caged.

Alexander Throckmorton

In youth my wings were strong and tireless,
But I did not know the mountains.
In age I knew the mountains
But my weary wings could not follow my vision.
Genius is wisdom and youth.

Jonathan Swift Somers

After you have enriched your soul
To the highest point,
With books, thought, suffering, the understanding of many
    personalities,
The power to interpret glances, silences,
The pauses in momentous transformations,
The genius of divination and prophecy,
So that you feel able at times to hold the world
In the hollow of your hand;
Then, if, by the crowding of so many powers
Into the compass of your soul,
Your soul takes fire,
And in the conflagration of your soul
The evil of the world is lighted up and made clear—
Be thankful if in that hour of supreme vision
Life does not fiddle.

Widow McFarlane

I was the Widow McFarlane,
Weaver of carpets for all the village.
And I pity you still at the loom of life,
You who are singing to the shuttle
And lovingly watching the work of your hands,
If you reach the day of hate, of terrible truth.
For the cloth of life is woven, you know,
To a pattern hidden under the loom—
A pattern you never see!
And you weave high-hearted, singing, singing,
You guard the threads of love and friendship
For noble figures in gold and purple.
And long after other eyes can see
You have woven a moon-white strip of cloth,
You laugh in your strength, for Hope o'erlays it
With shapes of love and beauty.
The loom stops short! The pattern's out!
You're alone in the room! You have woven a shroud!
And hate of it lays you in it!

Carl Hamblin

The press of the Spoon River *Clarion* was wrecked,
And I was tarred and feathered,
For publishing this on the day the Anarchists were hanged
    in Chicago:
"I saw a beautiful woman with bandaged eyes
Standing on the steps of a marble temple.
Great multitudes passed in front of her,
Lifting their faces to her imploringly.
In her left hand she held a sword.
She was brandishing the sword,
Sometimes striking a child, again a laborer,
Again a slinking woman, again a lunatic.
In her right hand she held a scale;
Into the scale pieces of gold were tossed
By those who dodged the strokes of the sword.
A man in a black gown read from a manuscript:
'She is no respecter of persons.'
Then a youth wearing a red cap
Leaped to her side and snatched away the bandage.
And lo, the lashes had been eaten away
From the oozy eye-lids;
The eye-balls were seared with a milky mucus;
The madness of a dying soul
Was written on her face —
But the multitude saw why she wore the bandage."

Editor Whedon

To be able to see every side of every question;
To be on every side, to be everything, to be nothing long;
To pervert truth, to ride it for a purpose,
To use great feelings and passions of the human family
For base designs, for cunning ends,
To wear a mask like the Greek actors—
Your eight-page paper—behind which you huddle,
Brawling through the megaphone of big type:
"This is I, the giant."
Thereby also living the life of a sneak-thief,
Poisoned with the anonymous words
Of your clandestine soul.
To scratch dirt over scandal for money,
And exhume it to the winds for revenge,
Or to sell papers,
Crushing reputations, or bodies, if need be,
To win at any cost, save your own life.
To glory in demoniac power, ditching civilization,
As a paranoiac boy puts a log on the track
And derails the express train.
To be an editor, as I was.
Then to lie here close by the river over the place
Where the sewage flows from the village,
And the empty cans and garbage are dumped,
And abortions are hidden.

Eugene Carman

Rhodes' slave! Selling shoes and gingham,
Flour and bacon, overalls, clothing, all day long
For fourteen hours a day for three hundred and thirteen days
For more than twenty years,
Saying "Yes'm" and "Yes, sir" and "Thank you"
A thousand times a day, and all for fifty dollars a month.
Living in this stinking room in the rattle-trap "Commercial."
And compelled to go to Sunday School, and to listen
To the Rev. Abner Peet one hundred and four times a year
For more than an hour at a time,
Because Thomas Rhodes ran the church
As well as the store and the bank.
So while I was tying my neck-tie that morning
I suddenly saw myself in the glass:
My hair all gray, my face like a sodden pie.
So I cursed and cursed: You damned old thing!
You cowardly dog! You rotten pauper!
You Rhodes' slave! Till Roger Baughman
Thought I was having a fight with someone,
And looked through the transom just in time
To see me fall on the floor in a heap
From a broken vein in my head.

Clarence Fawcett

The sudden death of Eugene Carman
Put me in line to be promoted to fifty dollars a month,
And I told my wife and children that night.
But it didn't come, and so I thought
Old Rhodes suspected me of stealing
The blankets I took and sold on the side
For money to pay a doctor's bill for my little girl.
Then like a bolt old Rhodes accused me,
And promised me mercy for my family's sake
If I confessed, and so I confessed,
And begged him to keep it out of the papers,
And I asked the editors, too.
That night at home the constable took me
And every paper, except the *Clarion*,
Wrote me up as a thief
Because old Rhodes was an advertiser
And wanted to make an example of me.
Oh! well, you know how the children cried,
And how my wife pitied and hated me,
And how I came to lie here.

W. Lloyd Garrison Standard

Vegetarian, non-resistant, free-thinker, in ethics a Christian;
Orator apt at the rhinestone rhythm of Ingersoll;
Carnivorous, avenger, believer and pagan;
Continent, promiscuous, changeable, treacherous, vain,
Proud, with the pride that makes struggle a thing for laughter;
With heart cored out by the worm of theatric despair;
Wearing the coat of indifference to hide the shame of defeat;
I, child of the abolitionist idealism—
A sort of Brand in a birth of half-and-half.
What other thing could happen when I defended
The patriot scamps who burned the court house,
That Spoon River might have a new one,
Than plead them guilty? When Kinsey Keene drove through
The card-board mask of my life with a spear of light,
What could I do but slink away, like the beast of myself
Which I raised from a whelp, to a corner and growl.
The pyramid of my life was nought but a dune,
Barren and formless, spoiled at last by the storm.

Professor Newcomer

Everyone laughed at Col. Prichard
For buying an engine so powerful
That it wrecked itself, and wrecked the grinder
He ran it with.
But here is a joke of cosmic size:
The urge of nature that made a man
Evolve from his brain a spiritual life—
Oh miracle of the world!—
The very same brain with which the ape and wolf
Get food and shelter and procreate themselves.
Nature has made man do this,
In a world where she gives him nothing to do
After all—(though the strength of his soul goes round
In a futile waste of power,
To gear itself to the mills of the gods)—
But get food and shelter and procreate himself!

Ralph Rhodes

All they said was true;
I wrecked my father's bank with my loans
To dabble in wheat; but this was true—
I was buying wheat for him as well,
Who couldn't margin the deal in his name
Because of his church relationship.
And while George Reece was serving his term
I chased the will-o'-the-wisp of women,
And the mockery of wine in New York.
It's deathly to sicken of wine and women
When nothing else is left in life.
But suppose your head is gray, and bowed
On a table covered with acrid stubs
Of cigarettes and empty glasses,
And a knock is heard, and you know it's the knock
So long drowned out by popping corks
And the peacock screams of demireps—
And you look up, and there's your Theft,
Who waited until your head was gray,
And your heart skipped beats to say to you:
"The game is ended. I've called for you.
Go out on Broadway and be run over;
They'll ship you back to Spoon River."

Mickey M'Grew

It was just like everything else in life:
Something outside myself drew me down,
My own strength never failed me.
Why, there was the time I earned the money
With which to go away to school,
And my father suddenly needed help
And I had to give him all of it.
Just so it went till I ended up
A man-of-all-work in Spoon River.
Thus when I got the water-tower cleaned,
And they hauled me up the seventy feet,
I unhooked the rope from my wrist,
And laughingly flung my giant arms
Over the smooth steel lips of the top of the tower—
But they slipped from the treacherous slime,
And down, down, down, I plunged
Through bellowing darkness!

Rosie Roberts

I was sick, but more than that, I was mad
At the crooked police, and the crooked game of life.
So I wrote to the Chief of Police at Peoria:
"I am here in my girlhood home in Spoon River,
Gradually wasting away.
But come and take me; I killed the son
Of the merchant prince, in Madam Lou's,
And the papers that said he killed himself
In his home while cleaning a hunting gun
Lied like the devil to hush up scandal,
For the bribe of advertising.
In my room I shot him, at Madam Lou's,
Because he knocked me down when I said
That, in spite of all the money he had,
I'd see my lover that night."

Oscar Hummel

I staggered on through darkness,
There was a hazy sky, a few stars
Which I followed as best I could.
It was nine o'clock, I was trying to get home.
But somehow I was lost,
Though really keeping the road.
Then I reeled through a gate and into a yard,
And called at the top of my voice:
"Oh, Fiddler! Oh, Mr. Jones!"
(I thought it was his house and he would show me the way home.)
But who should step out but A. D. Blood,
In his night shirt, waving a stick of wood,
And roaring about the cursed saloons
And the criminals they made?
"You drunken Oscar Hummel," he said,
As I stood there weaving to and fro,
Taking the blows from the stick in his hand
Till I dropped down dead at his feet.

Roscoe Purkapile

She loved me. Oh! how she loved me!
I never had a chance to escape
From the day she first saw me.
But then after we were married I thought
She might prove her mortality and let me out,
Or she might divorce me.
But few die, none resign.
Then I ran away and was gone a year on a lark.
But she never complained. She said all would be well,
That I would return. And I did return.
I told her that while taking a row in a boat
I had been captured near Van Buren Street
By pirates on Lake Michigan,
And kept in chains, so I could not write her.
She cried and kissed me, and said it was cruel,
Outrageous, inhuman!
I then concluded our marriage
Was a divine dispensation
And could not be dissolved,
Except by death.
I was right.

Mrs. Purkapile

He ran away and was gone for a year.
When he came home he told me the silly story
Of being kidnapped by pirates on Lake Michigan
And kept in chains so he could not write me.
I pretended to believe it, though I knew very well
What he was doing, and that he met
The milliner, Mrs. Williams, now and then
When she went to the city to buy goods, as she said.
But a promise is a promise
And marriage is marriage,
And out of respect for my own character
I refused to be drawn into a divorce
By the scheme of a husband who had merely grown tired
Of his marital vow and duty.

Josiah Tompkins

I was well known and much beloved
And rich, as fortunes are reckoned
In Spoon River, where I had lived and worked.
That was the home for me,
Though all my children had flown afar—
Which is the way of Nature—all but one.
The boy, who was the baby, stayed at home,
To be my help in my failing years
And the solace of his mother.
But I grew weaker, as he grew stronger,
And he quarreled with me about the business,
And his wife said I was a hindrance to it;
And he won his mother to see as he did,
Till they tore me up to be transplanted
With them to her girlhood home in Missouri.
And so much of my fortune was gone at last,
Though I made the will just as he drew it,
He profited little by it.

Mrs. Kessler

Mr. Kessler, you know, was in the army,
And he drew six dollars a month as a pension,
And stood on the corner talking politics,
Or sat at home reading Grant's *Memoirs;*
And I supported the family by washing,
Learning the secrets of all the people
From their curtains, counterpanes, shirts and skirts.
For things that are new grow old at length,
They're replaced with better or none at all:
People are prospering or falling back.
And rents and patches widen with time;
No thread or needle can pace decay,
And there are stains that baffle soap,
And there are colors that run in spite of you,
Blamed though you are for spoiling a dress.
Handkerchiefs, napery, have their secrets—
The laundress, Life, knows all about it.
And I, who went to all the funerals
Held in Spoon River, swear I never
Saw a dead face without thinking it looked
Like something washed and ironed.

Harmon Whitney

Out of the lights and roar of cities,
Drifting down like a spark in Spoon River,
Burnt out with the fire of drink, and broken,
The paramour of a woman I took in self-contempt,
But to hide a wounded pride as well.
To be judged and loathed by a village of little minds—
I, gifted with tongues and wisdom,
Sunk here to the dust of the justice court,
A picker of rags in the rubbage of spites and wrongs,—
I, whom fortune smiled on! I in a village,
Spouting to gaping yokels pages of verse,
Out of the lore of golden years,
Or raising a laugh with a flash of filthy wit
When they bought the drinks to kindle my dying mind.
To be judged by you,
The soul of me hidden from you,
With its wound gangrened
By love for a wife who made the wound,
With her cold white bosom, treasonous, pure and hard,
Relentless to the last, when the touch of her hand,
At any time, might have cured me of the typhus,
Caught in the jungle of life where many are lost.
And only to think that my soul could not re-act,
Like Byron's did, in song, in something noble,
But turned on itself like a tortured snake—
Judge me this way, O world!

Bert Kessler

I winged my bird,
Though he flew toward the setting sun;
But just as the shot rang out, he soared
Up and up through the splinters of golden light,
Till he turned right over, feathers ruffled,
With some of the down of him floating near,
And fell like a plummet into the grass.
I tramped about, parting the tangles,
Till I saw a splash of blood on a stump,
And the quail lying close to the rotten roots.
I reached my hand, but saw no brier,
But something pricked and stung and numbed it.
And then, in a second, I spied the rattler—
The shutters wide in his yellow eyes,
The head of him arched, sunk back in the rings of him,
A circle of filth, the color of ashes,
Or oak leaves bleached under layers of leaves.
I stood like a stone as he shrank and uncoiled
And started to crawl beneath the stump,
When I fell limp in the grass.

Lambert Hutchins

I have two monuments besides this granite obelisk:
One, the house I built on the hill,
With its spires, bay windows, and roof of slate;
The other, the lake-front in Chicago,
Where the railroad keeps a switching yard,
With whistling engines and crunching wheels,
And smoke and soot thrown over the city,
And the crash of cars along the boulevard,—
A blot like a hog-pen on the harbor
Of a great metropolis, foul as a sty.
I helped to give this heritage
To generations yet unborn, with my vote
In the House of Representatives,
And the lure of the thing was to be at rest
From the never-ending fright of need,
And to give my daughters gentle breeding,
And a sense of security in life.
But, you see, though I had the mansion house
And traveling passes and local distinction,
I could hear the whispers, whispers, whispers,
Wherever I went, and my daughters grew up
With a look as if someone were about to strike them;
And they married madly, helter-skelter,
Just to get out and have a change.
And what was the whole of the business worth?
Why, it wasn't worth a damn!

Lillian Stewart

I was the daughter of Lambert Hutchins,
Born in a cottage near the grist-mill,
Reared in the mansion there on the hill,
With its spires, bay windows, and roof of slate.
How proud my mother was of the mansion!
How proud of father's rise in the world!
And how my father loved and watched us,
And guarded our happiness.
But I believe the house was a curse,
For father's fortune was little beside it;
And when my husband found he had married
A girl who was really poor,
He taunted me with the spires,
And called the house a fraud on the world,
A treacherous lure to young men, raising hopes
Of a dowry not to be had;
And a man while selling his vote
Should get enough from the people's betrayal
To wall the whole of his family in.
He vexed my life till I went back home
And lived like an old maid till I died,
Keeping house for father.

Hortense Robbins

My name used to be in the papers daily
As having dined somewhere,
Or traveled somewhere,
Or rented a house in Paris,
Where I entertained the nobility.
I was forever eating or traveling,
Or taking the cure at Baden-Baden.
Now I am here to do honor
To Spoon River, here beside the family whence I sprang.
No one cares now where I dined,
Or lived, or whom I entertained,
Or how often I took the cure at Baden-Baden!

Batterton Dobyns

Did my widow flit about
From Mackinac to Los Angeles,
Resting and bathing and sitting an hour
Or more at the table over soup and meats
And delicate sweets and coffee?
I was cut down in my prime
From overwork and anxiety.
But I thought all along, whatever happens
I've kept my insurance up,
And there's something in the bank,
And a section of land in Manitoba.
But just as I slipped I had a vision
In a last delirium:
I saw myself lying nailed in a box
With a white lawn tie and a boutonnière.
And my wife was sitting by a window
Some place afar overlooking the sea;
She seemed so rested, ruddy and fat,
Although her hair was white.
And she smiled and said to a colored waiter:
"Another slice of roast beef, George.
Here's a nickel for your trouble."

Jacob Godbey

How did you feel, you libertarians,
Who spent your talents rallying noble reasons
Around the saloon, as if Liberty
Was not to be found anywhere except at the bar
Or at a table, guzzling?
How did you feel, Ben Pantier, and the rest of you,
Who almost stoned me for a tyrant,
Garbed as a moralist,
And as a wry-faced ascetic frowning upon Yorkshire pudding,
Roast beef and ale and good will and rosy cheer—
Things you never saw in a grog-shop in your life?
How did you feel after I was dead and gone,
And your goddess, Liberty, unmasked as a strumpet,
Selling out the streets of Spoon River
To the insolent giants
Who manned the saloons from afar?
Did it occur to you that personal liberty
Is liberty of the mind,
Rather than of the belly?

Walter Simmons

My parents thought that I would be
As great as Edison or greater:
For as a boy I made balloons
And wondrous kites and toys with clocks
And little engines with tracks to run on
And telephones of cans and thread.
I played the cornet and painted pictures,
Modeled in clay and took the part
Of the villain in the *Octoroon*.
But then at twenty-one I married
And had to live, and so, to live
I learned the trade of making watches
And kept the jewelry store on the square,
Thinking, thinking, thinking, thinking,—
Not of business, but of the engine
I studied the calculus to build.
And all Spoon River watched and waited
To see it work, but it never worked.
And a few kind souls believed my genius
Was somehow hampered by the store.
It wasn't true. The truth was this:
I didn't have the brains.

Tom Beatty

I was a lawyer like Harmon Whitney
Or Kinsey Keene or Garrison Standard,
For I tried the rights of property,
Although by lamp-light, for thirty years,
In that poker room in the opera house.
And I say to you that Life's a gambler
Head and shoulders above us all.
No mayor alive can close the house.
And if you lose, you can squeal as you will;
You'll not get back your money.
He makes the percentage hard to conquer;
He stacks the cards to catch your weakness
And not to meet your strength.
And he gives you seventy years to play:
For if you cannot win in seventy
You cannot win at all.
So, if you lose, get out of the room—
Get out of the room when your time is up.
It's mean to sit and fumble the cards,
And curse your losses, leaden-eyed,
Whining to try and try.

Roy Butler

If the learned Supreme Court of Illinois
Got at the secret of every case
As well as it does a case of rape
It would be the greatest court in the world.
A jury, of neighbors mostly, with "Butch" Weldy
As foreman, found me guilty in ten minutes
And two ballots on a case like this:
Richard Bandle and I had trouble over a fence,
And my wife and Mrs. Bandle quarreled
As to whether Ipava was a finer town than Table Grove.
I awoke one morning with the love of God
Brimming over my heart, so I went to see Richard
To settle the fence in the spirit of Jesus Christ.
I knocked on the door, and his wife opened;
She smiled and asked me in; I entered—
She slammed the door and began to scream,
"Take your hands off, you low down varlet!"
Just then her husband entered.
I waved my hands, choked up with words.
He went for his gun, and I ran out.
But neither the Supreme Court nor my wife
Believed a word she said.

Searcy Foote

I wanted to go away to college
But rich Aunt Persis wouldn't help me.
So I made gardens and raked the lawns
And bought John Alden's books with my earnings
And toiled for the very means of life.
I wanted to marry Delia Prickett,
But how could I do it with what I earned?
And there was Aunt Persis more than seventy,
Who sat in a wheel-chair half alive,
With her throat so paralyzed, when she swallowed
The soup ran out of her mouth like a duck —
A gourmand yet, investing her income
In mortgages, fretting all the time
About her notes and rents and papers.
That day I was sawing wood for her,
And reading Proudhon in between.
I went in the house for a drink of water,
And there she sat asleep in her chair,
And Proudhon lying on the table,
And a bottle of chloroform on the book,
She used sometimes for an aching tooth.
I poured the chloroform on a handkerchief
And held it to her nose till she died. —
Oh, Delia, Delia, you and Proudhon
Steadied my hand, and the coroner
Said she died of heart failure.
I married Delia and got the money —
A joke on you, Spoon River?

Edmund Pollard

I would I had thrust my hands of flesh
Into the disk-flowers bee-infested,
Into the mirror-like core of fire
Of the light of life, the sun of delight.
For what are anthers worth or petals
Or halo-rays? Mockeries, shadows
Of the heart of the flower, the central flame!
All is yours, young passer-by;
Enter the banquet room with the thought;
Don't sidle in as if you were doubtful
Whether you're welcome—the feast is yours!
Nor take but a little, refusing more
With a bashful "Thank you," when you're hungry.
Is your soul alive? Then let it feed!
Leave no balconies where you can climb;
Nor milk-white bosoms where you can rest;
Nor golden heads with pillows to share;
Nor wine cups while the wine is sweet;
Nor ecstasies of body or soul.
You will die, no doubt, but die while living
In depths of azure, rapt and mated,
Kissing the queen-bee, Life!

Thomas Trevelyan

Reading in Ovid the sorrowful story of Itys,
Son of the love of Tereus and Procne, slain
For the guilty passion of Tereus for Philomela,
The flesh of him served to Tereus by Procne,
And the wrath of Tereus, the murderess pursuing
Till the gods made Philomela a nightingale,
Lute of the rising moon, and Procne a swallow!
Oh livers and artists of Hellas centuries gone,
Sealing in little thuribles dreams and wisdom,
Incense beyond all price, forever fragrant,
A breath whereof makes clear the eyes of the soul!
How I inhaled its sweetness here in Spoon River!
The thurible opening when I had lived and learned
How all of us kill the children of love, and all of us,
Knowing not what we do, devour their flesh;
And all of us change to singers, although it be
But once in our lives, or change—alas!—to swallows,
To twitter amid cold winds· and falling leaves!

Percival Sharp

Observe the clasped hands!
Are they hands of farewell or greeting,
Hands that I helped or hands that helped me?
Would it not be well to carve a hand
With an inverted thumb, like Elagabalus?
And yonder is a broken chain,
The weakest-link idea perhaps—
But what was it?
And lambs, some lying down,
Others standing, as if listening to the shepherd—
Others bearing a cross, one foot lifted up—
Why not chisel a few shambles?
And fallen columns! Carve the pedestal, please,
Or the foundations; let us see the cause of the fall.
And compasses and mathematical instruments,
In irony of the under tenants' ignorance
Of determinants and the calculus of variations.
And anchors, for those who never sailed.
And gates ajar—yes, so they were;
You left them open and stray goats entered your garden.
And an eye watching like one of the Arimaspi—
So did you—with one eye.
And angels blowing trumpets—you are heralded—
It is your horn and your angel and your family's estimate.
It is all very well, but for myself I know
I stirred certain vibrations in Spoon River
Which are my true epitaph, more lasting than stone.

Hiram Scates

I tried to win the nomination
For president of the County Board
And I made speeches all over the county
Denouncing Solomon Purple, my rival,
As an enemy of the people,
In league with the master-foes of man.
Young idealists, broken warriors,
Hobbling on one crutch of hope,
Souls that stake their all on the truth,
Losers of worlds at heaven's bidding,
Flocked about me and followed my voice
As the savior of the county.
But Solomon won the nomination;
And then I faced about,
And rallied my followers to his standard,
And made him victor, made him King
Of the Golden Mountain with the door
Which closed on my heels just as I entered,
Flattered by Solomon's invitation,
To be the County Board's secretary.
And out in the cold stood all my followers:
Young idealists, broken warriors
Hobbling on one crutch of hope —
Souls that staked their all on the truth,
Losers of worlds at heaven's bidding,
Watching the Devil kick the Millennium
Over the Golden Mountain.

Peleg Poague

Horses and men are just alike.
There was my stallion, Billy Lee,
Black as a cat and trim as a deer,
With an eye of fire, keen to start,
And he could hit the fastest speed
Of any racer around Spoon River.
But just as you'd think he couldn't lose,
With his lead of fifty yards or more,
He'd rear himself and throw the rider,
And fall back over, tangled up,
Completely gone to pieces.
You see he was a perfect fraud:
He couldn't win, he couldn't work,
He was too light to haul or plow with,
And no one wanted colts from him.
And when I tried to drive him—well,
He ran away and killed me.

Jeduthan Hawley

There would be a knock at the door
And I would arise at midnight and go to the shop,
Where belated travelers would hear me hammering
Sepulchral boards and tacking satin.
And often I wondered who would go with me
To the distant land, our names the theme
For talk, in the same week, for I've observed
Two always go together.
Chase Henry was paired with Edith Conant;
And Jonathan Somers with Willie Metcalf;
And Editor Hamblin with Francis Turner,
When he prayed to live longer than Editor Whedon;
And Thomas Rhodes with widow McFarlane;
And Emily Sparks with Barry Holden;
And Oscar Hummel with Davis Matlock;
And Editor Whedon with Fiddler Jones;
And Faith Matheny with Dorcas Gustine.
And I, the solemnest man in town,
Stepped off with Daisy Fraser.

Abel Melveny

I bought every kind of machine that's known —
Grinders, shellers, planters, mowers,
Mills and rakes and ploughs and threshers —
And all of them stood in the rain and sun,
Getting rusted, warped and battered,
For I had no sheds to store them in,
And no use for most of them.
And toward the last, when I thought it over,
There by my window, growing clearer
About myself, as my pulse slowed down,
And looked at one of the mills I bought,
Which I didn't have the slightest need of,
As things turned out, and I never ran —
A fine machine, once brightly varnished,
And eager to do its work,
Now with its paint washed off —
I saw myself as a good machine
That Life had never used.

Oaks Tutt

My mother was for woman's rights
And my father was the rich miller at London Mills.
I dreamed of the wrongs of the world and wanted to right them.
When my father died, I set out to see peoples and countries
In order to learn how to reform the world.
I traveled through many lands.
I saw the ruins of Rome,
And the ruins of Athens,
And the ruins of Thebes.
And I sat by moonlight amid the necropolis of Memphis.
There I was caught up by wings of flame,
And a voice from heaven said to me:
"Injustice, Untruth destroyed them. Go forth!
Preach Justice! Preach Truth!"
And I hastened back to Spoon River
To say farewell to my mother before beginning my work.
They all saw a strange light in my eye.
And by and by, when I talked, they discovered
What had come in my mind.
Then Jonathan Swift Somers challenged me to debate
The subject, (I taking the negative):
"Pontius Pilate, the Greatest Philosopher of the World."
And he won the debate by saying at last,
"Before you reform the world, Mr. Tutt,
Please answer the question of Pontius Pilate:
'What is Truth?' "

Elliott Hawkins

I looked like Abraham Lincoln.
I was one of you, Spoon River, in all fellowship,
But standing for the rights of property and for order.
A regular church attendant,
Sometimes appearing in your town meetings to warn you
Against the evils of discontent and envy,
And to denounce those who tried to destroy the Union,
And to point to the peril of the Knights of Labor.
My success and my example are inevitable influences
In your young men and in generations to come,
In spite of attacks of newspapers like the *Clarion;*
A regular visitor at Springfield,
When the Legislature was in session,
To prevent raids upon the railroads,
And the men building up the state.
Trusted by them and by you, Spoon River, equally
In spite of the whispers that I was a lobbyist.
Moving quietly through the world, rich and courted.
Dying at last, of course, but lying here
Under a stone with an open book carved upon it
And the words "Of such is the Kingdom of Heaven."
And now, you world-savers, who reaped nothing in life
And in death have neither stones nor epitaphs,
How do you like your silence from mouths stopped
With the dust of my triumphant career?

Voltaire Johnson

Why did you bruise me with your rough places
If you did not want me to tell you about them?
And stifle me with your stupidities,
If you did not want me to expose them?
And nail me with the nails of cruelty,
If you did not want me to pluck the nails forth
And fling them in your faces?
And starve me because I refused to obey you,
If you did not want me to undermine your tyranny?
I might have been as soul serene
As William Wordsworth except for you!
But what a coward you are, Spoon River,
When you drove me to stand in a magic circle
By the sword of Truth described!
And then to whine and curse your burns,
And curse my power who stood and laughed
Amid ironical lightning!

English Thornton

Here! You sons of the men
Who fought with Washington at Valley Forge,
And whipped Black Hawk at Starved Rock,
Arise! Do battle with the descendants of those
Who bought land in the Loop when it was waste sand,
And sold blankets and guns to the army of Grant,
And sat in legislatures in the early days,
Taking bribes from the railroads!
Arise! Do battle with the fops and bluffs,
The pretenders and figurantes of the society column,
And the yokel souls whose daughters marry counts;
And the parasites on great ideas,
And the noisy riders of great causes,
And the heirs of ancient thefts.
Arise! And make the city yours,
And the state yours—
You who are sons of the hardy yeomanry of the forties!
By God! If you do not destroy these vermin
My avenging ghost will wipe out
Your city and your state.

Enoch Dunlap

How many times, during the twenty years
I was your leader, friends of Spoon River,
Did you neglect the convention and caucus,
And leave the burden on my hands
Of guarding and saving the people's cause?—
Sometimes because you were ill;
Or your grandmother was ill;
Or you drank too much and fell asleep;
Or else you said: "He is our leader,
All will be well; he fights for us;
We have nothing to do but follow."
But oh, how you cursed me when I fell,
And cursed me, saying I had betrayed you,
In leaving the caucus room for a moment,
When the people's enemies, there assembled,
Waited and watched for a chance to destroy
The Sacred Rights of the People.
You common rabble! I left the caucus
To go to the urinal!

Ida Frickey

Nothing in life is alien to you.
I was a penniless girl from Summum
Who stepped from the morning train in Spoon River.
All the houses stood before me with closed doors
And drawn shades—I was barred out;
I had no place or part in any of them.
And I walked past the old McNeely mansion,
A castle of stone 'mid the walks and gardens,
With workmen about the place on guard,
And the county and state upholding it
For its lordly owner, full of pride.
I was so hungry I had a vision:
I saw a giant pair of scissors
Dip from the sky, like the beam of a dredge,
And cut the house in two like a curtain.
But at the "Commercial" I saw a man,
Who winked at me as I asked for work—
It was Wash McNeely's son.
He proved the link in the chain of title
To half my ownership of the mansion,
Through a breach of promise suit—the scissors.
So, you see, the house, from the day I was born,
Was only waiting for me.

Seth Compton

When I died, the circulating library
Which I built up for Spoon River,
And managed for the good of inquiring minds,
Was sold at auction on the public square,
As if to destroy the last vestige
Of my memory and influence.
For those of you who could not see the virtue
Of knowing Volney's *Ruins* as well as Butler's *Analogy,*
And *Faust* as well as *Evangeline,*
Were really the power in the village,
And often you asked me,
"What is the use of knowing the evil in the world?"
I am out of your way now, Spoon River.
Choose your own good and call it good.
For I could never make you see
That no one knows what is good
Who knows not what is evil;
And no one knows what is true
Who knows not what is false.

Felix Schmidt

It was only a little house of two rooms—
Almost like a child's play-house—
With scarce five acres of ground around it;
And I had so many children to feed
And school and clothe, and a wife who was sick
From bearing children.
One day lawyer Whitney came along
And proved to me that Christian Dallman,
Who owned three thousand acres of land,
Had bought the eighty that adjoined me
In eighteen hundred and seventy-one
For eleven dollars, at a sale for taxes,
While my father lay in his mortal illness.
So the quarrel arose and I went to law.
But when we came to the proof,
A survey of the land showed clear as day
That Dallman's tax deed covered my ground
And my little house of two rooms.
It served me right for stirring him up.
I lost my case and lost my place.
I left the court room and went to work
As Christian Dallman's tenant.

Schroeder the Fisherman

I sat on the bank above Bernadotte
And dropped crumbs in the water,
Just to see the minnows bump each other,
Until the strongest got the prize.
Or I went to my little pasture
Where the peaceful swine were asleep in the wallow,
Or nosing each other lovingly,
And emptied a basket of yellow corn,
And watched them push and squeal and bite,
And trample each other to get the corn.
And I saw how Christian Dallman's farm,
Of more than three thousand acres,
Swallowed the patch of Felix Schmidt,
As a bass will swallow a minnow.
And I say if there's anything in man—
Spirit, or conscience, or breath of God—
That makes him different from the fishes or hogs,
I'd like to see it work!

Richard Bone

When I first came to Spoon River
I did not know whether what they told me
Was true or false.
They would bring me the epitaph
And stand around the shop while I worked
And say "He was so kind," "He was wonderful,"
"She was the sweetest woman," "He was a consistent Christian."
And I chiseled for them whatever they wished,
All in ignorance of its truth.
But later, as I lived among the people here,
I knew how near to the life
Were the epitaphs that were ordered for them as they died.
But still I chiseled whatever they paid me to chisel
And made myself party to the false chronicles
Of the stones,
Even as the historian does who writes
Without knowing the truth,
Or because he is influenced to hide it.

Silas Dement

It was moon-light, and the earth sparkled
With new-fallen frost.
It was midnight and not a soul was abroad.
Out of the chimney of the court-house
A grey-hound of smoke leapt and chased
The northwest wind.
I carried a ladder to the landing of the stairs
And leaned it against the frame of the trap-door
In the ceiling of the portico,
And I crawled under the roof and amid the rafters
And flung among the seasoned timbers
A lighted handful of oil-soaked waste.
Then I came down and slunk away.
In a little while the fire-bell rang—
Clang! Clang! Clang!
And the Spoon River ladder company
Came with a dozen buckets and began to pour water
On the glorious bonfire, growing hotter,
Higher and brighter, till the walls fell in,
And the limestone columns where Lincoln stood
Crashed like trees when the woodman fells them . . .
When I came back from Joliet
There was a new court-house with a dome.
For I was punished like all who destroy
The past for the sake of the future.

Dillard Sissman

The buzzards wheel slowly
In wide circles, in a sky
Faintly hazed as from dust from the road.
And a wind sweeps through the pasture where I lie
Beating the grass into long waves.
My kite is above the wind,
Though now and then it wobbles,
Like a man shaking his shoulders;
And the tail streams out momentarily,
Then sinks to rest.
And the buzzards wheel and wheel,
Sweeping the zenith with wide circles
Above my kite. And the hills sleep.
And a farm house, white as snow,
Peeps from green trees—far away.
And I watch my kite,
For the thin moon will kindle herself ere long,
Then she will swing like a pendulum dial
To the tail of my kite.
A spurt of flame like a water-dragon
Dazzles my eyes—
I am shaken as a banner!

Jonathan Houghton

There is the caw of a crow,
And the hesitant song of a thrush.
There is the tinkle of a cowbell far away,
And the voice of a plowman on Shipley's hill.
The forest beyond the orchard is still
With midsummer stillness;
And along the road a wagon chuckles,
Loaded with corn, going to Atterbury.
And an old man sits under a tree asleep,
And an old woman crosses the road,
Coming from the orchard with a bucket of blackberries.
And a boy lies in the grass
Near the feet of the old man,
And looks up at the sailing clouds,
And longs, and longs, and longs
For what, he knows not:
For manhood, for life, for the unknown world!
Then thirty years passed,
And the boy returned worn out by life
And found the orchard vanished,
And the forest gone,
And the house made over,
And the roadway filled with dust from automobiles—
And himself desiring The Hill!

E. C. Culbertson

Is it true, Spoon River,
That in the hall-way of the new court-house
There is a tablet of bronze
Containing the embossed faces
Of Editor Whedon and Thomas Rhodes?
And is it true that my successful labors
In the County Board, without which
Not one stone would have been placed on another,
And the contributions out of my own pocket
To build the temple, are but memories among the people,
Gradually fading away, and soon to descend
With them to this oblivion where I lie?
In truth, I can so believe.
For it is a law of the Kingdom of Heaven
That whoso enters the vineyard at the eleventh hour
Shall receive a full day's pay.
And it is a law of the Kingdom of this World
That those who first oppose a good work
Seize it and make it their own,
When the corner-stone is laid,
And memorial tablets are erected.

Shack Dye

The white men played all sorts of jokes on me.
They took big fish off my hook
And put little ones on, while I was away
Getting a stringer, and made me believe
I hadn't seen aright the fish I had caught.
When Burr Robbins circus came to town
They got the ring master to let a tame leopard
Into the ring, and made me believe
I was whipping a wild beast like Samson
When I, for an offer of fifty dollars,
Dragged him out to his cage.
One time I entered my blacksmith shop
And shook as I saw some horse-shoes crawling
Across the floor, as if alive—
Walter Simmons had put a magnet
Under the barrel of water.
Yet every one of you, you white men,
Was fooled about fish and about leopards too,
And you didn't know any more than the horse-shoes did
What moved you about Spoon River.

Hildrup Tubbs

I made two fights for the people.
First I left my party, bearing the gonfalon
Of independence, for reform, and was defeated.
Next I used my rebel strength
To capture the standard of my old party—
And I captured it, but I was defeated.
Discredited and discarded, misanthropical,
I turned to the solace of gold
And I used my remnant of power
To fasten myself like a saprophyte
Upon the putrescent carcass
Of Thomas Rhodes' bankrupt bank,
As assignee of the fund.
Everyone now turned from me.
My hair grew white,
My purple lusts grew gray,
Tobacco and whisky lost their savor,
And for years Death ignored me
As he does a hog.

Henry Tripp

The bank broke and I lost my savings.
I was sick of the tiresome game in Spoon River
And I made up my mind to run away
And leave my place in life and my family;
But just as the midnight train pulled in,
Quick off the steps jumped Cully Green
And Martin Vise, and began to fight
To settle their ancient rivalry,
Striking each other with fists that sounded
Like the blows of knotted clubs.
Now it seemed to me that Cully was winning,
When his bloody face broke into a grin
Of sickly cowardice, leaning on Martin
And whining out "We're good friends, Mart,
You know that I'm your friend."
But a terrible punch from Martin knocked him
Around and around and into a heap.
And then they arrested me as a witness,
And I lost my train and stayed in Spoon River
To wage my battle of life to the end.
Oh, Cully Green, you were my savior—
You, so ashamed and drooped for years,
Loitering listless about the streets,
And tying rags 'round your festering soul,
Who failed to fight it out.

Granville Calhoun

I wanted to be County Judge
One more term, so as to round out a service
Of thirty years.
But my friends left me and joined my enemies,
And they elected a new man.
Then a spirit of revenge seized me,
And I infected my four sons with it,
And I brooded upon retaliation,
Until the great physician, Nature,
Smote me through with paralysis
To give my soul and body a rest.
Did my sons get power and money?
Did they serve the people or yoke them
To till and harvest fields of self?
For how could they ever forget
My face at my bedroom window,
Sitting helpless amid my golden cages
Of singing canaries,
Looking at the old court-house?

Henry C. Calhoun

I reached the highest place in Spoon River,
But through what bitterness of spirit!
The face of my father, sitting speechless,
Child-like, watching his canaries,
And looking at the court-house window
Of the county judge's room,
And his admonitions to me to seek
My own in life, and punish Spoon River
To avenge the wrong the people did him,
Filled me with furious energy
To seek for wealth and seek for power.
But what did he do but send me along
The path that leads to the grove of the Furies?
I followed the path and I tell you this:
On the way to the grove you'll pass the Fates,
Shadow-eyed, bent over their weaving.
Stop for a moment, and if you see
The thread of revenge leap out of the shuttle,
Then quickly snatch from Atropos
The shears and cut it, lest your sons,
And the children of them and their children,
Wear the envenomed robe.

Alfred Moir

Why was I not devoured by self-contempt,
And rotted down by indifference
And impotent revolt like Indignation Jones?
Why, with all of my errant steps,
Did I miss the fate of Willard Fluke?
And why, though I stood at Burchard's bar,
As a sort of decoy for the house to the boys
To buy the drinks, did the curse of drink
Fall on me like rain that runs off,
Leaving the soul of me dry and clean?
And why did I never kill a man
Like Jack McGuire?
But instead I mounted a little in life,
And I owe it all to a book I read.
But why did I go to Mason City,
Where I chanced to see the book in a window,
With its garish cover luring my eye?
And why did my soul respond to the book,
As I read it over and over?

Perry Zoll

My thanks, friends of the County Scientific Association,
For this modest boulder,
And its little tablet of bronze.
Twice I tried to join your honored body,
And was rejected,
And when my little brochure
On the intelligence of plants
Began to attract attention
You almost voted me in.
After that I grew beyond the need of you
And your recognition.
Yet I do not reject your memorial stone,
Seeing that I should, in so doing,
Deprive you of honor to yourselves.

Dippold the Optician

What do you see now?
Globes of red, yellow, purple.
Just a moment! And now?
My father and mother and sisters.
Yes! And now?
Knights at arms, beautiful women, kind faces.
Try this.
A field of grain—a city.
Very good! And now?
A young woman with angels bending over her.
A heavier lens! And now?
Many women with bright eyes and open lips.
Try this.
Just a goblet on a table.
Oh I see! Try this lens!
Just an open space—I see nothing in particular.
Well, now!
Pine trees, a lake, a summer sky.
That's better. And now?
A book.
Read a page for me.
I can't. My eyes are carried beyond the page.
Try this lens.
Depths of air.
Excellent! And now?
Light, just light, making everything below it a toy world.
Very well, we'll make the glasses accordingly.

Magrady Graham

Tell me, was Altgeld elected Governor?
For when the returns began to come in
And Cleveland was sweeping the East,
It was too much for you, poor old heart,
Who had striven for democracy
In the long, long years of defeat.
And like a watch that is worn
I felt you growing slower until you stopped.
Tell me, was Altgeld elected,
And what did he do?
Did they bring his head on a platter to a dancer,
Or did he triumph for the people?
For when I saw him
And took his hand,
The child-like blueness of his eyes
Moved me to tears,
And there was an air of eternity about him,
Like the cold, clear light that rests at dawn
On the hills!

Archibald Higbie

I loathed you, Spoon River. I tried to rise above you,
I was ashamed of you. I despised you
As the place of my nativity.
And there in Rome, among the artists,
Speaking Italian, speaking French,
I seemed to myself at times to be free
Of every trace of my origin.
I seemed to be reaching the heights of art
And to breathe the air that the masters breathed,
And to see the world with their eyes.
But still they'd pass my work and say:
"What are you driving at, my friend?
Sometimes the face looks like Apollo's,
At others it has a trace of Lincoln's."
There was no culture, you know, in Spoon River,
And I burned with shame and held my peace.
And what could I do, all covered over
And weighted down with western soil,
Except aspire, and pray for another
Birth in the world, with all of Spoon River
Rooted out of my soul?

Tom Merritt

At first I suspected something—
She acted so calm and absent-minded.
And one day I heard the back door shut,
As I entered the front, and I saw him slink
Back of the smokehouse into the lot,
And run across the field.
And I meant to kill him on sight.
But that day, walking near Fourth Bridge,
Without a stick or a stone at hand,
All of a sudden I saw him standing,
Scared to death, holding his rabbits,
And all I could say was, "Don't, Don't, Don't,"
As he aimed and fired at my heart.

Mrs. Merritt

Silent before the jury,
Returning no word to the judge when he asked me
If I had aught to say against the sentence,
Only shaking my head.
What could I say to people who thought
That a woman of thirty-five was at fault
When her lover of nineteen killed her husband?
Even though she had said to him over and over,
"Go away, Elmer, go far away,
I have maddened your brain with the gift of my body:
You will do some terrible thing."
And just as I feared, he killed my husband;
With which I had nothing to do, before God!
Silent for thirty years in prison!
And the iron gates of Joliet
Swung as the gray and silent trusties
Carried me out in a coffin.

Elmer Karr

What but the love of God could have softened
And made forgiving the people of Spoon River
Toward me who wronged the bed of Thomas Merritt
And murdered him beside?
Oh, loving hearts that took me in again
When I returned from fourteen years in prison!
Oh, helping hands that in the church received me,
And heard with tears my penitent confession,
Who took the sacrament of bread and wine!
Repent, ye living ones, and rest with Jesus.

Elizabeth Childers

Dust of my dust,
And dust with my dust,
O, child who died as you entered the world,
Dead with my death!
Not knowing breath, though you tried so hard,
With a heart that beat when you lived with me,
And stopped when you left me for Life.
It is well, my child. For you never traveled
The long, long way that begins with school days,
When little fingers blur under the tears
That fall on the crooked letters.
And the earliest wound, when a little mate
Leaves you alone for another;
And sickness, and the face of Fear by the bed;
The death of a father or mother;
Or shame for them, or poverty;
The maiden sorrow of school days ended;
And eyeless Nature that makes you drink
From the cup of Love, though you know it's poisoned;
To whom would your flower-face have been lifted?
Botanist, weakling? Cry of what blood to yours?—
Pure or foul, for it makes no matter,
It's blood that calls to our blood.
And then your children—oh, what might they be?
And what your sorrow? Child! Child!
Death is better than Life!

Edith Conant

We stand about this place—we, the memories;
And shade our eyes because we dread to read:
"June 17th, 1884, aged 21 years and 3 days."
And all things are changed.
And we—we, the memories—stand here for ourselves alone,
For no eye marks us, or would know why we are here.
Your husband is dead, your sister lives far away,
Your father is bent with age;
He has forgotten you, he scarcely leaves the house
Any more.
No one remembers your exquisite face,
Your lyric voice!
How you sang, even on the morning you were stricken,
With piercing sweetness, with thrilling sorrow,
Before the advent of the child which died with you.
It is all forgotten, save by us, the memories,
Who are forgotten by the world.
All is changed, save the river and the hill—
Even they are changed.
Only the burning sun and the quiet stars are the same.
And we—we, the memories—stand here in awe,
Our eyes closed with the weariness of tears—
In immeasurable weariness!

Charles Webster

The pine woods on the hill,
And the farmhouse miles away,
Showed clear as though behind a lens
Under a sky of peacock blue!
But a blanket of cloud by afternoon
Muffled the earth. And you walked the road
And the clover field, where the only sound
Was the cricket's liquid tremolo.
Then the sun went down between great drifts
Of distant storms. For a rising wind
Swept clean the sky and blew the flames
Of the unprotected stars;
And swayed the russet moon,
Hanging between the rim of the hill
And the twinkling boughs of the apple orchard.
You walked the shore in thought
Where the throats of the waves were like whip-poor-wills
Singing beneath the water and crying
To the wash of the wind in the cedar trees,
Till you stood, too full for tears, by the cot,
And looking up saw Jupiter,
Tipping the spire of the giant pine,
And looking down saw my vacant chair,
Rocked by the wind on the lonely porch —
Be brave, Beloved!

Father Malloy

You are over there, Father Malloy,
Where holy ground is, and the cross marks every grave,
Not here with us on the hill—
Us of wavering faith, and clouded vision
And drifting hope, and unforgiven sins.
You were so human, Father Malloy,
Taking a friendly glass sometimes with us,
Siding with us who would rescue Spoon River
From the coldness and the dreariness of village morality.
You were like a traveler who brings a little box of sand
From the wastes about the pyramids
And makes them real and Egypt real.
You were a part of and related to a great past,
And yet you were so close to many of us.
You believed in the joy of life.
You did not seem to be ashamed of the flesh.
You faced life as it is,
And as it changes.
Some of us almost came to you, Father Malloy,
Seeing how your church had divined the heart,
And provided for it,
Through Peter the Flame,
Peter the Rock.

Ami Green

Not "a youth with hoary head and haggard eye,"
But an old man with smooth skin
And black hair!
I had the face of a boy as long as I lived,
And for years a soul that was stiff and bent,
In a world which saw me just as a jest,
To be hailed familiarly when it chose,
And loaded up as a man when it chose,
Being neither man nor boy.
In truth it was soul as well as body
Which never matured, and I say to you
That the much-sought prize of eternal youth
Is just arrested growth.

Calvin Campbell

Ye who are kicking against Fate,
Tell me how it is that on this hillside,
Running down to the river,
Which fronts the sun and the south wind,
This plant draws from the air and soil
Poison and becomes poison ivy?
And this plant draws from the same air and soil
Sweet elixirs and colors and becomes arbutus?
And both flourish?
You may blame Spoon River for what it is,
But whom do you blame for the will in you
That feeds itself and makes you dock-weed,
Jimpson, dandelion or mullen
And which can never use any soil or air
So as to make you jessamine or wistaria?

Henry Layton

Whoever thou art who passest by
Know that my father was gentle,
And my mother was violent,
While I was born the whole of such hostile halves,
Not intermixed and fused,
But each distinct, feebly soldered together.
Some of you saw me as gentle,
Some as violent,
Some as both.
But neither half of me wrought my ruin.
It was the falling assunder of halves,
Never a part of each other,
That left me a lifeless soul.

Harlan Sewall

You never understood, O unknown one,
Why it was I repaid
Your devoted friendship and delicate ministrations
First with diminished thanks,
Afterward by gradually withdrawing my presence from you,
So that I might not be compelled to thank you,
And then with silence which followed upon
Our final separation.
You had cured my diseased soul. But to cure it
You saw my disease, you knew my secret,
And that is why I fled from you.
For though when our bodies rise from pain
We kiss forever the watchful hands
That gave us wormwood, while we shudder
For thinking of the wormwood,
A soul that's cured is a different matter,
For there we'd blot from memory
The soft-toned words, the searching eyes,
And stand forever oblivious,
Not so much of the sorrow itself
As of the hand that healed it.

Ippolit Konovaloff

I was a gun-smith in Odessa.
One night the police broke in the room
Where a group of us were reading Spencer
And seized our books and arrested us.
But I escaped and came to New York
And thence to Chicago, and then to Spoon River,
Where I could study my Kant in peace
And eke out a living repairing guns!
Look at my moulds! My architectonics!
One for a barrel, one for a hammer,
And others for other parts of a gun!
Well, now suppose no gun-smith living
Had anything else but duplicate moulds
Of these I show you—well, all guns
Would be just alike, with a hammer to hit
The cap and a barrel to carry the shot,
All acting alike for themselves, and all
Acting against each other alike.
And there would be your world of guns!
Which nothing could ever free from itself
Except a Moulder with different moulds
To mould the metal over.

Henry Phipps

I was the Sunday school superintendent,
The dummy president of the wagon works
And the canning factory,
Acting for Thomas Rhodes and the banking clique;
My son the cashier of the bank,
Wedded to Rhodes' daughter,
My week days spent in making money,
My Sundays at church and in prayer.
In everything a cog in the wheel of things-as-they-are:
Of money, master and man, made white
With the paint of the Christian creed.
And then:
The bank collapsed. I stood and looked at the wrecked machine —
The wheels with blow-holes stopped with putty and painted;
The rotten bolts, the broken rods;
And only the hopper for souls fit to be used again
In a new devourer of life, when newspapers, judges and money-
    magicians
Build over again.
I was stripped to the bone, but I lay in the Rock of Ages,
Seeing now through the game, no longer a dupe,
And knowing "the upright shall dwell in the land
But the years of the wicked shall be shortened."
Then suddenly, Dr. Meyers discovered
A cancer in my liver.
I was not, after all, the particular care of God!
Why, even thus standing on a peak
Above the mists through which I had climbed,
And ready for larger life in the world,
Eternal forces
Moved me on with a push.

Harry Wilmans

I was just turned twenty-one,
And Henry Phipps, the Sunday school superintendent,
Made a speech in Bindle's Opera House.
"The honor of the flag must be upheld," he said,
"Whether it be assailed by a barbarous tribe of Tagalogs
Or the greatest power in Europe."
And we cheered and cheered the speech and the flag he waved
As he spoke.
And I went to the war in spite of my father,
And followed the flag till I saw it raised
By our camp in a rice field near Manila,
And all of us cheered and cheered it.
But there were flies and poisonous things;
And there was the deadly water,
And the cruel heat,
And the sickening, putrid food;
And the smell of the trench just back of the tents
Where the soldiers went to empty themselves;
And there were the whores who followed us, full of syphilis;
And beastly acts between ourselves or alone,
With bullying, hatred, degradation among us,
And days of loathing and nights of fear
To the hour of the charge through the steaming swamp,
Following the flag,
Till I fell with a scream, shot through the guts.
Now there's a flag over me in Spoon River!
A flag! A flag!

John Wasson

Oh! the dew-wet grass of the meadow in North Carolina
Through which Rebecca followed me wailing, wailing,
One child in her arms, and three that ran along wailing,
Lengthening out the farewell to me off to the war with the British,
And then the long, hard years down to the day of Yorktown.
And then my search for Rebecca,
Finding her at last in Virginia,
Two children dead in the meanwhile.
We went by oxen to Tennessee,
Thence after years to Illinois,
At last to Spoon River.
We cut the buffalo grass,
We felled the forests,
We built the school houses, built the bridges,
Leveled the roads and tilled the fields,
Alone with poverty, scourges, death—
If Harry Wilmans who fought the Filipinos
Is to have a flag on his grave,
Take it from mine!

Many Soldiers

The idea danced before us as a flag;
The sound of martial music;
The thrill of carrying a gun;
Advancement in the world on coming home;
A glint of glory, wrath for foes;
A dream of duty to country or to God.
But these were things in ourselves, shining before us,
They were not the power behind us,
Which was the Almighty hand of Life,
Like fire at earth's center making mountains,
Or pent up waters that cut them through.
Do you remember the iron band
The blacksmith, Shack Dye, welded
Around the oak on Bennet's lawn,
From which to swing a hammock,
That daughter Janet might repose in, reading
On summer afternoons?
And that the growing tree at last
Sundered the iron band?
But not a cell in all the tree
Knew aught save that it thrilled with life,
Nor cared because the hammock fell
In the dust with Milton's Poems.

Godwin James

Harry Wilmans! You who fell in a swamp
Near Manila, following the flag,
You were not wounded by the greatness of a dream,
Or destroyed by ineffectual work,
Or driven to madness by Satanic snags;
You were not torn by aching nerves,
Nor did you carry great wounds to your old age.
You did not starve, for the government fed you.
You did not suffer yet cry "forward"
To an army which you led
Against a foe with mocking smiles,
Sharper than bayonets. You were not smitten down
By invisible bombs. You were not rejected
By those for whom you were defeated.
You did not eat the savorless bread
Which a poor alchemy had made from ideals.
You went to Manila, Harry Wilmans,
While I enlisted in the bedraggled army
Of bright-eyed, divine youths,
Who surged forward, who were driven back and fell,
Sick, broken, crying, shorn of faith,
Following the flag of the Kingdom of Heaven.
You and I, Harry Wilmans, have fallen
In our several ways, not knowing
Good from bad, defeat from victory,
Nor what face it is that smiles
Behind the demoniac mask.

Lyman King

You may think, passer-by, that Fate
Is a pit-fall outside of yourself,
Around which you may walk by the use of foresight
And wisdom.
Thus you believe, viewing the lives of other men,
As one who in God-like fashion bends over an anthill,
Seeing how their difficulties could be avoided.
But pass on into life:
In time you shall see Fate approach you
In the shape of your own image in the mirror;
Or you shall sit alone by your own hearth,
And suddenly the chair by you shall hold a guest,
And you shall know that guest,
And read the authentic message of his eyes.

Caroline Branson

With our hearts like drifting suns, had we but walked,
As often before, the April fields till star-light
Silkened over with viewless gauze the darkness
Under the cliff, our trysting place in the wood,
Where the brook turns! Had we but passed from wooing,
Like notes of music that run together, into winning,
In the inspired improvisation of love!
But to put back of us as a canticle ended
The rapt enchantment of the flesh,
In which our souls swooned, down, down,
Where time was not, nor space, nor ourselves—
Annihilated in love!
To leave these behind for a room with lamps:
And to stand with our Secret mocking itself,
And hiding itself amid flowers and mandolins,
Stared at by all between salad and coffee.
And to see him tremble, and feel myself
Prescient, as one who signs a bond—
Not flaming with gifts and pledges heaped
With rosy hands over his brow.
And then, O night! deliberate! unlovely!
With all of our wooing blotted out by the winning,
In a chosen room in an hour that was known to all!
Next day he sat so listless, almost cold,
So strangely changed, wondering why I wept,
Till a kind of sick despair and voluptuous madness
Seized us to make the pact of death.

A stalk of the earth-sphere,
Frail as star-light;
Waiting to be drawn once again
Into creation's stream.
But next time to be given birth
Gazed at by Raphael and St. Francis
Sometimes as they pass.
For I am their little brother,

To be known clearly face to face
Through a cycle of birth hereafter run.
You may know the seed and the soil;
You may feel the cold rain fall,
But only the earth-sphere, only heaven
Knows the secret of the seed
In the nuptial chamber under the soil.
Throw me into the stream again,
Give me another trial—
Save me, Shelley!

Anne Rutledge

Out of me unworthy and unknown
The vibrations of deathless music:
"With malice toward none, with charity for all."
Out of me the forgiveness of millions toward millions,
And the beneficent face of a nation
Shining with justice and truth.
I am Anne Rutledge who sleep beneath these weeds,
Beloved in life of Abraham Lincoln,
Wedded to him, not through union,
But through separation.
Bloom forever, O Republic,
From the dust of my bosom!

Hamlet Micure

In a lingering fever many visions come to you:
I was in the little house again
With its great yard of clover
Running down to the board-fence,
Shadowed by the oak tree,
Where we children had our swing.
Yet the little house was a manor hall
Set in a lawn, and by the lawn was the sea.
I was in the room where little Paul
Strangled from diphtheria,
But yet it was not this room —
It was a sunny verandah enclosed
With mullioned windows,
And in a chair sat a man in a dark cloak,
With a face like Euripides.
He had come to visit me, or I had gone to visit him —
I could not tell.
We could hear the beat of the sea, the clover nodded
Under a summer wind, and little Paul came
With clover blossoms to the window and smiled.
Then I said: "What is 'divine despair,' Alfred?"
"Have you read 'Tears, Idle Tears'?" he asked.
"Yes, but you do not there express divine despair."
"My poor friend," he answered, "that was why the despair
Was divine."

Mabel Osborne

Your red blossoms amid green leaves
Are drooping, beautiful geranium!
But you do not ask for water.
You cannot speak! You do not need to speak—
Everyone knows that you are dying of thirst,
Yet they do not bring water!
They pass on, saying:
"The geranium wants water."
And I, who had happiness to share
And longed to share your happiness;
I who loved you, Spoon River,
And craved your love,
Withered before your eyes, Spoon River—
Thirsting, thirsting,
Voiceless from chasteness of soul to ask you for love,
You who knew and saw me perish before you,
Like this geranium which someone has planted over me,
And left to die.

William H. Herndon

There by the window in the old house
Perched on the bluff, overlooking miles of valley,
My days of labor closed, sitting out life's decline,
Day by day did I look in my memory,
As one who gazes in an enchantress' crystal globe,
And I saw the figures of the past,
As if in a pageant glassed by a shining dream,
Move through the incredible sphere of time.
And I saw a man arise from the soil like a fabled giant
And throw himself over a deathless destiny,
Master of great armies, head of the republic,
Bringing together into a dithyramb of recreative song
The epic hopes of a people;
At the same time Vulcan of sovereign fires,
Where imperishable shields and swords were beaten out
From spirits tempered in heaven.
Look in the crystal! See how he hastens on
To the place where his path comes up to the path
Of a child of Plutarch and Shakespeare.
O Lincoln, actor indeed, playing well your part,
And Booth, who strode in a mimic play within the play,
Often and often I saw you,
As the cawing crows winged their way to the wood
Over my house-top at solemn sunsets,
There by my window,
Alone.

Rebecca Wasson

Spring and Summer, Fall and Winter and Spring
After each other drifting, past my window drifting!
And I lay so many years watching them drift and counting
The years till a terror came in my heart at times,
With the feeling that I had become eternal; at last
My hundredth year was reached! And still I lay
Hearing the tick of the clock, and the low of cattle
And the scream of a jay flying through falling leaves!
Day after day alone in a room of the house
Of a daughter-in-law stricken with age and gray.
And by night, or looking out of the window by day,
My thought ran back, it seemed, through infinite time
To North Carolina and all my girlhood days,
And John, my John, away to the war with the British,
And all the children, the deaths, and all the sorrows.
And that stretch of years like a prairie in Illinois
Through which great figures passed like hurrying horsemen:
Washington, Jefferson, Jackson, Webster, Clay.
O beautiful young republic for whom my John and I
Gave all of our strength and love!
And O my John!
Why, when I lay so helpless in bed for years,
Praying for you to come, was your coming delayed?
Seeing that with a cry of rapture, like that I uttered
When you found me in old Virginia after the war,
I cried when I beheld you there by the bed,
As the sun stood low in the west growing smaller and fainter
In the light of your face!

Rutherford McDowell

They brought me ambrotypes
Of the old pioneers to enlarge.
And sometimes one sat for me—
Someone who was in being
When giant hands from the womb of the world
Tore the republic.
What was it in their eyes?—
For I could never fathom
That mystical pathos of drooped eyelids,
And the serene sorrow of their eyes.
It was like a pool of water,
Amid oak trees at the edge of a forest,
Where the leaves fall,
As you hear the crow of a cock
From a far-off farm house, seen near the hills
Where the third generation lives, and the strong men
And the strong women are gone and forgotten.
And these grand-children and great grand-children
Of the pioneers!
Truly did my camera record their faces, too,
With so much of the old strength gone,
And the old faith gone,
And the old mastery of life gone,
And the old courage gone,
Which labors and loves and suffers and sings
Under the sun!

Hannah Armstrong

I wrote him a letter asking him for old times' sake
To discharge my sick boy from the army;
But maybe he couldn't read it.
Then I went to town and had James Garber,
Who wrote beautifully, write him a letter;
But maybe that was lost in the mails.
So I traveled all the way to Washington.
I was more than an hour finding the White House.
And when I found it they turned me away,
Hiding their smiles. Then I thought:
"Oh, well, he ain't the same as when I boarded him
And he and my husband worked together
And all of us called him Abe, there in Menard."
As a last attempt I turned to a guard and said:
"Please say it's old Aunt Hannah Armstrong
From Illinois, come to see him about her sick boy
In the army."
Well, just in a moment they let me in!
And when he saw me he broke in a laugh,
And dropped his business as president,
And wrote in his own hand Doug's discharge,
Talking the while of the early days,
And telling stories.

Lucinda Matlock

I went to the dances at Chandlerville,
And played snap-out at Winchester.
One time we changed partners,
Driving home in the moonlight of middle June,
And then I found Davis.
We were married and lived together for seventy years,
Enjoying, working, raising the twelve children,
Eight of whom we lost
Ere I had reached the age of sixty.
I spun, I wove, I kept the house, I nursed the sick,
I made the garden, and for holiday
Rambled over the fields where sang the larks,
And by Spoon River gathering many a shell,
And many a flower and medicinal weed—
Shouting to the wooded hills, singing to the green valleys.
At ninety-six I had lived enough, that is all,
And passed to a sweet repose.
What is this I hear of sorrow and weariness,
Anger, discontent and drooping hopes?
Degenerate sons and daughters,
Life is too strong for you—
It takes life to love Life.

Davis Matlock

Suppose it is nothing but the hive:
That there are drones and workers
And queens, and nothing but storing honey—
(Material things as well as culture and wisdom)—
For the next generation, this generation never living,
Except as it swarms in the sun-light of youth,
Strengthening its wings on what has been gathered,
And tasting, on the way to the hive
From the clover field, the delicate spoil.
Suppose all this, and suppose the truth:
That the nature of man is greater
Than nature's need in the hive;
And you must bear the burden of life,
As well as the urge from your spirit's excess—
Well, I say to live it out like a god
Sure of immortal life, though you are in doubt,
Is the way to live it.
If that doesn't make God proud of you,
Then God is nothing but gravitation,
Or sleep is the golden goal.

Herman Altman

Did I follow Truth wherever she led,
And stand against the whole world for a cause,
And uphold the weak against the strong?
If I did I would be remembered among men
As I was known in life among the people,
And as I was hated and loved on earth.
Therefore, build no monument to me,
And carve no bust for me,
Lest, though I become not a demi-god,
The reality of my soul be lost,
So that thieves and liars,
Who were my enemies and destroyed me,
And the children of thieves and liars,
May claim me and affirm before my bust
That they stood with me in the days of my defeat.
Build me no monument
Lest my memory be perverted to the uses
Of lying and oppression.
My lovers and their children must not be dispossessed of me;
I would be the untarnished possession forever
Of those for whom I lived.

Jennie M'Grew

Not, where the stairway turns in the dark,
A hooded figure, shriveled under a flowing cloak!
Not yellow eyes in the room at night,
Staring out from a surface of cobweb gray!
And not the flap of a condor wing,
When the roar of life in your ears begins
As a sound heard never before!
But on a sunny afternoon,
By a country road,
Where purple rag-weeds bloom along a straggling fence,
And the field is gleaned, and the air is still,
To see against the sun-light something black,
Like a blot with an iris rim—
That is the sign to eyes of second sight. . . .
And that I saw!

Columbus Cheney

This weeping willow!
Why do you not plant a few
For the millions of children not yet born,
As well as for us?
Are they not non-existent, or cells asleep
Without mind?
Or do they come to earth, their birth
Rupturing the memory of previous being?
Answer! The field of unexplored intuition is yours.
But in any case why not plant willows for them,
As well as for us?

Wallace Ferguson

There at Geneva where Mt. Blanc floated above
The wine-hued lake like a cloud, when a breeze was blown
Out of an empty sky of blue, and the roaring Rhone
Hurried under the bridge through chasms of rock;
And the music along the cafés was part of the splendor
Of dancing water under a torrent of light;
And the purer part of the genius of Jean Rousseau
Was the silent music of all we saw or heard—
There at Geneva, I say, was the rapture less
Because I could not link myself with the I of yore,
When twenty years before I wandered about Spoon River?
Nor remember what I was nor what I felt?
We live in the hour all free of the hours gone by.
Therefore, O soul, if you lose yourself in death,
And wake in some Geneva by some Mt. Blanc,
What do you care if you know not yourself as the you
Who lived and loved in a little corner of earth
Known as Spoon River ages and ages vanished?

Marie Bateson

You observe the carven hand
With the index finger pointing heavenward.
That is the direction, no doubt
But how shall one follow it?
It is well to abstain from murder and lust,
To forgive, do good to others, worship God
Without graven images.
But these are external means after all
By which you chiefly do good to yourself.
The inner kernel is freedom,
It is light, purity—
I can no more.
Find the goal or lose it, according to your vision.

Tennessee Claflin Shope

I was the laughing-stock of the village,
Chiefly of the people of good sense, as they call themselves—
Also of the learned, like Rev. Peet, who read Greek
The same as English.
For instead of talking free trade,
Or preaching some form of baptism;
Instead of believing in the efficacy
Of walking cracks, picking up pins the right way,
Seeing the new moon over the right shoulder,
Or curing rheumatism with blue glass,
I asserted the sovereignty of my own soul.
Before Mary Baker G. Eddy even got started
With what she called science
I had mastered the *Bhagavad Gita,*
And cured my soul, before Mary
Began to cure bodies with souls—
Peace to all worlds!

Plymouth Rock Joe

Why are you running so fast hither and thither
Chasing midges or butterflies?
Some of you are standing solemnly scratching for grubs;
Some of you are waiting for corn to be scattered.
This is life, is it?
Cock-a-doodle-do! Very well, Thomas Rhodes,
You are cock of the walk no doubt.
But here comes Elliott Hawkins,
Gluck, Gluck, Gluck, attracting political followers.
Quah! quah! quah! why so poetical, Minerva,
This gray morning?
Kittie—quah—quah! for shame, Lucius Atherton,
The raucous squawk you evoked from the throat
Of Aner Clute will be taken up later
By Mrs. Benjamin Pantier as a cry
Of votes for women: Ka dook—dook!
What inspiration has come to you, Margaret Fuller Slack?
And why does your gooseberry eye
Flit so liquidly, Tennessee Clafflin Shope?
Are you trying to fathom the esotericism of an egg?
Your voice is very metallic this morning, Hortense Robbins—
Almost like a guinea hen's!
Quah! That was a guttural sigh, Isaiah Beethoven;
Did you see the shadow of the hawk,
Or did you step upon the drumsticks
Which the cook threw out this morning?
Be chivalric, heroic, or aspiring,
Metaphysical, religious, or rebellious,
You shall never get out of the barnyard
Except by way of over the fence
Mixed with potato peelings and such into the trough!

Immanuel Ehrenhardt

I began with Sir Willian Hamilton's lectures.
Then studied Dugald Stewart,
And then John Locke on the Understanding,
And then Descartes, Fichte and Schelling,
Kant and then Schopenhauer—
Books I borrowed from old Judge Somers.
All read with rapturous industry,
Hoping it was reserved to me
To grasp the tail of the ultimate secret,
And drag it out of its hole.
My soul flew up ten thousand miles,
And only the moon looked a little bigger.
Then I fell back, how glad of the earth!
All through the soul of William Jones
Who showed me a letter of John Muir.

Samuel Gardner

I who kept the greenhouse,
Lover of trees and flowers,
Oft in life saw this umbrageous elm,
Measuring its generous branches with my eye,
And listened to its rejoicing leaves
Lovingly patting each other
With sweet aeolian whispers.
And well they might:
For the roots had grown so wide and deep
That the soil of the hill could not withhold
Aught of its virtue, enriched by rain,
And warmed by the sun;
But yielded it all to the thrifty roots,
Through which it was drawn and whirled to the trunk,
And thence to the branches, and into the leaves,
Wherefrom the breeze took life and sang.
Now I, an under-tenant of the earth, can see
That the branches of a tree
Spread no wider than its roots.
And how shall the soul of a man
Be larger than the life he has lived?

Dow Kritt

Samuel is forever talking of his elm,
But I did not need to die to learn about roots—
I, who dug all the ditches about Spoon River.
Look at my elm!
Sprung from as good a seed as his,
Sown at the same time,
It is dying at the top:
Not from lack of life, nor fungus,
Nor destroying insect, as the sexton thinks.
Look, Samuel, where the roots have struck rock,
And can no further spread.
And all the while the top of the tree
Is tiring itself out, and dying,
Trying to grow.

William Jones

Once in a while a curious weed unknown to me,
Needing a name from my books;
Once in a while a letter from Yeomans.
Out of the mussel-shells gathered along the shore
Sometimes a pearl with a glint like meadow rue:
Then betimes a letter from Tyndall in England,
Stamped with the stamp of Spoon River.
I, lover of Nature, beloved for my love of her,
Held such converse afar with the great
Who know her better than I.
Oh, there is neither lesser nor greater,
Save as we make her greater and win from her keener delight.
With shells from the river cover me, cover me.
I lived in wonder, worshipping earth and heaven.
I have passed on the march eternal of endless life.

William Goode

To all in the village I seemed, no doubt,
To go this way and that way, aimlessly.
But here by the river you can see at twilight
The soft-winged bats fly zig-zag here and there—
They must fly so to catch their food.
And if you have ever lost your way at night,
In the deep wood near Miller's Ford,
And dodged this way and now that,
Wherever the light of the Milky Way shone through,
Trying to find the path,
You should understand I sought the way
With earnest zeal, and all my wanderings
Were wanderings in the quest.

J. Milton Miles

Whenever the Presbyterian bell
Was rung by itself, I knew it as the Presbyterian bell.
But when its sound was mingled
With the sound of the Methodist, the Christian,
The Baptist and the Congregational,
I could no longer distinguish it,
Nor any one from the others, or either of them.
And as many voices called to me in life,
Marvel not that I could not tell
The true from the false,
Nor even, at last, the voice that I should have known.

Faith Matheny

At first you will know not what they mean,
And you may never know,
And we may never tell you:
These sudden flashes in your soul,
Like lambent lightning on snowy clouds
At midnight when the moon is full.
They come in solitude, or perhaps
You sit with your friend, and all at once
A silence falls on speech, and his eyes
Without a flicker glow at you:
You two have seen the secret together,
He sees it in you, and you in him.
And there you sit thrilling lest the Mystery
Stand before you and strike you dead
With a splendor like the sun's.
Be brave, all souls who have such visions!
As your body's alive as mine is dead,
You're catching a little whiff of the ether
Reserved for God Himself.

Scholfield Huxley

God! ask me not to record your wonders;
I admit the stars and the suns
And the countless worlds.
But I have measured their distances
And weighed them and discovered their substances.
I have devised wings for the air,
And keels for water,
And horses of iron for the earth.
I have lengthened the vision you gave me a million times,
And the hearing you gave me a million times.
I have leaped over space with speech,
And taken fire for light out of the air.
I have built great cities and bored through the hills,
And bridged majestic waters.
I have written the *Iliad* and *Hamlet;*
And I have explored your mysteries,
And searched for you without ceasing,
And found you again after losing you
In hours of weariness—
And I ask you:
How would you like to create a sun
And the next day have the worms
Slipping in and out between your fingers?

Willie Metcalf

I was Willie Metcalf.
They used to call me "Doctor Meyers"
Because, they said, I looked like him.
And he was my father, according to Jack McGuire.
I lived in the livery stable,
Sleeping on the floor
Side by side with Roger Baughman's bulldog,
Or sometimes in a stall.
I could crawl between the legs of the wildest horses
Without getting kicked—we knew each other.
On spring days I tramped through the country
To get the feeling, which I sometimes lost,
That I was not a separate thing from the earth.
I used to lose myself, as if in sleep,
By lying with eyes half-open in the woods.
Sometimes I talked with animals—even toads and snakes—
Anything that had a eye to look into.
Once I saw a stone in the sunshine
Trying to turn into jelly.
In April days in this cemetery
The dead people gathered all about me,
And grew still, like a congregation in silent prayer.
I never knew whether I was a part of the earth
With flowers growing in me, or whether I walked—
Now I know.

Willie Pennington

They called me the weakling, the simpleton,
For my brothers were strong and beautiful,
While I, the last child of parents who had aged,
Inherited only their residue of power.
But they, my brothers, were eaten up
In the fury of the flesh, which I had not,
Made pulp in the activity of the senses, which I had not,
Hardened by the growth of the lusts, which I had not,
Through making names and riches for themselves.
Then I, the weak one, the simpleton,
Resting in a little corner of life,
Saw a vision, and through me many saw the vision,
Not knowing it was through me.
Thus a tree sprang
From me, a mustard seed.

The Village Atheist

Ye young debaters over the doctrine
Of the soul's immortality,
I who lie here was the village atheist,
Talkative, contentious, versed in the arguments
Of the infidels.
But through a long sickness
Coughing myself to death
I read the *Upanishads* and the poetry of Jesus.
And they lighted a torch of hope and intuition
And desire which the Shadow,
Leading me swiftly through the caverns of darkness,
Could not extinguish.
Listen to me, ye who live in the senses
And think through the senses only:
Immortality is not a gift,
Immortality is an achievement;
And only those who strive mightily
Shall possess it.

John Ballard

In the lust of my strength
I cursed God, but he paid no attention to me:
I might as well have cursed the stars.
In my last sickness I was in agony, but I was resolute
And I cursed God for my suffering;
Still He paid no attention to me;
He left me alone, as He had always done.
I might as well have cursed the Presbyterian steeple.
Then, as I grew weaker, a terror came over me:
Perhaps I had alienated God by cursing him.
One day Lydia Humphrey brought me a bouquet
And it occurred to me to try to make friends with God,
So I tried to make friends with Him;
But I might as well have tried to make friends with the bouquet.
Now I was very close to the secret,
For I really could make friends with the bouquet
By holding close to me the love in me for the bouquet,
And so I was creeping upon the secret, but—

Julian Scott

Toward the last
The truth of others was untruth to me;
The justice of others injustice to me;
Their reasons for death, reasons with me for life;
Their reasons for life, reasons with me for death;
I would have killed those they saved,
And saved those they killed.
And I saw how a god, if brought to earth,
Must act out what he saw and thought,
And could not live in this world of men
And act among them side by side
Without continual clashes.
The dust's for crawling, heaven's for flying—
Wherefore, O soul, whose wings are grown,
Soar upward to the sun!

Alfonso Churchill

They laughed at me as "Prof. Moon,"
As a boy in Spoon River, born with the thirst
Of knowing about the stars.
They jeered when I spoke of the lunar mountains,
And the thrilling heat and cold,
And the ebon valleys by silver peaks,
And Spica quadrillions of miles away,
And the littleness of man.
But now that my grave is honored, friends,
Let it not be because I taught
The lore of the stars in Knox College,
But rather for this: that through the stars
I preached the greatness of man,
Who is none the less a part of the scheme of things
For the distance of Spica or the Spiral Nebulae;
Nor any the less a part of the question
Of what the drama means.

Zilpha Marsh

At four o'clock in late October
I sat alone in the country school-house
Back from the road 'mid stricken fields,
And an eddy of wind blew leaves on the pane,
And crooned in the flue of the cannon-stove,
With its open door blurring the shadows
With the spectral glow of a dying fire.
In an idle mood I was running the planchette—
All at once my wrist grew limp,
And my hand moved rapidly over the board,
Till the name of "Charles Guiteau" was spelled,
Who threatened to materialize before me.
I rose and fled from the room bare-headed
Into the dusk, afraid of my gift.
And after that the spirits swarmed—
Chaucer, Caesar, Poe and Marlowe,
Cleopatra and Mrs. Surrat—
Wherever I went, with messages,—
Mere trifling twaddle, Spoon River agreed.
You talk nonsense to children, don't you?
And suppose I see what you never saw
And never heard of and have no word for,
I must talk nonsense when you ask me
What it is I see!

James Garber

Do you remember, passer-by, the path
I wore across the lot where now stands the opera house,
Hasting with swift feet to work through many years?
Take its meaning to heart:
You too may walk, after the hills at Miller's Ford
Seem no longer far away;
Long after you see them near at hand,
Beyond four miles of meadow;
And after woman's love is silent,
Saying no more: "I will save you."
And after the faces of friends and kindred
Become as faded photographs, pitifully silent,
Sad for the look which means: "We cannot help you."
And after you no longer reproach mankind
With being in league against your soul's uplifted hands—
Themselves compelled at midnight and at noon
To watch with steadfast eye their destinies.
After you have these understandings, think of me
And of my path, who walked therein and knew
That neither man nor woman, neither toil,
Nor duty, gold nor power
Can ease the longing of the soul,
The loneliness of the soul!

Lydia Humphrey

Back and forth, back and forth, to and from the church,
With my Bible under my arm
Till I was gray and old;
Unwedded, alone in the world,
Finding brothers and sisters in the congregation,
And children in the church.
I know they laughed and thought me queer.
I knew of the eagle souls that flew high in the sunlight,
Above the spire of the church, and laughed at the church,
Disdaining me, not seeing me.
But if the high air was sweet to them, sweet was the church to
    me.
It was the vision, vision, vision of the poets
Democratized!

Le Roy Goldman

"What will you do when you come to die,
If all your life long you have rejected Jesus,
And know as you lie there, He is not your friend?"
Over and over I said, I, the revivalist.
Ah, yes! but there are friends and friends.
And blessed are you, say I, who know all now,
You who have lost, ere you pass,
A father or mother, or old grandfather or mother,
Some beautiful soul that lived life strongly,
And knew you all through, and loved you ever,
Who would not fail to speak for you,
And give God an intimate view of your soul,
As only one of your flesh could do it.
That is the hand your hand will reach for,
To lead you along the corridor
To the court where you are a stranger!

Gustav Richter

After a long day of work in my hot-houses
Sleep was sweet, but if you sleep on your left side
Your dreams may be abruptly ended.
I was among my flowers where someone
Seemed to be raising them on trial,
As if after-while to be transplanted
To a larger garden of freer air.
And I was disembodied vision
Amid a light, as it were the sun
Had floated in and touched the roof of glass
Like a toy balloon and softly bursted,
And etherealized in golden air.
And all was silence, except the splendor
Was immanent with thought as clear
As a speaking voice, and I, as thought,
Could hear a Presence think as he walked
Between the boxes pinching off leaves,
Looking for bugs and noting values,
With an eye that saw it all:—
"Homer, oh yes! Pericles, good.
Caesar Borgia, what shall be done with it?
Dante, too much manure, perhaps.
Napoleon, leave him awhile as yet.
Shelley, more soil. Shakespeare, needs spraying—"
Clouds, eh!—

Arlo Will

Did you ever see an alligator
Come up to the air from the mud,
Staring blindly under the full glare of noon?
Have you seen the stabled horses at night
Tremble and start back at the sight of a lantern?
Have you ever walked in darkness
When an unknown door was open before you
And you stood, it seemed, in the light of a thousand candles
Of delicate wax?
Have you walked with the wind in your ears
And the sunlight about you
And found it suddenly shine with an inner splendor?
Out of the mud many times,
Before many doors of light,
Through many fields of splendor,
Where around your steps a soundless glory scatters
Like new-fallen snow,
Will you go through earth, O strong of soul,
And through unnumbered heavens
To the final flame!

Captain Orlando Killion

Oh, you young radicals and dreamers,
You dauntless fledglings
Who pass by my headstone,
Mock not its record of my captaincy in the army
And my faith in God!
They are not denials of each other.
Go by reverently, and read with sober care
How a great people, riding with defiant shouts
The centaur of Revolution,
Spurred and whipped to frenzy,
Shook with terror, seeing the mist of the sea
Over the precipice they were nearing,
And fell from his back in precipitate awe
To celebrate the Feast of the Supreme Being.
Moved by the same sense of vast reality
Of life and death, and burdened as they were
With the fate of a race,
How was I, a little blasphemer,
Caught in the drift of a nation's unloosened flood,
To remain a blasphemer,
And a captain in the army?

Jeremy Carlisle

Passer-by, sin beyond any sin
Is the sin of blindness of souls to other souls.
And joy beyond any joy is the joy
Of having the good in you seen, and seeing the good
At the miraculous moment!
Here I confess to a lofty scorn,
And an acrid skepticism.
But do you remember the liquid that Penniwit
Poured on tintypes, making them blue
With a mist like hickory smoke?
Then how the picture began to clear
Till the face came forth like life?
So you appeared to me, neglected ones,
And enemies too, as I went along
With my face growing clearer to you as yours
Grew clearer to me.
We were ready then to walk together
And sing in chorus and chant the dawn
Of life that is wholly life.

Joseph Dixon

Who carved this shattered harp on my stone?
I died to you, no doubt. But how many harps and pianos
Wired I and tightened and disentangled for you,
Making them sweet again — with tuning fork or without?
Oh well! A harp leaps out of the ear of a man, you say,
But whence the ear that orders the length of the strings
To a magic of numbers flying before your thought
Through a door that closes against your breathless wonder?
Is there no Ear round the ear of a man, that it senses
Through strings and columns of air the soul of sound?
I thrill as I call it a tuning fork that catches
The waves of mingled music and light from afar,
The antennae of Thought that listens through utmost space.
Surely the concord that ruled my spirit is proof
Of an Ear that tuned me, able to tune me over
And use me again if I am worthy to use.

Judson Stoddard

On a mountain top above the clouds
That streamed like a sea below me
I said that peak is the thought of Buddah,
And that one is the prayer of Jesus,
And this one is the dream of Plato,
And that one there the song of Dante,
And this is Kant and this is Newton,
And this is Milton and this is Shakespeare,
And this the hope of the Mother Church,
And this—why all these peaks are poems,
Poems and prayers that pierce the clouds.
And I said "What does God do with mountains
That rise almost to heaven?"

Russell Kincaid

In the last spring I ever knew,
In those last days,
I sat in the forsaken orchard
Where beyond fields of greenery shimmered
The hills at Miller's Ford,
Just to muse on the apple tree
With its ruined trunk and blasted branches,
And shoots of green whose delicate blossoms
Were sprinkled over the skeleton tangle,
Never to grow in fruit.
And there was I with my spirit girded
By the flesh half dead, the senses numb,
Yet thinking of youth and the earth in youth,—
Such phantom blossoms palely shining
Over the lifeless boughs of Time.
O earth that leaves us ere heaven takes us!
Had I been only a tree to shiver
With dreams of spring and a leafy youth,
Then I had fallen in the cyclone
Which swept me out of the soul's suspense
Where it's neither earth nor heaven.

Aaron Hatfield

Better than granite, Spoon River,
Is the memory-picture you keep of me
Standing before the pioneer men and women
There at Concord Church on Communion day,
Speaking in broken voice of the peasant youth
Of Galilee who went to the city
And was killed by bankers and lawyers;
My voice mingling with the June wind
That blew over wheat fields from Atterbury,
While the white stones in the burying ground
Around the Church shimmered in the summer sun.
And there, though my own memories
Were too great to bear, were you, O pioneers,
With bowed heads breathing forth your sorrow
For the sons killed in battle and the daughters
And little children who vanished in life's morning,
Or at the intolerable hour of noon.
But in those moments of tragic silence,
When the wine and bread were passed,
Came the reconciliation for us—
Us the ploughmen and the hewers of wood,
Us the peasants, brothers of the peasant of Galilee—
To us came the Comforter
And the consolation of tongues of flame!

Isaiah Beethoven

They told me I had three months to live,
So I crept to Bernadotte,
And sat by the mill for hours and hours
Where the gathered waters deeply moving
Seemed not to move:
O world, that's you!
You are but a widened place in the river
Where Life looks down and we rejoice for her
Mirrored in us, and so we dream
And turn away, but when again
We look for the face, behold the low-lands
And blasted cotton-wood trees where we empty
Into the larger stream!
But here by the mill the castled clouds
Mocked themselves in the dizzy water;
And over its agate floor at night
The flame of the moon ran under my eyes
Amid a forest stillness broken
By a flute in a hut on the hill.
At last when I came to lie in bed
Weak and in pain, with the dreams about me,
The soul of the river had entered my soul,
And the gathered power of my soul was moving
So swiftly it seemed to be at rest
Under cities of cloud and under
Spheres of silver and changing worlds—
Until I saw a flash of trumpets
Above the battlements over Time!

Elijah Browning

I was among multitudes of children
Dancing at the foot of a mountain.
A breeze blew out of the east and swept them as leaves,
Driving some up the slopes. . . . All was changed.
Here were flying lights, and mystic moons, and dream-music.
A cloud fell upon us. When it lifted all was changed.
I was now amid multitudes who were wrangling.
Then a figure in shimmering gold, and one with a trumpet,
And one with a scepter stood before me.
They mocked me and danced a rigadoon and vanished. . . .
All was changed again. Out of a bower of poppies
A woman bared her breasts and lifted her open mouth to mine.
I kissed her. The taste of her lips was like salt.
She left blood on my lips. I fell exhausted.
I arose and ascended higher, but a mist as from an iceberg
Clouded my steps. I was cold and in pain.
Then the sun streamed on me again,
And I saw the mists below me hiding all below them.
And I, bent over my staff, knew myself
Silhouetted against the snow. And above me
Was the soundless air, pierced by a cone of ice,
Over which hung a solitary star!
A shudder of ecstasy, a shudder of fear
Ran through me. But I could not return to the slopes—
Nay, I wished not to return.
For the spent waves of the symphony of freedom
Lapped the ethereal cliffs about me.
Therefore I climbed to the pinnacle.
I flung away my staff.
I touched that star
With my outstretched hand.
I vanished utterly.
For the mountain delivers to Infinite Truth
Whosoever touches the star!

Webster Ford

Do you remember, O delphic Apollo,
The sunset hour by the river, when Mickey M'Grew
Cried, "There's a ghost," and I, "It's Delphic Apollo";
And the son of the banker derided us, saying, "It's light
By the flags at the water's edge, you half-witted fools,"
And from thence, as the wearisome years rolled on, long after
Poor Mickey fell down in the water tower to his death,
Down, down, through bellowing darkness, I carried
The vision which perished with him like a rocket which falls
And quenches its light in earth, and hid it for fear
Of the son of the banker, calling on Plutus to save me?
Avenged were you for the shame of a fearful heart,
Who left me alone till I saw you again in an hour
When I seemed to be turned to a tree with trunk and branches
Growing indurate, turning to stone, yet burgeoning
In laurel leaves, in hosts of lambent laurel,
Quivering, fluttering, shrinking, fighting the numbness
Creeping into their veins from the dying trunk and branches!
'Tis vain, O youth, to fly the call of Apollo.
Fling yourselves in the fire, die with a song of spring,
If die you must in the spring. For none shall look
On the face of Apollo and live, and choose you must
'Twixt death in the flame and death after years of sorrow,
Rooted fast in the earth, feeling the grisly hand,
Not so much in the trunk as in the terrible numbness
Creeping up to the laurel leaves that never cease
To flourish until you fall. O leaves of me
Too sere for coronal wreaths, and fit alone
For urns of memory, treasured, perhaps, as themes
For hearts heroic, fearless singers and livers—
Delphic Apollo!

THE SPOONIAD

[The late Mr. Jonathan Swift Somers, laureate of Spoon River (see page 210), planned The Spooniad *as an epic in twenty-four books, but unfortunately did not live to complete even the first book. The fragment was found among his papers by William Marion Reedy and was for the first time published in* Reedy's Mirror *of December 18th, 1914.]*

The Spooniad

Of John Cabanis' wrath and of the strife
Of hostile parties, and his dire defeat
Who led the common people in the cause
Of freedom for Spoon River, and the fall
Of Rhodes' bank that brought unnumbered woes
And loss to many, with engendered hate
That flamed into the torch in Anarch hands
To burn the court-house, on whose blackened wreck
A fairer temple rose and Progress stood—
Sing, muse, that lit the Chian's face with smiles
Who saw the ant-like Greeks and Trojans crawl
About Scamander, over wall, pursued
Or else pursuing, and the funeral pyres
And sacred hecatombs, and first because
Of Helen who with Paris fled to Troy
As soul-mate; and the wrath of Peleus' son,
Decreed, to lose Chryseis, lovely spoil
Of war, and dearest concubine.
                                        Say first,
Thou son of night, called Momus, from whose eyes
No secret hides, and Thalia, smiling one,
What bred 'twixt Thomas Rhodes and John Cabanis
The deadly strife? His daughter Flossie, she,
Returning from her wandering with a troop
Of strolling players, walked the village streets,
Her bracelets tinkling and with sparkling rings
And words of serpent wisdom and a smile
Of cunning in her eyes. Then Thomas Rhodes,
Who ruled the church and ruled the bank as well,
Made known his disapproval of the maid;
And all Spoon River whispered and the eyes
Of all the church frowned on her, till she knew
They feared her and condemned.
                                        But them to flout
She gave a dance to viols and to flutes,
Brought from Peoria, and many youths,

335

But lately made regenerate through the prayers
Of zealous preachers and of earnest souls,
Danced merrily, and sought her in the dance,
Who wore a dress so low of neck that eyes
Down straying might survey the snowy swale
Till it was lost in whiteness.
                              With the dance
The village changed to merriment from gloom.
The milliner, Mrs. Williams, could not fill
Her orders for new hats, and every seamstress
Plied busy needles making gowns; old trunks
And chests were opened for their store of laces
And rings and trinkets were brought out of hiding
And all the youths fastidious grew of dress;
Notes passed, and many a fair one's door at eve
Knew a bouquet, and strolling lovers thronged
About the hills that overlooked the river.
Then, since the mercy seats more empty showed,
One of God's chosen lifted up his voice:
"The woman of Babylon is among us; rise
Ye sons of light and drive the wanton forth!"
So John Cabanis left the church and left
The hosts of law and order with his eyes
By anger cleared, and him the liberal cause
Acclaimed as nominee to the mayoralty
To vanquish A. D. Blood.
                              But as the war
Waged bitterly for votes and rumors flew
About the bank, and of the heavy loans
Which Rhodes' son had made to prop his loss
In wheat, and many drew their coin and left
The bank of Rhodes more hollow, with the talk
Among the liberals of another bank
Soon to be chartered, lo, the bubble burst
'Mid cries and curses; but the liberals laughed
And in the hall of Nicholas Bindle held
Wise converse and inspiriting debate.

High on a stage that overlooked the chairs

Where dozens sat, and where a pop-eyed daub
Of Shakespeare, very like the hired man
Of Christian Dallmann, brow and pointed beard,
Upon a drab proscenium outward stared,
Sat Harmon Whitney, to that eminence,
By merit raised in ribaldry and guile,
And to the assembled rebels thus he spake:
"Whether to lie supine and let a clique
Cold-blooded, scheming, hungry, singing psalms,
Devour our substance, wreck our banks and drain
Our little hoards for hazards on the price
Of wheat or pork, or yet to cower beneath
The shadow of a spire upreared to curb
A breed of lackeys and to serve the bank
Coadjutor in greed, that is the question.
Shall we have music and the jocund dance,
Or tolling bells? Or shall young romance roam
These hills about the river, flowering now
To April's tears, or shall they sit at home,
Or play croquet where Thomas Rhodes may see,
I ask you? If the blood of youth runs o'er
And riots 'gainst this regimen of gloom,
Shall we submit to have these youths and maids
Branded as libertines and wantons?"
                                        Ere
His words were done a woman's voice called "No!"
Then rose a sound of moving chairs, as when
The numerous swine o'er-run the replenished troughs;
And every head was turned, as when a flock
Of geese back-turning to the hunter's tread
Rise up with flapping wings; then rang the hall
With riotous laughter, for with battered hat
Tilted upon her saucy head, and fist
Raised in defiance, Daisy Fraser stood.
Headlong she had been hurled from out the hall
Save Wendell Bloyd, who spoke for woman's rights,
Prevented, and the bellowing voice of Burchard.
Then 'mid applause she hastened toward the stage
And flung both gold and silver to the cause

337

And swiftly left the hall.
                      Meantime upstood
A giant figure, bearded like the son
Of Alcmene, deep-chested, round of paunch,
And spoke in thunder: "Over there behold
A man who for the truth withstood his wife—
Such is our spirit—when that A. D. Blood
Compelled me to remove Dom Pedro—"
                              Quick
Before Jim Brown could finish, Jefferson Howard
Obtained the floor and spake: "Ill suits the time
For clownish words, and trivial is our cause
If naught's at stake but John Cabanis' wrath,
He who was erstwhile of the other side
And came to us for vengeance. More's at stake
Than triumph for New England or Virginia.
And whether rum be sold, or for two years
As in the past two years, this town be dry
Matters but little—Oh yes, revenue
For sidewalks, sewers; that is well enough!
I wish to God this fight were now inspired
By other passion than to salve the pride
Of John Cabanis or his daughter. Why
Can never contests of great moment spring
From worthy things, not little? Still, if men
Must always act so, and if rum must be
The symbol and the medium to release
From life's denial and from slavery,
Then give me rum!"
                    Exultant cries arose.
Then, as George Trimble had o'ercome his fear
And vacillation and begun to speak,
The door creaked and the idiot, Willie Metcalf,
Breathless and hatless, whiter than a sheet,
Entered and cried: "The marshal's on his way
To arrest you all. And if you only knew
Who's coming here to-morrow; I was listening
Beneath the window where the other side
Are making plans."

                    So to a smaller room
To hear the idiot's secret some withdrew
Selected by the Chair; the Chair himself
And Jefferson Howard, Benjamin Pantier,
And Wendell Bloyd, George Trimble, Adam Weirauch,
Immanuel Ehrenhardt, Seth Compton, Godwin James
And Enoch Dunlap, Hiram Scates, Roy Butler,
Carl Hamblin, Roger Heston, Ernest Hyde
And Penniwit, the artist, Kinsey Keene,
And E. C. Culbertson and Franklin Jones,
Benjamin Fraser, son of Benjamin Pantier
By Daisy Fraser, some of lesser note,
And secretly conferred.
                    But in the hall
Disorder reigned and when the marshal came
And found it so, he marched the hoodlums out
And locked them up.
                    Meanwhile within a room
Back in the basement of the church, with Blood
Counseled the wisest heads. Judge Somers first,
Deep learned in life, and next him, Elliott Hawkins
And Lambert Hutchins; next him Thomas Rhodes
And Editor Whedon; next him Garrison Standard,
A traitor to the liberals, who with lip
Upcurled in scorn and with a bitter sneer:
"Such strife about an insult to a woman—
A girl of eighteen"—Christian Dallman too,
And others unrecorded. Some there were
Who frowned not on the cup but loathed the rule
Democracy achieved thereby, the freedom
And lust of life it symbolized.

Now morn with snowy fingers up the sky
Flung like an orange at a festival
The ruddy sun, when from their hasty beds
Poured forth the hostile forces, and the streets
Resounded to the rattle of the wheels,
That drove this way and that to gather in
The tardy voters, and the cries of chieftains

Who manned the battle. But at ten o'clock
The liberals bellowed fraud, and at the polls
The rival candidates growled and came to blows.
Then proved the idiot's tale of yester-eve
A word of warning. Suddenly on the streets
Walked hog-eyed Allen, terror of the hills
That looked on Bernadotte ten miles removed.
No man of this degenerate day could lift
The boulders which he threw, and when he spoke
The windows rattled, and beneath his brows,
Thatched like a shed with bristling hair of black,
His small eyes glistened like a maddened boar.
And as he walked the boards creaked, as he walked
A song of menace rumbled. Thus he came,
The champion of A. D. Blood, commissioned
To terrify the liberals. Many fled
As when a hawk soars o'er the chicken yard.
He passed the polls and with a playful hand
Touched Brown, the giant, and he fell against,
As though he were a child, the wall; so strong
Was hog-eyed Allen. But the liberals smiled.
For soon as hog-eyed Allen reached the walk,
Close on his steps paced Bengal Mike, brought in
By Kinsey Keene, the subtle-witted one,
To match the hog-eyed Allen. He was scarce
Three-fourths the other's bulk, but steel his arms,
And with a tiger's heart. Two men he killed
And many wounded in the days before,
And no one feared.
                              But when the hog-eyed one
Saw Bengal Mike his countenance grew dark,
The bristles o'er his red eyes twitched with rage,
The song he rumbled lowered. Round and round
The court-house paced he, followed stealthily
By Bengal Mike, who jeered him every step:
"Come, elephant, and fight! Come, hog-eyed coward!
Come, face about and fight me, lumbering sneak!
Come, beefy bully, hit me, if you can!
Take out your gun, you duffer, give me reason

To draw and kill you. Take your billy out;
I'll crack your boar's head with a piece of brick!"
But never a word the hog-eyed one returned,
But trod about the court-house, followed both
By troops of boys and watched by all the men.
All day they walked the square. But when Apollo
Stood with reluctant look above the hills
As fain to see the end, and all the votes
Were cast, and closed the polls, before the door
Of Trainor's drug store Bengal Mike, in tones
That echoed through the village, bawled the taunt:
"Who was your mother, hog-eyed?" In a trice,
As when a wild boar turns upon the hound
That through the brakes upon an August day
Has gashed him with its teeth, the hog-eyed one
Rushed with his giant arms on Bengal Mike
And grabbed him by the throat. Then rose to heaven
The frightened cries of boys, and yells of men
Forth rushing to the street. And Bengal Mike
Moved this way and now that, drew in his head
As if his neck to shorten, and bent down
To break the death grip of the hog-eyed one;
'Twixt guttural wrath and fast-expiring strength
Striking his fists against the invulnerable chest
Of hog-eyed Allen. Then, when some came in
To part them, others stayed them, and the fight
Spread among dozens; many valiant souls
Went down from clubs and bricks.
                              But tell me, Muse,
What god or goddess rescued Bengal Mike?
With one last, mighty struggle did he grasp
The murderous hands and turning kick his foe.
Then, as if struck by lightning, vanished all
The strength from hog-eyed Allen, at his side
Sank limp those giant arms and o'er his face
Dread pallor and the sweat of anguish spread.
And those great knees, invincible but late,
Shook to his weight. And quickly as the lion
Leaps on its wounded prey, did Bengal Mike

Smite with a rock the temple of his foe,
And down he sank and darkness o'er his eyes
Passed like a cloud.
                              As when the woodman fells
Some giant oak upon a summer's day
And all the songsters of the forest shrill,
And one great hawk that has his nestling young
Amid the topmost branches croaks, as crash
The leafy branches through the tangled boughs
Of brother oaks, so fell the hog-eyed one
Amid the lamentations of the friends
Of A. D. Blood.
                              Just then, four lusty men
Bore the town marshal, on whose iron face
The purple pall of death already lay,
To Trainor's drug store, shot by Jack McGuire.
And cries went up of "Lynch him!" and the sound
Of running feet from every side was heard
Bent on the

EPILOGUE

(THE GRAVEYARD OF SPOON RIVER. TWO VOICES ARE HEARD BEHIND
A SCREEN DECORATED WITH DIABOLICAL AND ANGELIC FIG-
URES IN VARIOUS ALLEGORICAL RELATIONS. A FAINT LIGHT
SHOWS DIMLY THROUGH THE SCREEN AS IF IT WERE WOVEN
OF LEAVES, BRANCHES AND SHADOWS.)

FIRST VOICE

A game of checkers?

SECOND VOICE

Well, I don't mind.

FIRST VOICE

I move the Will.

SECOND VOICE

You're playing it blind.

FIRST VOICE

Then here's the Soul.

SECOND VOICE

Checked by the Will.

FIRST VOICE

Eternal Good!

SECOND VOICE

And Eternal Ill.

FIRST VOICE

I haste for the King row.

SECOND VOICE

Save your breath.

345

I was moving Life.

You're checked by Death.

Very good, here's Moses.

And here's the Jew.

My next move is Jesus.

St. Paul for you!

Yes, but St. Peter—

You might have foreseen—

You're in the King row—

With Constantine!

I'll go back to Athens.

Well, here's the Persian.

All right, the Bible.

SECOND VOICE

Pray now, what version?

FIRST VOICE

I take up Buddha.

SECOND VOICE

It never will work.

FIRST VOICE

From the corner Mahomet.

SECOND VOICE

I move the Turk.

FIRST VOICE

The game is tangled; where are we now?

SECOND VOICE

You're dreaming worlds. I'm in the King row.
Move as you will, if I can't wreck you
I'll thwart you, harry you, rout you, check you.

FIRST VOICE

I'm tired. I'll send for my Son to play.
I think he can beat you finally—

SECOND VOICE

Eh?

FIRST VOICE

I must preside at the stars' convention.

SECOND VOICE

Very well, my lord, but I beg to mention
I'll give this game my direct attention.

FIRST VOICE

A game indeed! But Truth is my quest.

Beaten, you walk away with a jest.
I strike the table, I scatter the checkers.

(A rattle of a falling table and checkers flying over a floor.)

Aha! You armies and iron deckers,
Races and states in a cataclysm—
Now for a day of atheism!

(The screen vanishes and BEELZEBUB *steps forward carrying a trumpet, which he blows faintly. Immediately* LOKI *and* YOGARINDRA *start up from the shadows of night.)*

BEELZEBUB

Good evening, Loki!

LOKI

The same to you!

BEELZEBUB

And Yogarindra!

YOGARINDRA

My greetings, too.

LOKI

Whence came you, comrade?

BEELZEBUB

From yonder screen.

YOGARINDRA

And what were you doing?

BEELZEBUB

Stirring His spleen.

LOKI

How did you do it?

348

BEELZEBUB

                    I made it rough
In a game of checkers.

LOKI

Good enough!

YOGARINDRA

I thought I heard the sounds of a battle.

BEELZEBUB

No doubt! I made the checkers rattle,
Turning the table over and strewing
The bits of wood like an army pursuing.

YOGARINDRA

I have a game! Let us make a man.

LOKI

My net is waiting him, if you can.

YOGARINDRA

And here's my mirror to fool him with—

BEELZEBUB

Mystery, falsehood, creed and myth.

LOKI

But no one can mold him, friend, but you.

BEELZEBUB

Then to the sport without more ado.

YOGARINDRA

Hurry the work ere it grow to day.

BEELZEBUB

I set me to it. Where is the clay?

(He scrapes the earth with his hands and begins to model.)

349

BEELZEBUB

Out of the dust,
Out of the slime,
A little rust,
And a little lime.
Muscle and gristle,
Mucin, stone
Brayed with a pestle,
Fat and bone.
Out of the marshes,
Out of the vaults,
Matter crushes
Gas and salts.
What is this you call a mind,
Flitting, drifting, pale and blind,
Soul of the swamp that rides the wind?
Jack-o'-lantern, here you are!
Dream of heaven, pine for a star,
Chase your brothers to and fro,
Back to the swamp at last you'll go.
Hilloo! Hilloo!

THE VALLEY

Hilloo! Hilloo!

(Beelzebub in scraping up the earth turns out a skull.)

BEELZEBUB

Old one, old one.
Now ere I break you,
Crush you and make you
Clay for my use,
Let me observe you:
You were a bold one
Flat at the dome of you,
Heavy the base of you.
False to the home of you,
Strong was the face of you,
Strange to all fears.
Yet did the hair of you

350

Hide what you were.
Now to re-nerve you —

(He crushes the skull between his hands and mixes it with the
clay.)

Now you are dust,
Limestone and rust.
I mold and I stir
And make you again.

THE VALLEY

Again? Again?

(In the same manner BEELZEBUB *has fashioned several figures,*
standing them against the trees.)

LOKI

Now for the breath of life. As I remember
You have done right to mold your creatures first,
And stand them up.

BEELZEBUB

From gravitation
I make the will.

YOGARINDRA

Out of sensation
Comes his ill.
Out of my mirror
Springs his error.
Who was so cruel
To make him the slave
Of me the sorceress, you the knave,
And you the plotter to catch his thought,
Whatever he did, whatever he sought?
With a nature dual
Of will and mind
A thing that sees, and a thing that's blind.
Come! to our dance! Something hated him
Made us over him, therefore fated him.
(They join hands and dance.)

351

LOKI

Passion, reason, custom, rules,
Creeds of the churches, lore of the schools,
Taint in the blood and strength of soul.
Flesh too weak for the will's control;
Poverty, riches, pride of birth,
Wailing, laughter, over the earth,
Here I have you caught again,
Enter my web, ye sons of men.

YOGARINDRA

Look in my mirror! Isn't it real?
What do you think now, what do you feel?
Here is treasure of gold heaped up;
Here is wine in the festal cup.
Tendrils blossoming, turned to whips,
Love with her breasts and scarlet lips.
Breathe in their nostrils.

BEELZEBUB

    Falsehood's breath,
Out of nothingness into death.
Out of the mold, out of the rocks
Wonder, mockery, paradox!
Soaring spirit, groveling flesh,
Bait the trap, and spread the mesh.
Give him hunger, lure him with truth,
Give him the iris hopes of Youth.
Starve him, shame him, fling him down,
Whirled in the vortex of the town.
Break him, age him, till he curse
The idiot face of the universe.
Over and over we mix the clay,—
What was dust is alive to-day.

THE THREE

Thus is the hell-born tangle wound
Swiftly, swiftly round and round.

BEELZEBUB

(Waving his trumpet.)

You live! Away!

ONE OF THE FIGURES

How strange and new!
I am I, and another, too.

ANOTHER FIGURE

I was a sun-dew's leaf, but now
What is this longing?—

ANOTHER FIGURE

Earth below
I was a seedling magnet-tipped
Drawn down earth—

ANOTHER FIGURE

And I was gripped
Electrons in a granite stone,
Now I think.

ANOTHER FIGURE

Oh, how alone!

ANOTHER FIGURE

My lips to thine. Through thee I find
Something alone by love divined!

BEELZEBUB

Begone! No, wait. I have bethought me, friends;
Let's give a play.

(He waves his trumpet.)

To yonder green rooms go.

(The figures disappear.)

353

YOGARINDRA

Oh, yes, a play! That's very well, I think,
But who will be the audience? I must throw
Illusion over all.

LOKI

And I must shift
The scenery, and tangle up the plot.

BEELZEBUB

Well, so you shall! Our audience shall come
From yonder graves.

*(He blows his trumpet slightly louder than before. The scene changes.
A stage arises among the graves. The curtain is down, con-
cealing the creatures just created, illuminated halfway up by
spectral lights.* BEELZEBUB *stands before the curtain.)*

BEELZEBUB

(A terrific blast of the trumpet.)

Who-o-o-o-o-o!

*(Immediately there is a rustling as of the shells of grasshoppers
stirred by a wind; and hundreds of the dead, including those
who have appeared in the Anthology, hurry to the sound of
the trumpet.)*

A VOICE

Gabriel! Gabriel!

MANY VOICES

The Judgment day!

BEELZEBUB

Be quiet, if you please
At least until the stars fall and the moon.

MANY VOICES

Save us! Save us!

(Beelzebub extends his hands over the audience with a benedictory motion and restores order.)

BEELZEBUB

Ladies and gentlemen, your kind attention
To my interpretation of the scene.
I rise to give your fancy comprehension,
And analyze the parts of the machine.
My mood is such that I would not deceive you,
Though still a liar and the father of it,
From judgment's frailty I would retrieve you,
Though falsehood is my art and though I love it.
Down in the habitations whence I rise,
The roots of human sorrow boundless spread.
Long have I watched them draw the strength that lies
In clay made richer by the rotting dead.
Here is a blossom, here a twisted stalk,
Here fruit that sourly withers ere its prime;
And here a growth that sprawls across the walk,
Food for the green worm, which it turns to slime.
The ruddy apple with a core of cork
Springs from a root which in a hollow dangles,
Not skillful husbandry nor laborious work
Can save the tree which lightning breaks and tangles.
Why does the bright nasturtium scarcely flower
But that those insects multiply and grow,
Which make it food, and in the very hour
In which the veinèd leafs and blossoms blow?
Why does a goodly tree, while fast maturing,
Turn crooked branches covered o'er with scale?
Why does the tree whose youth was not assuring
Prosper and bear while all its fellows fail?
I under the earth see much. I know the soil.
I know where mold is heavy and where thin.
I see the stones that thwart the plowman's toil,
The crooked roots of what the priests call sin.
I know all secrets, even to the core,
What seedlings will be upas, pine or laurel;
It cannot change howe'er the field's worked o'er.

Man's what he is and that's the devil's moral.
So with the souls of the ensuing drama:
They sprang from certain seed in certain earth.
Behold them in the devil's cyclorama,
Shown in their proper light for all they're worth.
Now to my task: I'll give an exhibition
Of mixing the ingredients of spirit.

(He waves his wand.)

Come, crucible, perform your magic mission,
Come, recreative fire, and hover near it!
I'll make a soul, or show how one is made.

(He waves his wand again. Parti-colored flames appear.)

This is the woman you shall see anon!

(A red flame appears.)

This hectic flame makes all the world afraid:
It was a soldier's scourge which ate the bone.
His daughter bore the lady of the action,
And died at thirty-nine of scrofula.
She was a creature of a sweet attraction,
Whose sex-obsession no one ever saw.

(A purple flame appears.)

Lo! this denotes aristocratic strains
Back in the centuries of France's glory.

(A blue flame appears.)

And this the will that pulls against the chains
Her father strove until his hair was hoary.
Sorrow and failure made his nature cold,
He never loved the child whose woe is shown,
And hence her passion for the things which gold
Brings in this world of pride, and brings alone.
The human heart that's famished from its birth
Turns to the grosser treasures, that is plain.
Thus aspiration fallen fills the earth
With jungle growths of bitterness and pain.

356

Of Celtic, Gallic fire our heroine!
Courageous, cruel, passionate and proud.
False, vengeful, cunning, without fear o' sin.
A head that oft is bloody, but not bowed.
Now if she meet a man—suppose our hero,
With whom her chemistry shall war yet mix,
As if she were her Borgia to his Nero,
'Twill look like one of Satan's little tricks!
However, it must be. The world's great garden
Is not all mine. I only sow the tares.
Wheat should be made immune, or else the Warden
Should stop their coming in the world's affairs.
But to our hero! Long ere he was born
I knew what would repel him and attract.
Such spirit mathematics, fig or thorn,
I can prognosticate before the fact.

(A yellow flame appears.)

This is a grandsire's treason in an orchard
Against a maid whose nature with his mated.

(Lurid flames appear.)

And this his memory distrait and tortured,
Which marked the child with hate because she hated.
Our heroine's grand dame was that maid's own cousin—
But never this our man and woman knew.
The child, in time, of lovers had a dozen,
Then wed a gentleman upright and true.
And thus our hero had a double nature:
One half of him was bad, the other good.
The devil must exhaust his nomenclature
To make this puzzle rightly understood.
But when our hero and our heroine met
They were at once attracted, the repulsion
Was hidden under Passion, with her net
Which must enmesh you ere you feel revulsion.
The virus coursing in the soldier's blood,
The orchard's ghost, the unknown kinship 'twixt them,
Our hero's mother's lovers round them stood,

Shadows that smiled to see how Fate had fixed them.
This twain pledge vows and marry, that's the play.
And then the tragic features rise and deepen.
He is a tender husband. When away
The serpents from the orchard slyly creep in.
Our heroine, born of spirit none too loyal,
Picks fruit of knowledge—leaves the tree of life.
Her fancy turns to France corrupt and royal,
Soon she forgets her duty as a wife.
You know the rest, so far as that's concerned,
She met exposure and her husband slew her.
He lost his reason, for the love she spurned.
He prized her as his own—how slight he knew her.

(He waves a wand, showing a man in a prison cell.)

Now here he sits condemned to mount the gallows—
He could not tell his story—he is dumb.
Love, says your poets, is a grace that hallows,
I call it suffering and martyrdom.
The judge with pointed finger says, "You killed her."
Well, so he did—but here's the explanation:
He could not give it. I, the drama-builder,
Show you the various truths and their relation.

(He waves his wand.)

Now, to begin. The curtain is ascending,
They meet at tea upon a flowery lawn.
Fair, is it not? How sweet their souls are blending—
The author calls the play "Laocoön."

A VOICE

Only an earth dream.

ANOTHER VOICE

With which we are done.
A flash of a comet
Upon the earth stream.

358

A dream twice removed,
A spectral confusion
Of earth's dread illusion.

A FAR VOICE

These are the ghosts
From the desolate coasts.
Would you go to them?
Only pursue them.
Whatever enshrined is
Within you is you.
In a place where no wind is,
Out of the damps,
Be ye as lamps.
Flame-like aspire,
To me alone true,
The Life and the Fire.

(BEELZEBUB, LOKI, *and* YOGARINDRA *vanish. The phantasmagoria fades out. Where the dead seemed to have assembled, only heaps of leaves appear. There is the light as of dawn. Voices of Spring.*)

FIRST VOICE

The springtime is come, the winter departed,
She wakens from slumber and dances light-hearted.
    The sun is returning,
    We are done with alarms,
    Earth lifts her face burning,
    Held close in his arms.
    The sun is an eagle
    Who broods o'er his young,
    The earth is his nursling
    In whom he has flung
    The life-flame in seed,
    In blossom desire,
    Till fire become life,
    And life become fire.

I slip and I vanish,
I baffle your eye;
I dive and I climb,
I change and I fly.
You have me, you lose me,
Who have me too well,
Now find me and use me—
I am here in a cell.

THIRD VOICE

You are there in a cell?
Oh, now for a rod
With which to divine you—

SECOND VOICE

Nay, child, I am God.

FOURTH VOICE

When the waking waters rise from their beds of snow, under the
    hill,
In little rooms of stone where they sleep when icicles reign,
The April breezes scurry through woodlands, saying "Fulfill!
Awaken roots under cover of soil—it is Spring again."

Then the sun exults, the moon is at peace, and voices
Call to the silver shadows to lift the flowers from their dreams.
And a longing, longing enters my heart of sorrow, my heart that
    rejoices
In the fleeting glimpse of a shining face, and her hair that gleams.

I arise and follow alone for hours the winding way by the river,
Hunting a vanishing light, and a solace for joy too deep.
Where do you lead me, wild one, on and on forever?
Over the hill, over the hill, and down to the meadows of sleep.

THE SUN

Over the soundless depths of space for a hundred million miles
Speeds the soul of me, silent thunder, struck from a harp of fire.
Before my eyes the planets wheel and a universe defiles,

I but a luminant speck of dust upborne in a vast desire.

What is my universe that obeys me — myself compelled to obey
A power that holds me and whirls me over a path that has no
     end?
And there are my children who call me great, the giver of life
     and day,
Myself a child who cry for life and know not whither I tend.

A million million suns above me, as if the curtain of night
Were hung before creation's flame, that shone through the weave
     of the cloth,
Each with its worlds and worlds and worlds crying upward for
     light,
For each is drawn in its course to what? — as the candle draws
     the moth.

THE MILKY WAY

Orbits unending,
Life never ending,
Power without end.

A VOICE

Wouldst thou be lord,
Not peace but a sword.
Not heart's desire —
Ever aspire.
Worship thy power,
Conquer thy hour,
Sleep not but strive,
So shalt thou live.

INFINITE DEPTHS

Infinite Law,
Infinite Life.

NOTES TO THE POEMS

The following annotations include textual variants—other than punctuation and spelling—that occur in the *Reedy's Mirror* (1914-15) version of the *Anthology* and in the typescripts of a few poems. For most of *Spoon River Anthology* there is no surviving text prior to *Reedy's Mirror*—and none prior to the 1916 edition for the thirty-one epitaph-poems and "Epilogue" that were added at that time. Since 1916 the text of the *Anthology* has not been changed through scores of printings, except in 1962 when the Collier Books paperback edition corrected a few typographical errors. The present edition includes a few more alterations of that kind, corrects alphabetizing errors in the table of contents, and makes a few small substantive changes, which are explained in the annotations. Also, the punctuation has been improved in several dozen places where it was extremely bad, and certain spellings have been regularized.

The real-life models for Masters's poems are indicated, if known, but it should be emphasized that some of his characterizations based on Petersburg and Lewistown people differ considerably from what local records and community memory reveal about those individuals. Of course, Masters was not writing local history, so even when a poem was substantially based on a person he had known, he frequently changed the characterization for artistic reasons. Masters derived scores of *Spoon River Anthology* surnames from family names in the Petersburg and Lewistown areas, but name sources are not included in the annotations unless the poet had a particular person in mind or the name has other significance. The birth and death dates of people reflected in the poems are from cemetery records, census records, and death certificates.

The annotations provided here owe much to the work of other scholars, especially Kimball Flaccus and Charles E. Burgess. The following works by Masters, studies by scholars, and materials by Lewistown residents are referred to in abbreviated form in the notes because they are cited more than once:

Burgess, Charles E. "Ancestral Lore in *Spoon River Anthology:* Fact and Fancy." *Papers on Language and Literature* 20 (1984): 185-204.

———. "Edgar Lee Masters: The Lawyer as Writer." In *The Vision of This Land: Studies of Vachel Lindsay, Edgar Lee Masters, and Carl Sandburg*, pp. 55-73. Edited by John E. Hallwas and Dennis J. Reader. Macomb: Western Illinois University, 1976.

———. "Edgar Lee Masters' Paternal Ancestry: A Pioneer Heritage and Influence." *Western Illinois Regional Studies* 7 (1984): 32-60.

———. Letter to John E. Hallwas, December 8, 1990. Edgar Lee Masters Collection. Archives and Special Collections, Western Illinois University Library.

———. "Masters and Some Mentors." *Papers on Language and Literature* 10 (1974): 175-201.

———. "Some Family Source Material for *Spoon River Anthology.*" *Western Illinois Regional Studies* 13 (1990): 80-89.

———. "*Spoon River:* Politics and Poetry." *Papers on Language and Literature* 23 (1987): 347-63.

———. "The Use of Local Lore in *Spoon River Anthology.*" Masters thesis, Southern Illinois University, Edwardsville, 1969.

Chandler, Josephine Craven. "The Spoon River Country." *Journal of the Illinois State Historical Society* 14 (1921-22): 252-329.

Flaccus, Kimball. "Edgar Lee Masters: A Biographical and Critical Study." Ph.D. diss., New York University, 1952.

Hallwas, John E. "Masters and the Pioneers: Four Epitaphs from *Spoon River Anthology.*" *The Old Northwest* 2 (1976): 389-99.

———. "Two Autobiographical Epitaphs in *Spoon River Anthology.*" *The Great Lakes Review* 3 (1976): 28-36.

Heylin, Jesse, ed. *History of Fulton County* (bound together with *Historical Encyclopedia of Illinois*, edited by Newton Bateman and Paul Selby). Chicago: Munsell, 1908.

History of Fulton County, Illinois. Peoria: Charles C. Chapman, 1879.

Hurt, James. "The Sources of the Spoon: Edgar Lee Masters and the *Spoon River Anthology.*" *The Centennial Review* 24 (1980): 403-31.

Kramer, Dale. *Chicago Renaissance.* New York: Appleton-Century, 1966.

Lewis, Mary B. Copy of *Spoon River Anthology* with annotations. Archives and Special Collections, Western Illinois University Library. (Lewis includes information supplied by several regional residents.)

Love, Francis. "Spoon River Names" (a list of models for *Spoon River Anthology* characters), in a July 14, 1953, letter to Kimball Flaccus from George P. Proctor. Folder 10, Box 4, Flaccus-Masters Archive. Special Collections Division, Georgetown University Library. (Proctor also comments on some of Love's identifications. Both Proctor and Love were Lewistown residents.)

Masters, Edgar Lee. *Across Spoon River: An Autobiography.* New York: Farrar and Rinehart, 1936.

―――. "Days in the Lincoln Country." *Journal of the Illinois State Historical Society* 18 (1925-26): 778-92.

―――. "The Genesis of Spoon River." *The American Mercury* 28 (January 1933): 38-55.

―――. *The Great Valley.* New York: Macmillan, 1916.

―――. *The Harmony of Deeper Music: Posthumous Poems of Edgar Lee Masters.* Edited by Frank K. Robinson. Austin: Humanities Research Center, University of Texas at Austin, 1976.

―――. "The Machine Age Comes to Spoon River." *Today,* April 14, 1934, pp. 8-9.

―――. *Mitch Miller.* New York: Macmillan, 1920.

―――. *The Sangamon.* New York: Farrar and Rinehart, 1942.

―――. *The Tale of Chicago.* New York: G. P. Putnam's Sons, 1933.

Narveson, Robert D. "Edgar Lee Masters' *Spoon River Anthology:* Background, Composition and Reputation." Ph.D. diss., University of Chicago, 1962.

Portrait and Biographical Album of Fulton County, Illinois. Chicago: Biographical Publishing, 1890.

Proctor, George P. "Questions for George P. Proctor, submitted by Kimball Flaccus." February 25, 1953. Folder 10, Box 4, Flaccus-Masters Archive. Special Collections Division, Georgetown University Library.

Wrenn, John H., and Margaret M. Wrenn. *Edgar Lee Masters.* Boston: Twayne, 1983.

The Hill

The title of this poem reflects Oak Hill Cemetery in Lewistown, which was commonly referred to as "The Hill" by local residents. In previous editions of the *Anthology* all of the lines were printed in italics. For this edition the lines spoken by the second, or inner, voice of the poet are printed in regular type. That voice starts to respond imaginatively at the end of the poem, launching the poet's spiritual quest, which continues throughout the series of epitaph-poems that follows. This important poem is discussed extensively in the introduction to this edition.

Where are: Wrenn and Wrenn suggest that Masters was indebted to the opening of Emerson's "Hamatreya" for the *ubi sunt* formula (p. 65). In that poem the speaker says, "Where are these men? Asleep beneath their grounds."

Uncle Isaac and Aunt Emily: Burgess indicates that this line refers to the poet's uncle and aunt, Isaac Bird Masters (1849-1923) and Emmeline Masters McLaughlin (1827-44), in "Some Family Source Material," pp. 81, 86.

old Towny Kincaid and Sevigne Houghton: Chandler points out that Sevigne Houghton's farm adjoined that of Masters's grandparents north of Petersburg and that the Kincaid family also lived in that neighborhood (p. 260). Her study includes a photograph of Houghton, facing page 260.

Major Walker: Major Newton Walker (1801-97) was a much-venerated Lewistown pioneer. He designed and supervised the construction of the third courthouse in Lewistown, which was burned by an incendiary in 1894 — an event reflected in "Silas Dement." Chandler discusses Walker and provides a photograph of him (pp. 298-301). See also the *History of Fulton County, Illinois*, pp. 775, 816, and William T. Davidson, "Major Newton Walker," Lewistown *Fulton Democrat,* September 20, 1899, p. 1.

Old Fiddler Jones: See "Fiddler Jones" and the note to that poem.

Clary's Grove: A frontier settlement two miles south of Petersburg near Lincoln's New Salem. Chandler points out that horse racing and fiddling were common activities there (p. 265).

Hod Putt

The speaker's name may be intended to reflect the southern pronunciation of "hard put," an idiom that means "faced with difficulty." It does describe the speaker's life.

Old Bill Piersol: William ("Bill") Phelps (1809-89) was an early Indian trader and store owner in Lewistown. See Chandler, pp. 293-98, and Flaccus, pp. 109-12. Phelps is buried in Lewistown's Oak Hill Cemetery.

Proctor's Grove: A thirteen-acre wooded tract located southwest of Lewistown. See Chandler, pp. 309-10.

Ollie McGee

This poem and "Fletcher McGee" are briefly discussed in the introduction to this edition.

These are driving him to the place where I lie: Although this line indicates that her husband is not dead, he is the speaker of the following epitaph. This discrepancy occurred because Masters wrote "Ollie McGee" in May 1914, and it appeared in *Reedy's Mirror* on May 29 as one of the seven poems that started the Spoon River Anthology series. "Fletcher McGee," written later, did not appear in *Reedy's Mirror* until October 9, 1914. He placed the two poems side by side in the 1915 edition but failed to change the line so as to reflect Fletcher's death.

Fletcher McGee

See the annotations to "Ollie McGee."

It was not mine, it was not hers: "It" has no clear referent, but McGee is referring to his wife's inner self, her tortured spirit, which resulted from his secret cruelty and thus was not entirely his creation or hers.

Robert Fulton Tanner

The speaker, a frustrated inventor, was ironically named for Robert Fulton (1765-1815), the great inventor and pioneer in steam navigation. According to Lewis, a man named Morris(?) Tanner owned a hardware store in Lewistown. See the introduction to this edition for a discussion of the "rat trap" metaphor in this poem.

Cassius Hueffer

The real-life model for this poem was a Lewistown resident named Cassius Whitney (1846-86), according to Lewis and Love, but they perhaps based their assertions on the first-name connection alone, since the poem evokes an inner life that the community was unaware of. As the introduction to this edition indicates, "Cassius Hueffer" reflects the poet's inner conflict. See also "Harmon Whitney" and the first note to that poem. In *Reedy's Mirror*, May 29, 1914, the poem is simply entitled "Cassius."

"His life was gentle . . .": The quotation is from Shakespeare's *Julius Caesar*, act 5, sc. 5. Mark Anthony is speaking about Brutus.

Serepta Mason

In *Reedy's Mirror*, May 29, 1914, this poem is entitled "Serepta the Scold."

Amanda Barker

According to Lewis and Love, this poem is based on the life of Elizabeth (Turner) Phelps (1865-90), the wife of Lewistown banker

Henry Phelps. She died in childbirth and is buried in Lewistown's Oak Hill Cemetery. The photograph section of this book includes a picture of her headstone. In *Reedy's Mirror,* May 29, 1914, the poem is entitled "Amanda."

Constance Hately

The speaker's name is allegorical: she was constantly hateful, as the last two lines of the poem indicate.

Chase Henry

Frank ("Chase") Henry (1855-1903) was the town drunkard in Lewistown, according to Flaccus, p. 202. He also set fire to the courthouse on December 14, 1894. See "Silas Dement" and the note to that poem. Henry died from chronic alcoholism and is buried in St. Mary's Cemetery at the edge of Lewistown.

the banker Nicholas: This refers to the Spoon River entrepreneur Nicholas Bindle, whose epitaph-poem was entitled "Nicholas, the Banker" in *Reedy's Mirror.* See the first note to "Nicholas Bindle."

Harry Carey Goodhue

The speaker's name is perhaps an allusion to Henry Charles Carey (1793-1879), an American economist, sociologist, and reformer who propounded the view that pursuit of self-interest would ultimately produce a harmony of interests of all social and economic classes. If so, the name is ironic. The word "harry" also means "to harass," which conveys this speaker's approach to community leaders.

the cherished jawbone of an ass: An allusion to the biblical story of Samson, who slew a thousand men with the jawbone of an ass (Judges 15:15).

Judge Somers

According to Lewis and Love, this poem is based on Judge John Winter (1826-1906), a Lewistown resident whose son Will was a friend of Masters. He is buried in Lewistown's Oak Hill Cemetery. See the *History of Fulton County, Illinois,* pp. 408, 818. See also the first note to "Seth Compton."

Blackstone and Coke: Sir William Coke (1723-80) wrote *Commentaries on the Laws of England* (1765-69), which is the most influential treatise on law in the English language, and it was widely read by law students in the nineteenth century. Sir Edward Coke (1552-1634) was an eminent British jurist who wrote various treatises on the law.

Justice Breese: Sidney Breese (1800-1878) was a noted justice of the Illinois Supreme Court (1841-43, 1857-78).

Kinsey Keene

Lewis asserts that Kinsey Thomas (1860-1913), a Lewistown lawyer, was the model for this poem, but it is probably based on the poet's father, Hardin W. Masters (1845-1925), who was also a lawyer, or on Lewis C. ("Lute") Breeden (1861-1914), a Lewistown newspaper editor and political leader. The poet viewed them both as heroic opponents of the repressive forces in the community. See "Jefferson Howard," "Enoch Dunlap," and the notes to those poems. Although none of these three figures is generally remembered for insulting community leaders, Masters recalled that Breeden once told off the leaders at a political caucus—apparently by saying they could all go to hell. That act was much-admired by the poet and his old friend Edwin P. Reese, who often swapped humorous insults in their correspondence. For example, in a 1925 letter Masters jokingly told Reese, "You can do what Lute Breeden said the caucus could do," and later, "you can follow the Lute Breeden injunction." See letter from Masters to Reese, December 17, 1925, Folder 1, Edgar Lee Masters Papers, Illinois State Historical Library.

Cambronne's dying words: "La garde muert at ne se rend pas" ("The guard dies but never surrenders") are the words incorrectly attributed by some to Count Pierre Jacques Etienne Cambronne (1770-1842), a French general at the Battle of Waterloo, when he was asked to surrender. However, this poem actually contains a scatological insult directed at the repressive forces of the community, for French tradition asserts that Cambronne's response was a single word: *"merde"* ("shit"). In France *merde* is commonly referred to as *"le mot de Cambronne."* See Bergen Evans, *Dictionary of Quotations* (New York: Delacorte, 1968), p. 735.

Waterloo: The location south of Brussels, Belgium, where the allies won a decisive victory over Napoleon in 1815. Mont St. Jean is nearby.

Maitland: Sir Frederick Lewis Maitland (1777-1839), a British naval officer.

Benjamin Pantier

This poem has been associated with Lewistown lawyer Kinsey Thomas (1860-1913) by Lewis and Love. The same local sources have asserted that "Mrs. Benjamin Pantier" is based on the lawyer's wife, Emogene Thomas. Both are buried in Lewistown's Oak Hill Cemetery.

It is also likely that these two "Pantier" poems reflect the conflict between Hardin W. Masters (1845-1925) and Emma Masters (1849-1926), the poet's parents, whose "marriage was the union of conflicting and irresistible forces" (*Across Spoon River*, p. 10). Since the poems are followed by "Reuben Pantier," which characterizes the Pantiers' son, and since local sources such as Lewis and Love assert that it reflects Masters himself, there is support for viewing the three "Pantier" poems as autobiographical in origin. Also, in "Jim Brown," Benjamin Pantier and his wife are associated with conflicting social forces, just as Masters views his parents in his autobiography. Hardin and Emma Masters are buried in Petersburg's Oakland Cemetery.

James Hurt suggests that these two "pantier" poems also reflect the conflict between Masters and his first wife: "Some of the tensions in Masters' first marriage replicated, perhaps not coincidentally, those in his parents' marriage, and certainly we can hear behind Mrs. Pantier's distaste for whiskey, onions, and sex the voice of Helen Jenkins, who made Masters serve a year of church-going and abstinence from whiskey and cigars before she would marry him" (p. 422).

Mrs. Benjamin Pantier

For a discussion of the background to this poem, see the note to "Benjamin Pantier."

Wordsworth's "Ode": William Wordsworth's famous poem, "Ode: Intimations of Immortality from Recollections of Early Childhood" (1807). The "Immortality Ode" directly contrasts with "Mortality" by Knox, mentioned below.

"Oh, why should the spirit of mortal be proud?": "Mortality" (c. 1825), a poem by William Knox, was better known by its first line, given here. As Masters certainly knew, this was Lincoln's favorite poem.

Reuben Pantier

This poem reflects the poet's appreciation for his favorite grammar school teacher, Esther Sparks. See "Emily Sparks" and the note to that poem.

Rue de Rivoli: A street in Paris.

cocotte: A French word meaning "loose woman" or "tart."

Emily Sparks

Masters told Kimball Flaccus that this poem was based on Esther Sparks (1833-91), his favorite grammar school teacher (Flaccus, p. 160).

For a recollection of her by another student of the same era, see George Proctor, "George Proctor's Memoirs," Lewistown *Fulton Democrat,* April 3, 1957, p. 7.

However, two scholars have also related the poem to Masters's favorite high school teacher, Mary Fisher (b. 1858), whose better students "took fire under her inspiration" (*Across Spoon River,* p. 59). See Chandler, "The Spoon River Country," p. 321, and Burgess, "Masters and Some Mentors," pp. 187-88.

Trainor, the Druggist

Burgess points out that the "actual pharmacist–drugstore operator in Lewistown during the Masters family's residence was Nathan Painter (1853-1919), who was a political ally of Hardin Masters" (letter to Hallwas, p. 2). However, there were other drugstore owners. Lewis suggests a connection with either Philip (James P.) or Eck (R. A.) Randall, who operated Randall Brothers Drug Store, which opened in 1886. Philip (1855-1906) was a widower for many years, and Eck (1857-1900) was apparently a bachelor. Both are buried in Lewistown's Oak Hill Cemetery.

Daisy Fraser

the "Q" railroad: The Chicago, Burlington, and Quincy Railroad, which ran through Lewistown, was commonly called the "Q."

Benjamin Fraser

This strange figure, who is obsessed by the feeling that spirits surround him, crying for life, is a symbolic reflection of the poet's realization that in writing the epitaph-poems, he gave life to people of the past who "beat upon" his own spirit. A passage in *Across Spoon River* reveals the autobiographical basis of the poem: "I did feel somehow by these months of exploring the souls of the dead, by this half-sacrilegious revelation of their secrets, that I had convoked about my head swarms of powers and beings who were watching me and protesting, and yet inpsiring me to go on" (p. 352). Masters apparently felt that, in effect, he seized and crushed the souls of the dead in order to express himself. Although writing is not mentioned in this poem, it is suggested by the imagery of wings and flame. Because the speaker used others for his own purposes, he was later punished by being condemned to lifeless isolation. In "The Spooniad" Masters refers to this figure as "Benjamin Fraser, son of Benjamin Pantier / By Daisy Fraser." This is a kind of private joke, for Benjamin Pantier is based on Masters's father, and Daisy

Fraser is a prostitute. Of course, Masters was not illegitimate, but he may have been asserting that his character was not like his mother's or that he suspected his father of philandering.

My soul made their spirits gilt: That is, the speaker's imaginative expression of those spirits gave them a kind of shining permanence, but "gilt" also implies a surface covering that obscures what lies beneath: the real selves of those people. Hence the word "gilt" also suggests the poet's sense of guilt for using the remembered selves of others to express himself.

Minerva Jones

Lewis and Love suggest two possible models for this poem: Marie Wheadon and Minnie Staton (b. 1871), both of Lewistown. Since the following poem, " 'Indignation' Jones," is based on Minnie's father, Jonas Staton, the connection with her seems likely. The controversial circumstances of Minerva Jones's death have not been explicitly associated with either woman. Also, Masters had an Aunt Minerva who had an interest in poetry and to whom he showed some of his early newspaper verse (*Across Spoon River,* p. 98). In *Reedy's Mirror,* June 19, 1914, this poem is simply entitled "Minerva." As Masters knew, Minerva was the name of the virgin goddess of wisdom and war in Roman mythology.

Yahoos: This unusual term, which originated in Swift's *Gulliver's Travels* (1726), has several meanings that relate to the poem: bumpkins, vicious men, and poor whites (or "white trash," as "Indignation" Jones puts it in the following poem).

"Butch" Weldy: In *Reedy's Mirror,* June 19, 1914, the man's name is " 'Butch' Weedy," but that is probably a typographical error.

"Indignation" Jones

Lewis and Love assert that this poem is based on Lewistown resident Jonas Staton (1833-1905). He was a house painter, and he is buried in Lewistown's Oak Hill Cemetery.

Doctor Meyers

Lewis connects this poem with Dr. David D. Talbott (1837-1919), a Lewistown physician, but she also adds that it is "not a true story." That comment apparently refers to the sensational details surrounding the disgrace and death of Dr. Meyers. In fact, since Dr. Talbott died after the poem was published, it is likely that the abortion death case does not relate to him. Talbott and his wife Amelia (1847-1935) are buried in Lewistown's Oak Hill Cemetery. See *Portrait and Bi-*

ographical *Album*, pp. 497-99. Burgess has noted that Dr. J. T. Miers was the first physician in Oakford, a village near Petersburg ("The Use of Local Lore," p. 141), but the only apparent connection with this poem is the similar name. See also the note to "Willie Metcalf."

A possible source for the details about the goodhearted doctor disgraced because of a death during an abortion is the case of Dr. John W. Aiken, a physician in McDonough County (adjacent to Fulton), who was tried and convicted of "murder by abortion" at Macomb in May of 1899 following the death of a female patient. That sensational murder case was widely reported in area newspapers. See John E. Hallwas, *McDonough County Heritage* (Macomb: Illinois Heritage Press, 1984), pp. 125-29.

Mrs. Meyers

See the note to "Doctor Meyers." In *Reedy's Mirror*, August 7, 1914, this poem is entitled "Mrs. Doctor Meyers."

"Butch" Weldy

This poem is based on the accidental death of Charles Beggs (d. July 31, 1889), a worker at the Ranny and Phelps canning factory in Lewistown. A newspaper account of the inquest survives: "The jury summoned to inquire into the death of Charles Beggs found the evidence insufficient to attach blame to anyone. Their verdict was simply death by accidental burning. It seems that one of the employees in the upper room, through a misunderstanding, neglected to put out the fire in the soldering stove. That is, the fire was out at the moment of the explosion, but had been extinguished but a moment before. . . . Let it suffice to say that when the top of the yard reservoir was unscrewed it produced a draft through the connecting pipes, which fanning the fire to life, exploded the gasoline. Charley Beggs, being in the act of pouring gasoline into the reservoir, was blown prostrate and actually cooked." See "From Lewistown," Canton *Fulton County Ledger*, August 8, 1889, p. 1. Masters apparently felt that the owners of the cannery were liable, despite what the jury at the inquest decided. Indeed, two weeks later a similar explosion occurred, in which no one was hurt, suggesting that the machinery was defective. Of course, Masters later represented clients in liability cases, so he undoubtedly had occasion to reflect on this event. The speaker's blindness is metaphorical for his earlier inability to see the true character of "Old Rhodes' son," the cannery owner.

the canning works: Masters mentions the Lewistown cannery in

"The Machine Age Comes to Spoon River," p. 9. See also, Burgess, "The Use of Local Lore," p. 108.

Old Rhodes' son: Henry Willis Phelps, the son of bank president Henry Phelps, was a partner in the Lewistown cannery. See the first note to "Ralph Rhodes."

Knowlt Hoheimer

the battle of Missionary Ridge: The final battle in the struggle for Chattanooga during the Civil War, November 25, 1863, and a Union victory. Burgess has pointed out that Masters had an uncle who was severely wounded at this battle. See "Edgar Lee Masters' Paternal Ancestry: A Pioneer Heritage and Influence," p. 50.

"Pro Patria": A Latin phrase meaning "for his country," here expressing an ironic misapprehension of the speaker's motive for serving in the war.

Frank Drummer

Lewis associates this poem with Frank Hummer, a Lewistown resident, and Masters did know the Hummer family well. However, it may also relate to the poet's high school days in Lewistown, when he spent his free time "reading incessantly" in the encyclopedia (*Across Spoon River,* p. 59).

Hare Drummer

Love suggests that this poem is based on Frank Ehrenhardt (1859-1945), a German farmer who lived west of Lewistown and is buried in Oak Hill Cemetery. Burgess quotes a letter indicating that Ehrenhardt "had an orchard and made cider," and he therefore suggests that Ehrenhardt might have been the model for both "Hare Drummer" and the following poem, "Conrad Siever" ("The Use of Local Lore," pp. 145-46). He is probably right about the latter, as the text of that poem and lines 1-2 of "Hare Drummer" suggest, but Ehrenhardt is probably not the model for the present poem. Lewis asserts that "Hare Drummer" is based on Henry ("Hare") Hummer, Masters's childhood friend, with whom he played, fished, and hunted. See *Across Spoon River,* pp. 62, 78. The poem may reflect Hummer, but it is surely based primarily on Masters's own memories of childhood days in the countryside near Petersburg and Lewistown. See the discussion of this poem in the introduction to this edition.

Siever's: Siever's woods were located in the southeast part of Lewistown, but this may refer to the Ehrenhardt farm.

Aaron Hatfield's farm: Aaron Hatfield was a neighbor of Masters's grandparents in the Sand Ridge area near Petersburg. In the poem "Aaron Hatfield," the poet characterizes his grandfather.

How many are with me: How many are in the cemetery.

Conrad Siever

See the first note to "Hare Drummer."

that wasted garden: The town cemetery.

northern-spy: Northern Spy apple tree.

Doc Hill

According to Love, this poem is based on Dr. Alexander Hull (1821-95), a Lewistown physician. Hull was the Masters family physician, and his expertise is recorded by the grateful poet in *Across Spoon River,* pp. 68-69, 93, 107. His commitment to the poor was emphasized in his obituary: "And the poor! How they loved the man! We have seen him on the bitterest days in winter stop to administer medicine to a street wanderer. . . . What a record of human love!" ("Dr. Alex Hull," Lewistown *Fulton Democrat,* Sept. 11, 1895, p. 1). A huge crowd attended his funeral, and he was buried in Oak Hill Cemetery. Although Hull is clearly the model for this poem, various details about the speaker's personal life may be fictitious. For example, instead of a son (line 5), Hull had a daughter, his only child. See also, *Portrait and Biographical Album,* pp. 190-93, which includes a lithograph of the doctor.

Em Stanton: According to Love, this refers to a Lewistown woman named Emma Miner.

Andy the Night-Watch

According to Love, the model for this poem was Lewistown resident Andrew Stevenson (1829-1919). He is buried in Oak Hill Cemetery.

Sarah Brown

Nirvana: In the Hindu religion "Nirvana" refers to spiritual reunion with Brahma and the final emancipation of the soul. In a more generalized sense, the word refers to a beatific spiritual condition.

Percy Bysshe Shelley

Chandler and others have identified the model for this poem as Lewistown resident William Cullen Bryant (1851-75), a relative of the famous poet. According to Chandler, he "was the victim of an accident, having been killed by the discharge of a gun while duck hunting on Thompson's Lake" (p. 329). He is buried at Lewistown's Oak Hill Cemetery, where his gravestone is a marble shaft topped by the statue of a woman. See the photograph in this edition.

Bert Kessler: According to Lewis, this is the actual name of Bryant's good friend, who also lived in Lewistown.

Thompson's Lake: Thompson Lake, located southeast of Lewistown along the Illinois River, was a noted area for waterfowl hunting until it was drained in about 1920.

an Italian artist: In *Reedy's Mirror,* June 19, 1914, the phrase is "some Italian artist."

the ashes of my namesake: The word "namesake" is used here in the general sense of "one having the same name," and it refers to Shelley, whose ashes were buried in the Protestant cemetery at Rome in the shadow of the massive sepulchral monument of Caius Cestius.

Flossie Cabanis

Lewis and Love assert that the model for this poem was Caroline Hull (1867-1923), a little-known actress who was raised in Lewistown. She was the daughter of Dr. Hull, the model for "Doc Hill," and she acted in plays at Beadle's Opera House before leaving for New York. She is buried in Lewistown's Oak Hill Cemetery.

Bindle's opera house: Beadle's Opera House in Lewistown. See "Nicholas Bindle" and the first note to that poem. In *Reedy's Mirror,* June 19, 1914, the poem refers to "McCune's opera house."

East Lynne: A very popular melodrama by Mrs. Henry Wood, *East Lynne* was first produced in 1863 and was later performed by many stock troupes. Local people performed it in Lewistown in 1885.

Ralph Barrett: Lawrence Barrett (1838-91), a noted American actor. In *Reedy's Mirror* the poem refers to "Clay Coleman," and in line nine the name is "Clay" rather than "Ralph."

Duse: Eleonora Duse (1859-1924), an Italian actress, famous for her tragic roles.

Julia Miller

This poem reflects the life of Margaret George Davidson (1869-97), the poet's early sweetheart in Lewistown, who later married newspaper editor William T. Davidson and died at age twenty-eight. Despite what this poem implies, she was happily married to Davidson—who was thirty-two years older than she was—and they already had one small child when she died of a heart condition that stemmed from a childhood illness. She was not pregnant when she married Davidson, nor did she commit suicide. Burgess discusses the background to this poem in "Masters and Some Mentors," pp. 191-93. See also "Margaret Gilman George-Davidson," Lewistown *Fulton Democrat,* December 1, 1897, p. 1, and part 2, p. 2. Margaret George is "Anne" in *Across Spoon River,* and she is buried in Lewistown's Oak Hill Cemetery. See also the notes to "Caroline Branson," "Amelia Garrick," "Louise Smith," and "Editor Whedon."

that estranged young soul: This is a reference to Masters, who broke off his relationship with Margaret George, to whom he felt he "owed marriage." He was later tormented by the fear that he had wronged her. See *Across Spoon River,* pp. 100-107, 111.

"And Jesus said . . . in paradise.": This is the response of Christ to one of the criminals crucified alongside him (Luke 23:43). According to Margaret George Davidson's obituary, she had been reading the Bible at the time she died ("Margaret Gilman George-Davidson," Lewistown *Fulton Democrat,* December 1, 1897, p. 1).

Johnnie Sayre

This poem is based on Masters's boyhood chum, George Mitchell ("Mitch") Miller, who was "killed while flipping [a ride on] a train" (*Across Spoon River,* p. 29). The boy was ten years old at the time, March 26, 1879. The words that close the poem were carved on the boy's gravestone in Petersburg's Oakland Cemetery. Mitch Miller's father was a Cumberland Presbyterian minister, Rev. Robert D. L. Miller, which helps to explain the religious cast of the poem. He was also the Menard County superintendent of schools for twenty-two years, which may have prompted Masters to stress the impact of truancy on the mind of his character. Masters also based his first novel, *Mitch Miller* (1920), on memories of his boyhood days with the tragic youth, whose death is also reflected there (pp. 247-51). Wrenn and Wrenn point out that the words that close this poem are also "the theme of Mitch Miller's funeral sermon in the later novel" (p. 49).

Charlie French

This poem is based on the death of a Lewistown boy named Charles ("Charley") Bell (1868-81). That tragic event was briefly described in the Canton newspaper: "Died, on Friday evening, July 11, from the effects of a wound received from the accidental discharge of a toy pistol, Charley Bell, aged 14 years. The accident occurred at Canton, July 4, producing lock-jaw a few days later, and finally resulting in the death of the victim on the date mentioned. The boy was an orphan. . . . Six boys of about Charley's age acted as pall bearers." See "From the County Seat," Canton *Fulton County Ledger,* July 17, 1884, p. 5. Bell is buried in Oak Hill Cemetery.

Captain Harris: Burgess suggests that this reference "probably is derived from the military career of Thomas L. Harris of Petersburg; his service, however, was in the Mexican War" (letter to Hallwas, p. 2).

Zenas Witt

According to Flaccus, this unusual name was derived by combining the first and last names of two signers of the Illinois Constitution of 1848, Zenas H. Vernon and Franklin Witt (p. 201). The poem apparently does not refer to the life of either man.

Theodore the Poet

Masters told novelist Theodore Dreiser (1871-1945), "I have you pickled in my Anthology as 'Theodore the Poet'" (letter to Dreiser, August 20, 1914, in the Theodore Dreiser Collection, Special Collections, Van Pelt Library, University of Pennsylvania). Dreiser's realism had a big impact on Masters, and they were friends long before the *Anthology* was written. See the discussion of Dreiser's influence in the introduction to this edition.

The Town Marshal

John E. Logan (d. 1887) was the marshal in Lewistown during the 1880s, and he was killed by a man named George ("Bones") Weldy. Masters describes the episode in *Across Spoon River,* pp. 94-95: "The annual issue in Lewistown was saloons or no saloons. And about 1888 . . . the saloons were voted out. A terrible man named John Logan was appointed town marshal by the prohibition mayor, with instructions to keep order on the streets and to hunt down the drinkers. . . . He was provided with a gun and a cane made of steel and knobbed with a ball of lead almost as large as an egg. . . . One day a man named Weldy, a fellow peaceable enough, returned from Havana and walked on one of the side streets toward home carrying a jug of whisky. He was a little intoxicated but not disorderly. . . . Logan struck him over the head with the lead-knobbed cane, knocking Weldy flat. Then he began to beat Weldy with the cane. Weldy finally got to his feet and drew a small thirty-two caliber revolver and fired it. The sound of the explosion was so slight that Logan did not hear it; nevertheless, the bullet penetrated his abdomen, and he soon sank on the sidewalk. . . . Thus came the end of Logan, who had killed two men in brawls and who, having joined the church, had become an avenging angel of the law." A mob gathered to lynch Weldy, but he was hurried out of town. The poet's father, Hardin W. Masters, defended Weldy and got him to plead guilty in return for a life sentence, which was handed down on August 30, 1887. As Masters recalled, "My father showed the facts in the Bones Weldy case . . . and there the question was whether a man should hang who had been beaten half to death by the town marshal before he fired a shot" (letter to Edwin P. Reese, undated, c. 1924, Folder 1, Edgar Lee Masters Papers, Illinois State Historical Library). Years later the elder Masters petitioned Governor John Peter Altgeld for a pardon, which was granted. See the following poem, "Jack McGuire," as well as "Oscar Hummel."

Maple Grove: Maple's Mill, located several miles northeast of Lewistown, had a sawmill in the later nineteenth century.

Jack McGuire

The model for this poem was George ("Bones") Weldy (1860-1940), who killed the Lewistown marshal in 1887. See "The Town Marshal" and the note to that poem. Weldy is buried in Lewistown's Oak Hill Cemetery.

Kinsey Keene: Weldy's lawyer was Hardin W. Masters, the poet's father. See "Kinsey Keene" and the first note to that poem. The deal between Keene and the judge has no factual basis.

Dorcas Gustine

That act of the Spartan boy . . . uncomplainingly.: This refers to a Greek folk tale that illustrates the Spartan ideal of manliness. In some versions the animal is a fox rather than a wolf. See Charles D. Shaw, *Stories of the Ancient Greeks* (Boston: Ginn, 1903), p. 134.

Nicholas Bindle

Masters indicated that "The opera house [in Lewistown] . . . had been built in 1876 at an expense of $50,000 by the man whose career I epitaphed under the name of Nicholas Bindle" ("The Genesis of Spoon River," p. 42). That man was Nathan Beadles (1811-92), who is buried in Lewistown's Oak Hill Cemetery. Beadle's Block, as the building was called, housed not only the opera house but the law office of Hardin W. Masters, the poet's father. See Flaccus, pp. 115-17, 134. For information on Beadles, see Heylin, pp. 782-83; *History of Fulton County, Illinois,* pp. 785-86; and *Portrait and Biographical Album,* pp. 621-22. In "The Spooniad" the liberals of

Spoon River meet at Bindle's Opera House. In *Reedy's Mirror,* June 26, 1914, this poem is entitled "Nicholas, the Banker."

the pipe-organ, which I gave to the church: In 1908 Henry Willis Phelps gave an organ to the Lewistown Presbyterian Church. For information about him, see the first note to "Ralph Rhodes." But Nathan Beadles also gave money to the Methodist Church, some of which may have been used for an organ.

Jacob Goodpasture

When Fort Sumter fell and the war came: Fort Sumter, in the harbor at Charleston, South Carolina, fell to the Confederates on April 13, 1861, starting the Civil War.

the Transfiguration: That is, the spiritual renewal of America — or the "new birth of freedom," as Lincoln put it in his Gettysburg Address.

Harold Arnett

Lewis and Love assert that this poem is based on a Lewistown resident, John Craig, Sr. (1858-85). However, Craig was shot by his wife. He is buried in Lewistown's Oak Hill Cemetery.

the coughing of John Yarnell: This curious reference suggests that Masters was recalling an actual circumstance. There is a John Yarnell buried in Oak Hill Cemetery. On April 23, 1867, he was indicted for shooting and killing James P. Goodwin, the Lewistown marshal. Yarnell was subsequently convicted and sentenced to fourteen years in prison. His death date is unknown.

Margaret Fuller Slack

This poem combines details associated with the two wives of Dr. William S. Strode, a physician and amateur naturalist of Bernadotte and, later, Lewistown. Strode was the model for "William Jones." His first wife, Amelia Steele, died of lockjaw on December 23, 1888, and Masters told Kimball Flaccus that her death was reflected in this poem (Flaccus, p. 201). Strode's second wife, Julia Brown (1866-1954), was an author, teacher, feminist, and friend of Masters. The poet discusses her briefly in *Across Spoon River,* p. 128. Lewis and Love assert that the poem reflects her life, although she was never married to a druggist. The speaker's name was apparently derived by combining the name of nineteenth-century feminist author Margaret Fuller (1810-50) with the last name of a lawyer, William Slack, whom Masters knew in Chicago. See also the first note to "Tennessee Claflin Shope."

George Eliot: Pseudonym of the famous nineteenth-century novelist, Mary Ann Evans (1819-80).

George Trimble

Lewis and Love assert that the model for this poem was a Lewistown resident named George Allen (b. 1855). He was a schoolteacher who had a wife and daughter, but nothing else is known about him. There was a George Trimble (b. 1835) in Lewistown, but since he was a teamster, it is unlikely that he inspired this poem.

free-silver: The free-silver movement of the late nineteenth century, championed by William Jennings Bryan (1860-1925), was an attempt to restore bimetallism by allowing silver to be minted in unlimited quantities, thereby greatly increasing the money supply and supposedly helping farmers and debtors. Burgess points out that Masters spoke in support of free silver and that his speech was printed by the press of the *Lewistown News* as *Bimetallism: Speech Delivered by Edgar L. Masters at Petersburg, Illinois, August 27, 1896* (letter to Hallwas, p. 2).

the single-tax of Henry George: Henry George (1839-97) was an American economist and reformer who founded the single-tax movement. He wrote *Progress and Poverty* (1880), a very influential book.

the Peerless Leader: William Jennings Bryan, who lost "the first battle" (his first presidential campaign) in 1896.

"Ace" Shaw

Lewis associates this poem with "Ace" Weldy, a Lewistown resident who was the brother of "Bones" Weldy, the model for "Jack McGuire." Nothing is known about him. In *Reedy's Mirror,* July 3, 1914, this poem is entitled " 'Ace' Breeden," which suggests that Masters may have had Lewis C. ("Lute") Breeden in mind, but whether the latter held such a view is unknown. On Breeden, see the note to "Enoch Dunlap."

Justice Arnett

Burgess asserts that this poem "Probably reflects . . . a political foe of Hardin Wallace Masters, Addison M. Barnett. His Oak Hill Cemetery dates are 1845-1920. He was elected Fulton County Judge 1890-94" (letter to Hallwas, p. 2).

Willard Fluke

The speaker's name suggests an effort of the "will"—his determination to save himself—that was initiated by the "fluke" or lucky chance of his sexual escapade with the loose woman. Of course, the "fluke" turned out to be very unlucky because he contracted venereal disease, which resulted in his child being born blind.

Aner Clute

Lewis asserts that the model for this poem was Elizabeth Clute, a Lewistown resident who was "always associated in gossip with Lute Ross." Nothing is known about Clute, but see the first note to "Lucius Atherton."

to lead the life: That is, the life of a prostitute. The second half of the poem asserts that she turned to prostitution because the people of Spoon River had stereotyped her as a loose woman following one sexual episode.

Lucius Atherton

According to Lewis and Love, this poem reflects the life of Lewis C. ("Lute") Ross (1848-1916), the son of Lewis W. Ross, a prominent Lewistown attorney and political leader. See also the note to "Washington McNeeley." Lute Ross was a bachelor and, apparently, a woman chaser. At one time he was a suitor for the hand of Madeline Masters, the poet's sister. In the previous poem, "Aner Clute," the speaker says that she was seduced by Lucius Atherton, as does the speaker in "Lucille Luck," a poem in *The New Spoon River* (1924). Ross is buried in Lewistown's Oak Hill Cemetery.

However, this poem also relates to a deep inner conflict in Masters between spiritual aspiration and sexuality. See the discussion of "Lucius Atherton" in the introduction to this edition, and see the passages in *Across Spoon River* on the poet's "pursuit of the eternal feminine" (pp. 170-71, 406-8). "Ezra Bartlett" also reflects this conflict.

Mayer's restaurant: Burgess identifies this as Lewistown's "Meyers restaurant" ("The Use of Local Lore," p. 102).

a mighty shade: Dante (1265-1321), the great Italian poet who celebrated his beloved Beatrice in the *Divine Comedy*.

Homer Clapp

the skating rink: Roller skating became very popular in the late nineteenth century, and many small towns, including Lewistown, had a rink.

Deacon Taylor

This poem reflects Masters's view of William Taylor Davidson (1837-1915), a Lewistown newspaper editor, religious exponent, and temperance advocate. He was a heavy drinker early in his life, but he later became an ardent prohibitionist. In 1884 he was the chief organizer of the local prohibition political party. As an editor he often accused drugstores of being "lawless dram sellers," which they probably were during periods when saloons were not licensed. He surely was not a secret drinker, nor did he die of cirrhosis of the liver caused by alcoholism. For more on Davidson and Masters's hatred of him, see the note to "Editor Whedon" and the introduction to this edition.

"Spiritus frumenti": A Latin phrase meaning "spirit of grain," here referring to alcohol.

Sam Hookey

According to Burgess, "In the 1870's and 1880's a circus wintered in Petersburg, to the delight of small boys. The epitaph 'Sam Hookey' was a result" ("The Use of Local Lore," p. 103).

Robespierre: Maximilien-François-Marie-Isidore de Robespierre (1758-95), the famous French revolutionist and leader of the Reign of Terror.

Cooney Potter

Red Eagle cigars: Lewis provides this humorous annotation: "Made by Frank Sayre of Lewistown—a local cigar. No wonder he died from smoking these."

Fiddler Jones

Masters indicated that "Fiddler Jones" was based on a real person of the Petersburg area, the brother of Hannah Armstrong ("The Genesis of Spoon River," p. 41). His name was John Jones, but he was always called "Fid" or "Fiddler." See Chandler, "The Spoon River Country," pp. 265-66. Burgess discusses other fiddlers of the Petersburg–New Salem area who may also have influenced this characterization ("The Use of Local Lore," p. 135).

Little Grove: A hamlet located several miles southwest of Petersburg.

Red-Head Sammy: Samuel Watkins (d. 1911), a musician who lived near Atterberry, northwest of Petersburg. Masters mentions him in *The Sangamon,* p. 69.

Louise Smith

This poem and "Herbert Marshall" reflect the end of Masters's love relationship with Margaret George in 1889. At that time he grew tired of the brilliant young woman, whom he had been seeing for several years, and became attracted to a lovely sixteen-year-old girl that he refers to as "Alfreda" in *Across Spoon River* (pp. 102-7, 111-14, 121, 127, 133). She is the basis for "Annabelle" in this poem, and her real name was Delia Proctor (b. 1869). See "Searcy Foote," which reflects the same period in Masters's life, and where the young woman is called "Delia Prickett." The introduction to this edition includes a brief discussion of Masters's troubled relationships with women, including this early episode. Other poems that reflect Margaret George are "Caroline Branson," "Amelia Garrick," and "Julia Miller."

the Seminary: A private secondary school.

Deadly ivy instead of clematis: That is, poison ivy instead of clematis. Both are vines, but the clematis produces a lovely flower.

Herbert Marshall

This poem is autobiographical. See the note to "Louise Smith."

George Gray

This poem is apparently based on Lucien Gray (b. 1867), the son of John A. Gray of Lewistown, a lawyer and circuit court judge. The younger Gray was a boyhood acquaintance of Masters and later a Lewistown lawyer. In a letter to Edwin P. Reese the poet refers to Gray in terms that are similar to the poem: "there in Lewistown he wore a sort of magnifying mist around him just as his father did, by not taking part in things and holding himself aloof" (letter to Edwin P. Reese, August 7, 1925, Folder 1, Edgar Lee Masters Papers, Illinois State Historical Library). For information on both Grays, see Heylin, pp. 890-91.

The speaker's name, Gray, symbolizes his inability to assert himself and hence his lack of self-realization.

Hon. Henry Bennett

Burgess points out a possible relationship between this poem and a Petersburg man: "John Bennett, a dry goods store and hotel operator in Petersburg, served as the first state representative from Menard County in the Illinois legislature, 1840-41. He was a friend of Squire Davis Masters. One of his sons, Henry, is described by ELM as a 'half-blind' regular on the Petersburg square during the poet's boyhood" (letter to Hallwas, p. 3).

at Georgie Kirby's: In *The Sangamon* Masters discusses George ("Georgie") Kirby, a neighbor and friend of his grandfather (pp. 113-

15), and one of his poems in *More People* (New York: D. Appleton-Century, 1939) is entitled "Old Georgie Kirby" (pp. 144-45).

Griffy the Cooper

Robert D. Narveson has pointed out that another, probably earlier, version of this poem, entitled "The Tub," was submitted to *Poetry* magazine and is now among the Harriet Monroe Papers at the University of Chicago Library. See "Masters's 'Griffy the Cooper,' Two Versions," *Midwestern Miscellany* 7 (1980): 39-43. "The Tub" does not have the first three lines of "Griffy the Cooper." Instead, it begins with "You think you know life" (a version of line four in "Griffy the Cooper") and does not include "perhaps" in the following line. It has another variation six lines later ("Taboos and rules and standards and falsehoods") and does not include the final line of "Griffy the Cooper." Although the two poems are substantially the same, Narveson finds the *Anthology* version to be more effective. He also points out that the name "Griffy" means "one who grasps onto things, in this case, ideas" (p. 41).

Sexsmith the Dentist

the "Battle Hymn of the Republic": The famous Civil War song written in 1861 by Julia Ward Howe (1819-1910), here used as a metaphor for northern victory in the war.

if the chattel slave / Had crowned the dominant dollar: That is, if the slave had been economically invaluable to the country.

Whitney's cotton gin: The cotton gin, which was invented by Eli Whitney (1765-1825), separated the fibers from the seed and thus made possible a great expansion in cotton planting.

Burchard's bar: There was a Burchard's saloon in Lewistown.

A. D. Blood

The model for this poem was apparently Lewistown banker Henry Phelps. See the note to "Thomas Rhodes." If "Reuben Pantier" reflects Masters himself, as several people have asserted, then this account of Reuben ("the worthless son of Benjamin Pantier") having sex on the grave of Spoon River's repressive mayor, A. D. Blood, is a kind of literary revenge against the forces Masters hated in Lewistown.

Robert Southey Burke

The speaker is named after Robert Southey (1774-1843), who was poet laureate of England for thirty years and the author of historical and biographical works as well. He was also interested in social reform. The speaker's last name may be an allusion to Edmund Burke (1729-97), the great British statesman and political philosopher who advocated conservative reform.

Dora Williams

Burgess asserts that this poem and "Hortense Robbins" may be based in part on the experiences of the poet's sister, Madeline Masters Stone (1870-1932), whose first husband died in 1907, after which she traveled much in Europe, where she married a fortune-hunting Danish diplomat (letter to Hallwas, p. 4).

the Champs Élysées: A famous avenue in Paris.

the Campo Santo: A famous cemetery in Pisa, Italy.

"Contessa Navigato / Implora eterna quiete": An Italian sentence that translates, "Countess Navigato begs for everlasting rest."

Mrs. Williams

Wrenn and Wrenn point out that in this poem "the lilting amphibrachs of W. S. Gilbert's operetta *Pinafore* (in which Masters saw his parents perform in Lewistown, with his mother in the role of Buttercup) are cleverly mimicked. The poem includes verbatim a line from 'Little Buttercup': 'To set off sweet faces' " (p. 66). Masters was so impressed by the local performance of the play that he later wrote a poem about it, entitled "Memories of *Pinafore,*" published in *The Harmony of Deeper Music,* p. 38.

William and Emily

Wrenn and Wrenn assert that Squire Davis and Lucinda Masters, the poet's beloved grandparents, were the prototypes for these two elderly lovers (p. 55). Appropriately, they speak in unison of their relationship. For information about their marriage, see the note to "Lucinda Matlock."

The Circuit Judge

Although this poem does not refer to historical specifics, it was undoubtedly inspired by a Lewistown circuit court judge whom Masters hated for opposing his father. He later described the man as an "insidious genius" (*Across Spoon River,* p. 232). His name was Simeon P. Shope (1836-1920), and he was a well-respected judge of the Sixth Judicial Circuit (1877-85) who was later an Illinois Supreme Court justice (1885-94). He is buried in Lewistown's Oak Hill Cemetery.

Nemesis: In classical mythology, Nemesis was the goddess of retribution and the equalizer of fortune and misfortune.

Blind Jack

"Susie Skinner": Masters provides some of the lyrics to this humorous folk song in *Mitch Miller,* p. 149.

a blind man: Homer (c. 700 B.C.), the legendary Greek poet who composed the *Iliad,* the great epic about "the fall of Troy." As this reference suggests, Masters viewed old-time fiddlers as bardic figures, interpreters of their native culture, and thus akin to Homer.

John Horace Burleson

Burgess connects this poem with Masters's father-in-law: "Some life details are different, but the epitaph strongly reflects Masters' father-in-law, Robert Jenkins, a corporate lawyer in Chicago. He was born in 1846 in rural Clark County, MO." (letter to Hallwas, p. 3). In *Reedy's Mirror,* July 24, 1914, this poem is entitled "A Leading Citizen."

"Roll on, thou deep and dark blue Ocean, roll!": A line from Canto 4, stanza 179, of *Childe Harold's Pilgrimage* (1818) by Lord Byron.

Nancy Knapp

We bought the farm . . . against the rest of them: Burgess has suggested that this account of family discord over a will reflects a dispute among the heirs of Squire Davis Masters, which occurred during 1910-14 ("Some Family Source Material," pp. 83-84).

Barry Holden

Burgess indicates that this poem reflects two sensational murder cases that occurred in 1883-84: "The first was the death by throat-cutting of a pregnant prostitute, Missouri 'Zura' Burns, in Logan County. The trial of the alleged murderer, Orrin Carpenter, was held in Petersburg, Menard County, on a change of venue. One of the best sources is Beverly Smith, 'Murder in a Rural Setting: Logan County Homicides 1865-1900,' *Western Illinois Regional Studies* 13 (1990): 75-76. As in the epitaph sequence of events, in *Past and Present of Menard County* (1905), Rev. Miller recounts that information about the trial prompted a farmer, Charles Houlden, to fatally stab, beat and axe his wife. Houlden was hanged May 15, 1885. The surname 'Duval' was a mischievous use of a Fulton County politician's name, in no way connected with the notorious homicides" (letter to Hallwas, p. 3).

State's Attorney Fallas

The speaker's last name, "Fallas," suggests that his life recapitulated the Fall of humankind. By realizing that minds and behavior are often shaped by forces beyond human control, he achieved a more profound knowledge of good and evil. In fact, that turned out to be a kind of "fortunate fall," to use a concept from Milton's *Paradise Lost,* for it led to the speaker's "deeds of charity." The following poem, "Wendell P. Bloyd," focuses explicitly on the biblical story of the Fall.

Driving the jury to hang the madman Holden: See the note to "Barry Holden."

books of science: This refers to books of Christian Science. The doctor's incompetence apparently turned him against traditional medicine. See "Tennessee Claflin Shope," where "science" is clearly used to mean "Christian Science."

Wendell P. Bloyd

"And God said . . . the garden of Eden.": Genesis 3:22-23.

Francis Turner

Wrenn and Wrenn point out that this poem reflects Masters's adolescent love, Margaret George, and is akin to his fictional treatment of their relationship in *Skeeters Kirby* (1923), his second novel (p. 55). The fifth line, "For scarlet-fever left my heart diseased," does describe the heart condition of Margaret George, and the romanticized outdoor love scene is in the same style as a scene in the novel, but there are no verbal parallels. See *Skeeters Kirby,* pp. 105-6.

John M. Church

In "Edgar Lee Masters: The Lawyer as Writer" (p. 67), Burgess points out that this poem depicts the kind of lawyer that Masters fought against in Chicago — "the hard, shrewd, money-grabbing corporation and business lawyers," as he said in *Across Spoon River,* p. 399. However, the poet asserted that such people operated in Lewistown too. See "The Machine Age Comes to Spoon River," pp. 8-9. In *Reedy's Mirror,* July 24, 1914, this poem is entitled "An Able Lawyer." The name Masters later provided, "Church," is, of course, ironic in view of the speaker's evil and corruption.

the "Q": The Chicago, Burlington, and Quincy Railroad ran through Lewistown and was commonly called "the Q."

But the rats devoured my heart / And a snake made a nest in my skull!: These images associated with physical corruption (decay) are symbolic of the speaker's spiritual corruption.

Russian Sonia

Weimar: A city that was the literary and artistic center of Germany in the nineteenth century.

passée: A French word meaning "past," used here in the sense of "no longer in vogue or popularity." The word also means "faded."

Isa Nutter

satyriasis: An insatiable sexual desire.

Barney Hainsfeather

Burgess comments on the background to this poem: "Masters is using religious persuasions to build an ironic joke. The Hainsfeathers were well-respected Jewish merchants in Petersburg (*The Sangamon,* p. 63); Dr. John Allen, an early settler, was founder of the Petersburg Presbyterian Church" (letter to Hallwas, p. 3).

ach!: A German word meaning "alas!"

Petit, the Poet

Masters told Kimball Flaccus that he had Ernest McGaffey in mind when he wrote this poem (Flaccus, p. 241). McGaffey (b. 1861) was a friend of the poet in Chicago during the 1890s and was briefly associated with the Scanlon and Masters law firm. He was also the author of several volumes of conventional, mediocre verse. The poet briefly describes him in *Across Spoon River,* where he is called "Maltravers" (pp. 147-48).

Despite Masters's comment, the poem is essentially autobiographical. It reflects Masters's momentous realization that his preoccupation with writing conventional poems prior to 1914 had simply blinded him to the great themes he was expressing in the Spoon River Anthology series. Homer and Whitman, mentioned in the final line, were two of Masters's favorite poets, chiefly because they expressed the national character and spirit of Greece and America. For a discussion of the poem, see Hallwas, "Two Autobiographical Epitaphs," pp. 34-35.

Triolets, villanelles, rondels, rondeaus, / Ballades: Artificial French verse forms. Masters was interested in those forms early in his life, and a few of his ballades are included in *A Book of Verses* (1898).

The snows and the roses of yesteryear are vanished: Robert D. Narveson points out that this line echoes the refrain of Villon's

"Ballade of Dead Ladies" (in the Rosetti translation): "Where are the snows of yesteryear?" See "*Spoon River Anthology:* An Introduction," *MidAmerica* 7 (1980): 62.

Pauline Barrett

And I did it looking there in the mirror—: That is, she committed suicide because she could not stand the change in herself.

Mrs. Charles Bliss

This speaker's name is ironic in view of her happy family life.
Reverend Wiley: A Methodist minister in Lewistown. See "Rev. Lemuel Wiley" and the note to that poem.

Mrs. George Reece

According to Lewis, this poem reflects the life of Moses Turner (1840-1904), who was the partner of Henry Phelps in the Turner, Phelps, and Company bank that failed in 1894, causing great financial hardship in Lewistown. Lewis comments, "He was really a god in Lewistown. All had faith in him." Masters apparently did not blame Turner, but he did blame Phelps (1837-1924) and his son, Henry Willis Phelps (b. 1863), who was the actual cashier. Those two are referred to in lines six and seven of the poem. Masters had much information about the bank failure because his father, Hardin W. Masters, assisted the state's attorney in prosecuting Turner and Phelps for embezzlement. Despite what the poem indicates, neither man went to prison. Turner is buried in Lewistown's Oak Hill Cemetery. See also the note to "Thomas Rhodes." For a discussion of the bank failure, see Burgess, "*Spoon River:* Politics and Poetry," pp. 354-56.

"Act well your part, there all the honor lies.": From Pope's *Essay on Man* (1734), Epistle 4, line 194. That section of the poem is entitled "Of the Nature and State of Man, with Respect to Happiness."

Rev. Lemuel Wiley

Fulton County historian Marjorie Turner-Rich Bordner indicates that Rev. W. R. Wiley was pastor of the Lewistown Methodist Church from 1887 to 1892 (letter to John E. Hallwas, November 23, 1990, in the Edgar Lee Masters Collection, Archives and Special Collections, Western Illinois University Library).

Thomas Ross, Jr.

Burgess suggests that this poem may reflect Harvey Lee Ross, Jr. (1817-1907), a son of the founder of Lewistown, Ossian M. Ross.

His two brothers were more ambitious, prosperous men (letter to Hallwas, p. 3). However, there is no evidence that Ross was damaged financially by one of his brothers.

Miller's Ford: Miller's Ferry, on the Sangamon River north of Petersburg.

Rev. Abner Peet

In "*Spoon River:* Politics and Poetry," Burgess comments, "The poet denied later that he had in mind the Rev. W. O. Peet, who served several Central Illinois parishes including the Methodist Episcopal Church at Petersburg from 1877 to 1879, which Squire Davis Masters and most of his children attended" (p. 353). Chandler refers to a Lewistown figure, "the Reverend Stephen Peet . . . a man of much distinction, editor of 'The American Antiquarian and Oriental Magazine'" (p. 283). It is likely that Masters recalled one or both of these ministers and at least borrowed the name for his own Reverend Peet in the *Anthology.* However, he apparently had in mind the preeminent Lewistown minister of his era in the community, Rev. Benjamin Y. George (d. 1920), the father of Masters's sweetheart, Margaret George. He was a talented writer and an outspoken opponent of saloons. Hence the fate of the speaker's sermons is ironic. See also the second note to "Tennessee Claflin Shope."

Burchard, the grog-keeper: In responding to a series of questions, Lewistown resident George Proctor told Kimball Flaccus, "I do remember Mr. Burchard, the saloon keeper" (Proctor, question 27).

Jefferson Howard

As Flaccus was the first to point out, this poem was based on Hardin W. Masters (1845-1925), the poet's father, a lawyer and politician who fought against the repressive forces—especially prohibition advocates—in Lewistown (p. 165). Masters idolized his father, who was also the model for "Kinsey Keene" in the *Anthology,* state's attorney Kirby in *Mitch Miller* (1920), and Leonard Westerfield in *The Tide of Time* (1937). For a brief discussion of the poem's background, see Hallwas, "Two Autobiographical Epitaphs," pp. 28-29, and the introduction to this edition.

The speaker's unusual first name was derived from the name of a circuit court judge, Jefferson Orr, who tried the arson case that stemmed from the burning of Lewistown's courthouse in 1894. The name also alludes to the Jeffersonian tradition of American democratic values to which Masters repeatedly asserted his allegiance.

Calvinists: Literally, followers of John Calvin (1509-64), the famous French theologian and reformer—and hence believers in predestination, total depravity, God's sovereignty, etc.—but Masters used the term in a more general and negative sense, to mean morally austere, repressive, joyless people.

Judge Selah Lively

Lewis asserts that this poem was based on Judge Andrew N. Barrett (1863-1919), especially because the opening lines reflect his life. Barrett is buried in Lewistown's Oak Hill Cemetery.

Eugenia Todd

the final sleep: Death. The speaker is asserting that spiritual problems will be worked through after death until the soul is healed.

Yee Bow

There was a Lewistown resident named Yee Bow. Masters mentions him in *Across Spoon River* (p. 138) and "Introduction to Chicago," *The American Mercury* 31 (January 1934): 50. On September 4, 1895, the following ad appeared in Lewistown's *Fulton Democrat:* "Yee Bow does the best laundry work ever seen in Lewistown. Call on him." He apparently was not killed, and one local newspaper article mentions that he was a highly regarded person who belonged to the Presbyterian Sunday School. See "From Lewistown," Canton *Fulton County Ledger,* November 14, 1889, p. 1. In response to a question by Kimball Flaccus about what finally happened to Yee Bow, Lewistown resident George Proctor commented, "I believe he went back to China" (Proctor, question 51).

Confucius: The great teacher, philosopher, and sage of ancient China, Confucius (551-479 B.C.) did not found a religion, but the philosophical system of Confucianism has been enormously influential. He encouraged filial piety, which blended well with the ancestor worship already practiced in China. See the closing line of the poem.

Pekin: A variant spelling of Peking (also called Beijing), the capital of the People's Republic of China and the cultural center of the country.

Washington McNeely

This poem is based on the life of Lewis W. Ross (1812-95), the son of the founder of Lewistown, Ossian M. Ross, and the man for whom Lewistown was named. A lawyer, he served in the Illinois legislature during the 1840s and in the U.S. House of Representatives from 1863 to 1869. He was a leading figure in the Democratic party in Illinois. The "great mansion-house" refers to the home he built in 1857, which Chandler describes at some length (pp. 313-14). She also provides a photograph of the house. According to Chandler, Ross sent his children to Notre Dame and Vassar (p. 313). Although three of their names are reflected in the poem—Mary, John, and Jennie—their fates do not correspond to the details in the poem. Ross's wife, Frances (1822-1902) did not precede him in death. Lewis and Frances Ross are buried in Lewistown's Oak Hill Cemetery. For information on Ross, see Heylin, pp. 1079-80; *History of Fulton County, Illinois,* pp. 809-10; and *Portrait and Biographical Album,* pp. 770-76.

There was also a prominent McNeely family in Petersburg, from whom Masters derived the speaker's last name. Thompson W. McNeely (b. 1835) was also a U.S. congressman (1868-72) and owned a mansion at the south edge of Petersburg, built in 1876. See the *Menard County Illinois History* (Petersburg: History of Menard County, Inc., 1988), pp. 154-55.

Paul McNeely

Masters indicated that in this poem he depicted the nurse who took care of him in 1915 when he was recovering from the collapse that brought the writing of *Spoon River Anthology* to an end (*Across Spoon River,* p. 359). Although he refers to her as "Jane" in his autobiography, her name was Bertha Bauman. Masters told Kimball Flaccus that she was connected with St. Luke's Hospital and that he tried to date her, unsuccessfully, after he got well ("Edgar Lee Masters" typescript, chapter 9, p. 12, Folder 36, Box 11, Kimball Flaccus Papers, Dartmouth College Library).

Mary McNeely

Since "Washington McNeely" was based on the life of Lewis W. Ross, this poem would seem to reflect his daughter Mary. However, she died as a small child.

Daniel M'Cumber

This poem was apparently based on Masters's love affair with Tennessee Mitchell. See the note to "Georgine Sand Miner."

Fourierist: French utopian theorist Charles Fourier (1772-1837) propounded a cooperative social system known as Fourierism, which had many "phalanxes" or colonies in America, including one short-lived effort at Canton Township, Illinois, not far from Lewistown.

Georgine Sand Miner

William L. Phillips was the first of several scholars to assert that this poem reflects Tennessee Mitchell (1874-1929), who was the poet's mistress for eighteen months in 1909 and 1910. See "How Sherwood Anderson wrote *Winesburg, Ohio*," *American Literature* 23 (1951): 17. Masters admitted to Phillips that Mitchell was "Deirdre" in *Across Spoon River*, pp. 295-313. On Mitchell, see also Kramer, pp. 174-75, and John H. Wrenn and Margaret M. Wrenn, " 'T. M.': The Forgotten Muse of Sherwood Anderson and Edgar Lee Masters," in *Sherwood Anderson: Centennial Studies* (Troy, N.Y.: Whitsun Publishing, 1976), pp. 175-84. "Daniel M'Cumber," then, reflects the poet's view of that love affair, which widened the breach between himself and his first wife. The imagery of a poisonous bite that occurs in these two poems is echoed in *Across Spoon River*, where Masters says, "It was three years before I extirpated Deirdre's poison from my blood" (p. 312). See also the note to "Tennessee Claflin Shope."

The speaker's name is an adaptation of "George Sand," the pseudonym of Amandine Aurore Lucie Dupin, Baroness Dudevant (1804-76), a noted French feminist, novelist, and playwright whose separation from her husband led to a series of love affairs.

Thomas Rhodes

Masters indicated that "In drawing the banker, Thomas Rhodes, I had in mind a Lewistown character who deserved all that I said about him, but the name Rhodes was never borne by anyone that I knew who played the mean part in life that Thomas Rhodes did" ("The Genesis of Spoon River," p. 50). That "Lewistown character" was Henry Phelps (1837-1924), a partner in the Phelps and Proctor store and the Turner and Phelps bank, which failed in 1894. See the note to "Mrs. George Reece." Phelps was also president of the village council in 1879 and superintendent of the Presbyterian Church Sunday School, and in those roles he was the model for "A. D. Blood" and "Henry Phipps." See Burgess, "The Use of Local Lore," p. 33, as well as the *History of Fulton County, Illinois*, pp. 807-8. In regard to the speaker's name, Burgess notes that "Walter Hancock Rhodes was an official of the Lewistown National Bank from 22 February 1894 until 2 May 1907" and that the bank "was a rival to one in which Hardin Wallace Masters [the poet's father] was a stockholder" ("*Spoon River*: Politics and Poetry," pp. 353-54).

Thomas Rhodes is the arch-villain in *Spoon River Anthology*. Mentioned in twenty epitaphs, he helps to provide continuity. See the discussion of this poem in the introduction to this edition.

Ida Chicken

The speaker's unusual name was derived from that of a maid who worked in the Masters' house at Lewistown during the 1880s, Em Chicken. In *Across Spoon River* the poet describes her as "a slattern" who had an illegitimate child (p. 30), so the poem apparently does not reflect her life.

Penniwit, the Artist

In response to a question by Kimball Flaccus, Lewistown resident George Proctor commented, "Above her [Mrs. Annie Hobbs] bookstore was the Pennington studio (Penniwit of the Anthology)" (Proctor, question 26). In the nineteenth century, photographers were commonly called "artists."

"I except": The word "except" is being used in an obsolete sense that was once common in the courtroom. The statement means "I object," and in this context the judge's facial expression conveys his objection to Penniwit's effort to reflect his soul in the photograph.

Jim Brown

In response to a question from Kimball Flaccus, Lewistown resident George Proctor indicated that "Jim Brown" was based on a real person, the uncle of Julia Brown Strode (Proctor, question 17). Brown (1844-1908) was a contractor for much of his life. The social conflict in this poem reflects the poet's dichotomous view of Lewistown, discussed in the introduction to this edition. See also the note to "Benjamin Pantier."

Dom Pedro: A horse used for breeding.

"Turkey in the straw" or *"There is a fountain filled with blood"*: These two well-known tunes represent what Masters once described as "the eternal struggle between those who want to live and those who want to save — those who want to enjoy this world and those who want to make it a hallway to another one" ("Tells Origin of 'Spoon River,'" *St. Louis Post-Dispatch,* March 29, 1918, p. 21). "Turkey in the Straw" is a lively tune that was once popular with fiddlers, whereas "There is a Fountain Filled with Blood" is a hymn that was common at camp meetings and church services.

over at Concord: The Concord Church was not far from the farm of Masters's grandparents, north of Petersburg.

Pinafore: H. M. S. *Pinafore* (1878), the tremendously popular comic opera by Gilbert and Sullivan, was performed in many communities, including Lewistown. See also the note to "Mrs. Williams."

They thought it a slam on colts: That is, they protested the move as undue criticism of young horses, striking a responsive chord in a culture substantially centered around the horse.

Robert Davidson
The speaker's last name and the very negative characterization suggest that this poem reflects Masters's view of William T. Davidson, a Lewistown newspaper editor, religious advocate, and political leader. See "Deacon Taylor," "Editor Whedon," and the notes to those poems.

nephritis: A disease of the kidneys.

Elsa Wertman
Gus Wertman: Burgess notes that "Wertman" is German for "worthy man" ("The Use of Local Lore," p. 76). Gus Wertman stands opposed to Thomas Greene, who simply took advantage of the speaker.

Hamilton Greene
Lewis asserts that this poem reflects the life of Judge Thomas A. Boyd (1830-97). Boyd was, in fact, a judge, a member of Congress, and a state political leader. See Heylin, pp. 798-99. There is no evidence that Boyd was an illegitimate child. He is buried in Lewistown's Oak Hill Cemetery.

Roger Heston
Burgess comments on this poem: "These youthful debaters are probably drawn from Masters himself and one of his chums—Edwin P. Reese or Will Winter. There were at least two Pricketts with farms near Lewistown c. 1890" (letter to Hallwas, p. 4).

Amos Sibley
In *Reedy's Mirror,* September 11, 1914, this poem is entitled "Rev. George Sibley."

Mrs. Sibley
My secret: Under a mound that you shall never find: The speaker is referring to an unwanted child, probably a fetus that was aborted and buried so as to conceal an adulterous relationship. See the first note to "Caroline Branson."

Adam Weirauch
Altgeld and Armour: John Peter Altgeld (1847-1902), a Cook County judge and a liberal, reformist governor of Illinois (1892-96), was

denounced in many newspapers for pardoning the surviving anarchists who had been convicted in the famous Haymarket Riot case. He was the model for "Herman Altman" in the *Anthology*. Philip Armour (1832-1901) was the famous industrial promoter who headed the Armour meat-packing company in Chicago.

sold my vote / On Charles T. Yerkes' street-car franchise: Yerkes (1837-1905) was an unscrupulous financier who controlled Chicago's street-railway system. When bills were introduced in the Illinois legislature to extend his monopolistic franchise in Chicago for ninety-nine years, Altgeld vetoed them. The speaker is depicted as a corrupt member of the legislature who sold his vote to Yerkes.

Ezra Bartlett

Lewis asserts that this poem reflects the life of U.S. Peterson (c. 1821-95), who served in the 103rd Illinois Infantry Regiment during the Civil War. According to the *Report of the Adjutant General of the State of Illinois* (Springfield: Phillips Brothers, 1901), 5:616, the man's name was William S. Peterson, and he was the chaplain of the 103rd Regiment. He enlisted at Canton, which is a dozen miles north of Lewistown, but he may well have been from the Lewistown area. Curiously, the *Report of the Adjutant General* indicates that he was "Dismissed for falsehood, April 17, 1863." Nothing else is known about him. On the inner conflict reflected in this poem, see the first note to "Lucius Atherton."

Amelia Garrick

Masters indicated that this poem and "Caroline Branson" were based on Margaret George (1869-97), the daughter of the Presbyterian minister in Lewistown ("The Genesis of Spoon River," p. 45). See also the notes to "Julia Miller," "Caroline Branson," "Louise Smith," and "Editor Whedon."

Siever's woods: Siever's woods were located in the southeast part of Lewistown.

And you, you are a leader in New York, / The wife: It is likely that Masters based this reference on himself but changed the sex of the speaker's former friend to female. Masters broke off his relationship with Margaret George, moved to the city, succeeded, and became "A name in the society columns." Moreover, she died but continued to have an impact on his life, as suggested by the poems based on her in the *Anthology* and his treatment of their relationship in *Skeeters Kirby* (1923), where she is portrayed as Winifred Hervey.

John Hancock Otis

This speaker, who is so concerned with the cause of liberty, is appropriately named after John Hancock (1737-93), the great American patriot who was president of the Continental Congress and the first signer of the Declaration of Independence. Like the speaker, Hancock had inherited wealth.

to the manor born": This is the text in *Reedy's Mirror,* January 1, 1915. The Macmillan text has "to the manner born," which is surely a typographical error. The correct phrase is "to the manor born," and it designates someone with inherited wealth and social standing.

John Cabanis

Burgess suggests that this poem reflects the liberal leadership of the poet's father, Hardin W. Masters, who was Mayor of Lewistown from 1899 to 1903 and from 1905 to 1907 (*"Spoon River:* Politics and Poetry," pp. 361-62). That may be true, but during the 1880s—the era in Lewistown to which so many epitaph-poems of community conflict relate—Masters regarded Lewis C. ("Lute") Breeden as the leader of the "liberal party." See the note to "Enoch Dunlap." Breeden was also a university-educated man who had a deep interest in Greek culture and literature, which is reflected in the reference here to Plato's *Republic.*

Plato's lofty guardians: In Plato's utopian work, *The Republic* (c. 375 B.C.), the rulers of the city are called the "Guardians." They are qualified to rule because they are the wisest; they are philosophers.

The Unknown

In the *Greek Anthology,* which had such an influence on Masters, the names of many speakers of the epitaphs are unknown.

Aaron Hatfield: The name of a wealthy farmer whose land was adjacent to the poet's grandparents' farm, north of Petersburg.

Hades: The place of the dead in classical mythology.

Jonathan Swift Somers

The speaker in this poem is a namesake of the famous satirist, Jonathan Swift (1667-1745). "The Spooniad," a mock-heroic work at the end of the *Anthology,* is attributed to Somers.

Carl Hamblin

This poem reflects the idealism of Lewis C. ("Lute") Breeden, editor of the *Lewistown News,* for whom Masters worked in the

1880s. For biographical information, see the note to "Enoch Dunlap." Although this poem appeared in *Reedy's Mirror* on September 18, 1914, and "Editor Whedon" did not appear until October 9, 1914, they were placed next to one another in the book version of the *Anthology* because the two speakers are editors of flatly contrasting moral character.

the day the Anarchists were hanged in Chicago: On November 11, 1887, four of the anarchists convicted in the Haymarket Riot case were hanged in Chicago. Masters viewed them as victims of injustice, which they surely were. See Masters, *The Tale of Chicago,* pp. 213-18. Not long after the hanging, a labor organization called "The Haymarketers" was formed in Lewistown, and the poet's father was a prominent member. See "From Lewistown," Canton *Fulton County Ledger,* February 6, 1890, p. 1.

a beautiful woman with bandaged eyes: The traditional personification of Justice, based on the Roman goddess Justitia.

Editor Whedon

Masters indicated that this poem was based on a Lewistown editor, "a fanatical and quarrelsome Prohibitionist of equivocal morality who accepted bribes for political support and then betrayed his bargains" ("The Genesis of Spoon River," p. 42). He also told Kimball Flaccus that the man was William T. Davidson (1837-1915), editor of *The Fulton Democrat,* not the actual "Editor Whedon . . . a mild, harmless man" (Flaccus, p. 130). The latter was Selah Wheadon, a Universalist preacher who took over the *Lewistown News* in January of 1884 and changed it from a Republican to a Democratic newspaper. He soon hired Masters as a printer's devil. A year or two later that newspaper passed into the hands of Lewis C. ("Lute") Breeden.

Masters disliked William T. Davidson for several reasons, the most important being that Davidson and Hardin W. Masters, the poet's father, were political enemies. As Lewistown's leading temperance advocate, Davidson clashed repeatedly with the elder Masters, who supported the licensing of saloons and was himself a drinker. In the poet's view, Davidson prevented his father from receiving a much-sought-after nomination to Congress. Masters's first published poem, "The Minotaur, Bill Davidson" (1884), was a satirical attack on the man, written soon after the would-be poet became a printer's devil at Wheadon's *Lewistown News* (reprinted in Flaccus, pp. 125-28). Lute Breeden was a close friend of Hardin Masters and shared the latter's dislike of Davidson, so he too probably influenced the poet's view. The conflict between Masters's father and Davidson is portrayed in *The Tide of Time* (1937), a novel in which the central figure, Leonard Westerfield Atterberry, is based on Hardin Masters and his chief opponent is "William T. Davis," editor of the *Frederick County Democrat.* In 1895 Davidson married Margaret George, who had been Masters's sweetheart during his teenage years. That increased the poet's hatred. For a discussion of that matter, see Burgess, "Masters and Some Mentors," pp. 192-200. See also the notes to "Julia Miller" and "Amelia Garrick."

Despite Masters's view, there is no evidence that Davidson lacked integrity, although he was an outspoken advocate of his political views who sometimes angered his opponents. He was, in fact, a highly regarded, public-spirited journalist and community leader, as pointed out in the introduction to this edition. See the tributes to Davidson by E. A. Snively and John R. Rowland in the *Journal of the Illinois State Historical Society* 8 (1915-16): 79-113, and the discussion of his life in John Leonard Conger and William E. Hull, *History of the Illinois River Valley* (Chicago: S. J. Clarke, 1932), 3:561-64. See also Heylin, pp. 849-51, and *Portrait and Biographical Album,* pp. 245-49. Davidson is buried in Lewistown's Oak Hill Cemetery. He is also the model for two other negative portraits in the *Anthology,* "Deacon Taylor" and "Robert Davidson."

Eugene Carman

According to Lewis and Love, the model for this poem was Lewistown resident Frank Stevens (b. 1845). In a 1957 memoir George Proctor of Lewistown recalls him: "Frank Stevens [was] a clerk in our store. He was a middle-aged bachelor.... One day, when he thought he was alone, as he stood before the mirror just over the wash stand in the back of the store, he was seen by a member of the family to shake his fist at his reflection in the glass, saying, 'Phelps and Proctor's slave!'" ("George Proctor's Memoirs," Lewistown *Fulton Democrat,* April 3, 1957, p. 7).

W. Lloyd Garrison Standard

According to Lewis, the model for this poem was Frank J. Standard (1871-1904) of Lewistown, who attended school with Masters. He was a vegetarian and freethinker, and he is buried in Lewistown's Oak Hill Cemetery. This speaker is also a namesake of William Lloyd Garrison (1805-79), the famous abolitionist leader.

the rhine-stone rhythm of Ingersoll: Robert G. Ingersoll (1833-99) was a famous freethinker and orator who influenced Masters. The poet told Flaccus that this comment infuriated Ingersoll's daughter, so he wrote a poem in praise of Ingersoll (Flaccus, p. 160). It appears in *The Great Valley* (p. 77).

A sort of Brand in a birth of half-and-half: This refers to the title character in *Brand* (1866), a play by Henrik Ibsen. Brand is a strong-willed idealist whose absolutism leads to his destruction. The speaker in this poem is suggesting that he is similarly driven but is also self-contradictory. In earlier editions of *Spoon River Anthology* the word "Brand" is italicized, but the speaker is clearly not referring to the play text, so italics were not used for this edition.

Professor Newcomer

This poem may reflect the views of Alphonso G. Newcomer (1864-1913), a poet and professor at Knox College in Galesburg from 1889 to 1892. Newcomer was devoted to Greek literature, taught it effectively, and undoubtedly influenced Masters's lifelong devotion to Greek culture and literature. He also gave talks on "skepticism and faith" and was "going through the same formative ideas" as the poet (*Across Spoon River*, p. 117), so this poem about the spiritual frustration of mankind may reflect Newcomer's views. When he died, Masters wrote a tribute to him: "In Memory of Professor Newcomer," *The Dial*, October 16, 1913, p. 299. See also "Alfonso Churchill" and the note to that poem.

Col. Prichard: Burgess asserts that lines 1-4 may refer to a Lewistown resident: "Robert Prichard, who served as Fulton County sheriff and Lewistown Township supervisor, operated a farm adjacent to Lewistown. His sketch in Heylin, p. 1046, refers to farm machinery: 'It is a saying with him that he got born fifty years too soon, as modern machinery has made the farmer's life easy'" (letter to Hallwas, p. 4).

He ran with it: Both the *Reedy's Mirror* text (September 13, 1914) and the Macmillan text of this poem print the line this way: "He ran it with." But that is clearly an error, which no doubt resulted from the haste with which Masters wrote. The engine ran the grinder rather than the other way around.

Ralph Rhodes

According to Lewis, the model for this poem was Henry Willis Phelps (b. 1863) of Lewistown. He was the son of Henry Phelps, partner in the Turner, Phelps, and Company bank that failed on January 9, 1894. Burgess points out that the younger Phelps later moved to New York, where he became president and chairman of the American Can Company ("*Spoon River:* Politics and Poetry," p. 355). As the final line of the poem suggests, Phelps was buried back in Lewistown, in Oak Hill Cemetery. See also the notes to "Mrs. George Reece" and "Thomas Rhodes."

demireps: Women with a reputation for loose sexual behavior.

your Theft: Your fate. The speaker views his death as a kind of long-awaited retribution for his unscrupulous financial dealings.

Mickey M'Grew

In response to a question by Kimball Flaccus, Lewistown resident George Proctor indicated that this poem was based on the death of Harry ("Mickey") McFall: "He had been in the tank for repair work. In climbing out he somehow lost his footing and fell back into the tower" (Proctor, question 15). McFall was a childhood friend of the poet, and in *Across Spoon River* Masters remembered him as "a powerful boy, whose arms were large and hard as iron" because he worked in his father's blacksmith shop (p. 64). McFall died on June 12, 1901, at age thirty-four, and is buried in Lewistown's Oak Hill Cemetery.

Rosie Roberts

According to Lewis, the speaker in this poem "Killed Marshall Field's son." Marshall Field, Jr., the only son of Chicago's famous "merchant prince" and wealthiest resident, died from a gunshot wound on November 27, 1905. There were rumors about murder and suicide, but the family made an effort to conceal the truth, and the verdict at the inquest was accidental death. This poem is obviously based on that event, but Masters reworked the story into an account of passion-based violence and hushed-up scandal. Rosie Roberts is a fictional figure. See John Tebbel, *The Marshall Fields* (New York: E. P. Dutton, 1947), pp. 104-9.

Oscar Hummel

This poem is based on the abusive tactics of John Logan, the Lewistown marshal who attacked the drunken George ("Bones") Weldy in 1887 and was shot dead in turn. Here Masters allows the brutality of a similar prohibition enforcer to succeed. See the note to "The Town Marshal."

Roscoe Purkapile

A descendant of the Purkapile family of Menard County told the poet's younger son, Hilary, that the Purkapile epitaphs were based on a family episode, according to Charles E. Burgess, "Hilary Masters," *Illinois Magazine* 28 (March-April 1989): 24.

Van Buren Street: A street in downtown Chicago, which does not run all the way east to Lake Michigan, however, but stops at Grant Park.

Mrs. Kessler

Grant's Memoirs: Personal Memoirs of U. S. Grant (1885-86).

Harmon Whitney

Lewis asserts that this poem reflects the life of Lewistown lawyer Cassius Whitney (1846-86). Also, another Lewistown lawyer, Harvey H. Atherton, wrote in a March 3, 1953, letter to Kimball Flaccus that Whitney "had the reputation of being a bright lawyer but died at an early age from excessive use of liquor" (Folder 7, Box 1, Flaccus-Masters Archive, Special Collections Division, Georgetown University Library). Someone, perhaps Masters, wrote a brief obituary about Whitney for the Canton newspaper, lamenting the untimely death of "this brilliant lawyer." See "From the County Seat," Canton *Fulton County Ledger,* July 1, 1886, p. 1. Whitney is buried in Lewistown's Oak Hill Cemetery. See also the first note to "Cassius Hueffer."

It is also not difficult to see Masters himself beneath this characterization, reacting to the aspects of his life that oppressed him: "a village of little minds" (his Lewistown background), "the justice court" (his work as a lawyer), and "a wife . . . pure and hard" (his first marriage).

my soul could not re-act, / Like Byron's did, in song: British poet Lord Byron (1788-1824) was famous for creating the Byronic hero, a moody, passionate figure who felt disdain for the common run of humanity, rather like the speaker in this poem. However, Byron responded to personal conflicts by creating great works like *Childe Harold's Pilgrimage* and *Manfred,* which dramatized his inner life, whereas Harmon Whitney is simply stifled and self-tormented.

Bert Kessler

This speaker was apparently based on a Lewistown resident of the same name who was a hunter. See "Percy Bysshe Shelley" and the notes to that poem.

Lambert Hutchins

Lewis and Love indicate that the model for this poem was Edward Laning (1834-1917) of Petersburg. He served in the Illinois House of Representatives (1869-72) and Senate (1881-84), and in 1875 he built a large home called The Oaks on a hill in Petersburg. He is buried in Petersburg's Oakland Cemetery.

the lake-front in Chicago, / Where the railroad keeps a switching yard: In 1851 the Illinois legislature gave Chicago lakefront property to the Illinois Central Railroad, and that act was controversial throughout the century as the Illinois railroad system developed.

Hortense Robbins

This poem may reflect the life of the poet's sister, Madeline Masters Stone. See the first note to "Dora Williams."

taking the cure at Baden-Baden: The baths at Baden Baden, in eastern Austria, were frequented by those afflicted with rheumatism, gout, and other ailments. They were a fashionable gathering place for the wealthy.

Jacob Godbey

This poem may reflect Masters's uncle, Rev. Bethuel Vincent (1834-1920), whom Masters describes in *Across Spoon River* as a man opposed to his father's liberal politics and "a prohibitionist with a false and exaggerated sense of my father's mode of life" (p. 97). "Ben Pantier," mentioned in the poem as one who typifies the liberal, bar-patronizing crowd, is a character based on Hardin W. Masters. See Burgess, "Some Family Source Material," p. 84, and see also the note to "Benjamin Pantier."

the insolent giant / Who manned the saloons from afar: The wealthy investors who controlled the saloons—and by implication, the town—through absentee ownership. This concern is also reflected in "McDowell Young" and "Ezra Fink" in *The New Spoon River* (1924).

Walter Simmons

the "Octoroon": The Octoroon (1859) was a famous antislavery melodrama by Dion Boucicault (1822?-90).

Roy Butler

whether Ipava was a finer town than Table Grove: Ipava and Table Grove are villages six miles apart, located west of Lewistown in Fulton County.

Searcy Foote

In a letter to Lewistown resident George Proctor, Kimball Flaccus commented on this poem: "This latter poem is autobiographical to a degree, for Masters had a rich aunt who was paralyzed and who would not help him financially to go to college. Masters had read John Alden's books as a boy, as mentioned in the poem. Of course, Masters did not murder his rich aunt.... Nor did he marry Delia. The name Delia he obviously took from your sister and applied to a generalized boyhood sweetheart" (Flaccus to Proctor, June 1, 1955, Folder 10, Box 4, Flaccus-Masters Archive, Special Collections Division, Georgetown University Library). See also the notes below.

rich Aunt Persis: As the note above suggests, this is probably a reference to the poet's aunt, but there was also an elderly woman named Persis Foote (1821-98) in Lewistown, so the description of "Aunt Persis" here may reflect her as well.

John Alden's books: John B. Alden (1827-1924) produced informational works like *Alden's Home Atlas of the World* (1888) and *Alden's Cyclopedia of Eminent Biography* (1892) as well as collections of poetry and prose.

Delia Prickett: In a May 15, 1955, letter to Kimball Flaccus, George Proctor indicated that this referred to his sister, Delia Proctor (b. 1869), who was the poet's early sweetheart, and he mentioned that again in a letter of June 23, 1955 (Folder 10, Box 4, Flaccus-Masters Archive, Special Collections Division, Georgetown University Library). The response of Flaccus to the earlier letter is quoted above. See also the note to "Louise Smith."

Proudhon: Pierre Joseph Proudhon (1809-65) was a French socialist and political theorist who edited journals and wrote books related to economic justice and social revolution.

Edmund Pollard

Like some other poems in the *Anthology* and many in *The New Spoon River* (1924), this poem expresses a philosophy of life. Hedonism was one facet of Masters's character, and it was expressed in his many love affairs. "Edmund Pollard," with its sexual imagery, is a kind of poetic argument for that perspective.

Thomas Trevelyan

Masters probably derived the last name of this lover of classical culture from one or both of England's famous historians named Trevelyan, George Otto Trevelyan (1838-1928) and George Macaulay Trevelyan (1876-1962).

Reading in Ovid the sorrowful story of Itys: The speaker interprets his own experience in terms of the famous Philomela story from Ovid's *Metamorphoses* (c. 8 A.D.), summarized in lines 1-7.

Hellas: Greece. Ovid was not a Greek writer, but the Philomela story was a Greek legend that he reinterpreted.

Percival Sharp

In her introduction to the 1962 paperback edition of *Spoon River Anthology,* May Swenson asserts that Masters provided his own epitaph with this poem because "the spirit of Percival Sharp comments ironically on the symbols of other tombs" (New York: Collier Books, 1962, p. 9). While there is nothing specifically autobiographical about the poem, Masters was interested in "the cause of the fall" of people and the "determinants" of their fate, as the *Anthology* demonstrates.

Elagabalus: A Roman emperor (c. 200 A.D.) and priest of the solar god by the same name.

Arimaspi: In Greek and Roman mythology, a race of one-eyed Scythian men who strove with gryphons for the gold they guarded.

Hiram Scates

This poem probably reflects the political leadership of Lewis C. ("Lute") Breeden, who was Masters's hero during the 1880s in Lewistown and who attracted a number of "young idealists" as his followers. Apparently some political compromise by Breeden later caused disenchantment. See the note to "Enoch Dunlap," which provides information on Breeden, who is the basis for several poems.

the Millennium: A Christian term referring to the thousand years of triumphant holiness prophesied in Revelations 20, but here used figuratively to indicate a time of good government and happiness — which did not occur.

Oaks Tutt

The speaker's name was derived from those of two signers of the 1848 Illinois Constitution, Oaks Turner and William Tutt, according to Flaccus, p. 202. Neither man's life is reflected in the poem.

London Mills: A village on the Spoon River, twenty miles north of Lewistown.

the necropolis of Memphis: The cemetery at Memphis, the early capital of ancient Egypt, on the west bank of the Nile.

'What is Truth?' ": Pilate's query to Jesus in John 18:38.

Elliott Hawkins

According to Lewis and Love, this poem reflects the life of Samuel P. Cummings of Lewistown. Burgess agrees and makes this comment:

"Samuel P. Cummings . . . resided in Lewistown and Astoria in Fulton County, was a disabled Civil War veteran, justice of the peace, county judge, and served in both the Illinois House and Senate. *Portrait and Biographical Album,* pp. 714-15, gives his birth date as Feb. 5, 1818, in Maine. Masters, in *The Sangamon,* p. 225, alludes to Cummings' lobbying activities in Springfield, mistakenly giving his home as the town of Vermont in Fulton County" (letter to Hallwas, p. 5).

the Knights of Labor: A secret order, constituted as a labor union, that planned to unite all skilled and unskilled workers. It had 700,000 members by 1886 and then declined. Some people criticized it for promoting strikes and discontent.

"Of such is the Kingdom of Heaven": A statement that occurs in two of the Beatitudes: "Blessed are the poor in spirit, for of such is the kingdom of heaven" and "Blessed are those who are persecuted for righteousness' sake, for of such is the kingdom of heaven" (Matthew 5: 3, 10). Both are ironic as applied to the speaker.

Voltaire Johnson

The speaker is a namesake of Voltaire (1694-1778), the great French writer and crusader for freedom of thought. The poem undoubtedly reflects Masters's view of himself—as a heroic, truth-loving opponent of society's evils, who is exposing them like Voltaire did in France.

English Thornton

Burgess comments, "The character may have been suggested by an anarchist orator, John Turner, an Englishman, whose deportation Darrow and Masters fought unsuccessfully in a 1903 case before the United States Supreme Court" ("Edgar Lee Masters: The Lawyer as Writer," p. 70). Masters refers to the case in *Across Spoon River,* pp. 274-75. See also the brief discussion of this poem in the introduction to this edition.

whipped Black Hawk at Starved Rock: The speaker is not historically accurate here. Black Hawk (1767-1838) did not fight a battle at Starved Rock, the famous bluff along the Illinois River.

the Loop: Chicago's principal business district, located in the heart of the city.

Enoch Dunlap

This poem is based on Lewis C. ("Lute") Breeden (1861-1914), the *Lewistown News* editor for whom Masters worked from 1885 to 1889. Although he was born and raised in Fulton County, Breeden came from a family with a Virginia background, and he was a friend and political ally of the poet's father. A leader in the county's Democratic Central Committee, he was a hero to Masters, and his death from alcoholism and Bright's disease occurred on October 1, 1914, while the *Anthology* was being written. His commitment to democratic ideals, outspoken opposition to repressive forces, and leadership in journalism and politics are reflected in "John Cabanis," "Carl Hamblin," and this poem—as well as perhaps in "Kinsey Keene," "Hiram Scates," and "Magrady Graham." See the notes to all these poems. Some of them were written before Breeden's death, but "Enoch Dunlap" and "Magrady Graham" were written in the weeks that followed his death, and they appeared in *Reedy's Mirror* on November 13 and December 11, respectively. Masters also wrote a few later poems about the death of a small-town idealist and reformer that are based on Breeden. See "Cato Braden" and "Will Boyden Lectures" in *The Great Valley*, pp. 106-28, and "Lute Crockett" and "Tom Barron" in *Poems of People* (New York: Appleton-Century, 1936), pp. 126-30.

"Enoch Dunlap" reflects Breeden's years of leadership in Fulton County politics, especially in political caucuses, where he was, in Masters's view, the guardian of the people's rights. (On this, see also the notes to "Kinsey Keene.") Breeden evidently underwent some kind of fall from favor, and perhaps change in character, for which Masters blamed the people of Lewistown. As he said in a December 26, 1926, letter to Edwin P. Reese, "they broke and degraded him; they took away his honor, his self-respect, his good-nature, and filled him with lice and filth from themselves" (letter to Reese, Folder 1, Edgar Lee Masters Papers, Illinois State Historical Library). Curiously, Masters says little about Breeden in *Across Spoon River* (pp. 74, 83), perhaps because as he got older he increasingly viewed his father as the only man of great integrity in Lewistown, further reshaping the past. On Breeden, see *Portrait and Biographical Album*, pp. 337-38.

Ida Frickey

Nothing in life is alien to you: This is similar to a famous line by the second-century B.C. Roman writer Terence: "Nothing human is alien to me."

Summum: A hamlet thirteen miles south of Lewistown.

the "Commercial": A hotel.

Seth Compton

This poem may reflect the life of Judge John Winter, a Lewistown freethinker whose personal library was made available to Masters and perhaps to others as well (*Across Spoon River,* pp. 81, 84). See the first note to "Judge Somers."

Of knowing Volney's Ruins as well as Butler's Analogy / And Faust as well as Evangeline: Volney's *Ruins* (1791) is a famous skeptical work, whereas Joseph Butler's *Analogy of Religion* (1736) is a work of religious apologetics; Goethe's *Faust* (1808; 1832) is a tragedy about enormous passion and a relentless quest for self-fulfillment, whereas Henry Wadsworth Longfellow's *Evangeline* (1847) is a sentimental narrative poem about a thwarted love relationship.

Who knows not what is false: The word "not" is omitted in the *Reedy's Mirror* text, November 20, 1914.

Schroeder the Fisherman

Bernadotte: A village on the Spoon River ten miles west of Lewistown, it was a noted fishing spot in the later nineteenth century.

if there's anything in man . . . / That makes him different from fishes or hogs: The speaker's philosophy is Social Darwinism, which was influential in the late nineteenth century. It comprehended society in terms of evolutionary principles and emphasized "survival of the fittest."

Silas Dement

This poem is based on the burning of the Fulton County Courthouse at Lewistown on December 14, 1894. The name of the incendiary was Frank ("Chase") Henry, who later confessed but did not serve time in the Illinois State Penitentiary at Joliet. The background to the poem is discussed by Chandler, pp. 301-4, and Burgess, "*Spoon River:* Politics and Poetry," pp. 356-57. See also Heylin, pp. 762x-762y, as well as newspaper accounts: "Indicted," Lewistown *Fulton Democrat,* August 31, 1895, pp. 1-2, and "The Conspiracy," *Fulton Democrat,* Sept. 4, 1895, p. 1. "Chase Henry" is based on the same individual. The name of this speaker, "Dement," means "to become insane."

Dillard Sissman

This poem is based on the poet's memories of his boyhood days at his grandparents' farm north of Petersburg. See *Across Spoon River,* pp. 58, 397, and *The Sangamon,* p. 23. For a discussion of the poem, see John E. Hallwas, "Masters' 'Dillard Sissman,'" *The Explicator* 36 (Spring 1978): 2-3.

A spurt of flame: This is apparently based on the poet's recollection of sunsets on the Masters farm, when "the fire of the sun dazzled in distant windows" (*Across Spoon River,* p. 403). However, some kind of visionary experience is being suggested.

Jonathan Houghton

This poem is autobiographical. It is based on Masters's recollection of his boyhood days at his grandparents' farm north of Petersburg. See *Across Spoon River,* p. 403. The old man and old woman in lines nine and ten are, then, Squire Davis and Lucinda Masters. The name "Houghton" was derived from a neighboring farmer, Sevigne Houghton, who is mentioned in "The Hill." Narveson has pointed out that an earlier version of the poem, entitled "Thirty Years After," was submitted to *Poetry* in 1915. It has a somewhat different, and less effective, conclusion:

> Now thirty years are gone,
> And the boy returns worn out by life.
> The orchard has vanished, the forest is cut away,
> The house is made over,
> And automobiles fill the road-way with dust.

See "Edgar Lee Masters' *Spoon River Anthology,*" p. 112. The poem was revised and entitled "Jonathan Houghton" for the 1916 edition of the *Anthology.* For discussions of the poem, see Hallwas, "Two Autobiographical Epitaphs," pp. 32-34, and the introduction to this edition.

Shipley's Hill: Shipley Hill was one mile east of the Masters farm. When the poet was about three years old, his family lived on the hill for a year, and he frequently saw and visited it afterward. See *Across Spoon River,* pp. 12-13.

Atterbury: Atterberry, a village four miles west of the Masters farm, where the poet's family moved when he was still very young. See *Across Spoon River,* pp. 13-14.

The Hill: The cemetery. See "The Hill," which opens the *Anthology.*

E. C. Culbertson

Lewis and Love assert that this poem reflects the life of Lewistown resident George W. Dick. Burgess points out that Dick was a Lewistown Township supervisor on the Fulton County Board in the mid-1890s and had "a role in decisions to build the new courthouse." But he also mentions that the poet's father, Hardin W. Masters, served on the board at the same time, so "the epitaph reflects him"

("*Spoon River*: Politics and Poetry," pp. 357-58; letter to Hallwas, p. 5).

That whoso enters the vineyard at the eleventh hour / Shall receive a full day's pay: This refers to the Parable of the Vineyard (Matthew 20:1-16). Its theme of spiritual reward contrasts with the account of self-serving participation that closes the poem.

Shack Dye

As Burgess has pointed out, Shack Dye was the real name of an African-American blacksmith in Petersburg ("The Use of Local Lore," p. 50).

When Burr Robbins circus came to town: In *Across Spoon River* Masters recalls his youth in Lewistown, "when the Burr Robbins circus came to town, with the elephants, the gaudy circus wagons, and the clowns" (p. 44).

Granville Calhoun

Lewis and Love assert that this poem reflects the life of David J. Waggoner (1822-83), who served several terms as sheriff of Fulton County but was defeated by a large margin the last time he ran for the office, in 1882. He died soon afterward and is buried in Lewistown's Oak Hill Cemetery. In a March 3, 1953, letter to Kimball Flaccus, Lewistown resident Harvey H. Atherton asserted that this poem was based on another figure, Thomas A. Boyd (1830-97), who was a Fulton County judge in the 1880s (Folder 7, Box 1, Flaccus-Masters Archive, Special Collections Division, Georgetown University Library). However, Boyd ended his judicial career by resigning in 1888, so the connection with him seems unlikely. He is also buried in Oak Hill Cemetery.

Henry C. Calhoun

Lewis indicates that this poem reflects the life of Harry M. Waggoner (1856-1935), a Lewistown resident who was the son of Sheriff David J. Waggoner, the model for "Granville Calhoun." He is buried in Lewistown's Oak Hill Cemetery.

the Furies: In classical mythology, the Furies were avenging goddesses who pursued wrongdoers through life and even beyond death, until they were punished. In this context, the speaker is saying that he made the purpose of the Furies his purpose with respect to the people of Spoon River, who had wronged his father.

the Fates: In classical mythology the Fates were a trio of weaving goddesses who determined the length of a person's life. One of them,

Atropos, snipped the thread of life, thus determining when that person would die. In the last eight lines the speaker is asserting that revenge is a readily transferable motive that can be instilled in younger members of a family, poisoning their lives, as was the case with his father and himself.

Alfred Moir

This poem reflects an incident in the poet's life that occurred in 1886, shortly after he had graduated from high school. While passing through Mason City, Illinois, which lies between Petersburg and Lewistown, he happened to see a beautifully decorated volume of Shelley's poems in a store window, so he bought it (*Across Spoon River,* pp. 76-77). Masters later told Kimball Flaccus about the impact of that book: "It changed the whole world for me. . . . Thereafter I devoted myself heart, soul, brain, lights, and liver to Shelley. I read everything I could find about him." See Flaccus, "Edgar Lee Masters," typescript, p. 70, Folder 35, Box 11, Kimball Flaccus Papers, Dartmouth College Library. For a brief discussion of the poem, see Herb Russell, "Alfred Moir," *The Explicator,* 3 (1973), item 54.

Burchard's bar: There was a Burchard's saloon in late nineteenth-century Lewistown.

Perry Zoll

the County Scientific Association: In the mid-1880s Masters joined the Fulton County Scientific Association, a group that provided him with much intellectual stimulation. However, membership was open to anyone.

Magrady Graham

This poem is perhaps based on Lewis C. ("Lute") Breeden, who was the Democratic leader that Masters most admired in Lewistown during his years there and who was a supporter of John Peter Altgeld. For information on Breeden, whose idealism made him akin to Altgeld, see the note to "Enoch Dunlap."

was Altgeld elected Governor?: John Peter Altgeld (1847-1902) was elected governor of Illinois in 1892 and served one four-year term. That election was the first time Democrats had carried the state since 1856. Masters, a Democrat, supported and revered Altgeld.

democracy: As Masters knew, the word "democracy" was often used in the nineteenth century to refer to the cause of the Democratic party, and it has that implication here.

his head on a platter to a dancer: An allusion to the biblical account in which the daughter of Herodias, who had pleased Herod with her dancing, asked for, and received, the head of John the Baptist on a platter (Mark 6:21-28). In reference to Altgeld, the speaker is asking whether he was destroyed by a corrupt society.

Archibald Higbie

This poem reflects an aspect of Masters's consciousness, his effort to "rise above" his culturally limited background (*Across Spoon River*, p. 114) and create significant literary art — here presented symbolically through the career of painter Archibald Higbie. See the discussion of this poem in the introduction to this edition.

Apollo's: Apollo was the Greek god of poetry and music, as well as other aspects of Greek culture. He personified manly youth and beauty, and that idealized image is apparently compromised by the trace of Lincoln's face, which symbolizes the artist's limited cultural background. Masters loved Greek culture, and he strove to serve the god of poetry. See "Webster Ford" and the notes to that poem.

weighted down with western soil: In the later nineteenth century the word "western" was still used in reference to midwestern culture, and artists in the Midwest often felt culturally disadvantaged in comparison to their eastern and European counterparts.

Tom Merritt

This poem and the two that follow it are based on a Fulton County murder case in which the poet's father, Hardin W. Masters, was a defense lawyer. On May 3, 1884, Elmer Lamb shot and killed John Lawson near the Vanliew crossing of the Narrow Gauge Railway at Fairview, twenty miles north of Lewistown. The case was sensational because Lamb was Mrs. Lawson's lover, although he was only nineteen years old and she was thirty-five. Both were convicted in late August and received lengthy prison sentences. There was no convincing evidence that Mrs. Lawson was an accessory to the murder, but the public was outraged by the illicit love affair — especially since she was old enough to be Lamb's mother. She was regarded as an older woman who had led the youth astray and hence was substantially responsible for what occurred, as the poem "Mrs. Merritt" indicates. The specifics of the case are given in a series of articles in the nearby Canton newspaper, the *Fulton County Ledger:* "John Lawson Shot," May 8, 1884, p. 8; "Mrs. Lawson Sent to Jail," May 15, 1884, p. 4; "From the County Seat," May 29, 1884, p. 1; "Elmer Lamb in Jail," May 29, 1884, p. 4; and "Mary and Her Lamb," September 4, 1884, p. 1.

Fourth Bridge: A bridge over the Spoon River, southwest of Lewistown. It is not close to where the murder actually took place.

Mrs. Merritt

See the first note to "Tom Merritt."
the iron gates of Joliet: The Illinois State Penitentiary was located at Joliet, thirty-five miles southwest of Chicago.

Elmer Karr

See the first note to "Tom Merritt." Whether this poem reflects the postprison experience of murderer Elmer Lamb is unknown.

Elizabeth Childers

This unusual poem, in which the speaker addresses an infant who died with her during childbirth, may reflect the problem of illegitimacy. The references to parental shame, "maiden sorrow," blood relationships, and a future generation with questionable identity contribute to that impression. In any case, Elizabeth Childers was apparently glad to die, and she views her infant who died at birth as fortunate in thereby avoiding the sorrows of life. As one who did not live to be a mother, the speaker's name is ironic. See also the note to "Edith Conant."
To whom would your face have been lifted?: Had the child lived, he or she would have been alone since Elizabeth Childers died in childbirth and apparently had no husband.

Edith Conant

This poem is unusual for two reasons — because the speaker's "memories" are personified as things that stand by the grave and recall the past and because what they recall relates so closely to the life of Elizabeth Childers, the speaker in the preceding poem. Evidently Masters wrote two very different poems based on the same person or situation — a young woman who died in childbirth — for "Elizabeth Childers" appeared in the October 2, 1914, issue of *Reedy's Mirror,* and "Edith Conant" was published the following week. The identical initials of the two women, "E. C.," suggest that he may have based the poems on the death of a young woman with those initials. He was apparently exploring ways to express the tragedy involved in such a double death of mother and baby. Because the two poems both refer to such a double death, and because Edith Conant's "memories" address her as "you," it may seem to the reader as though "Edith Conant" is a commentary on "Elizabeth Childers," but that is not the case since the two poems did not appear together in the magazine version of the *Anthology*. To avoid confusion, Masters should have separated them in the book version. Oddly enough, in *The New Spoon River* (1924) Edith Conant's child is portrayed as living a normal life span. See "Celestine Conant."

Charles Webster

The farmhouse, orchard, and nearby hill are suggestive of the poet's grandparents' farm at Sand Ridge. The poem may be based on a visit to the farm shortly after his grandfather's death in 1904. If so, the closing line is an imaginative expression of words of comfort from the old man to his bereaved grandson.

cot: Cottage; that is, the farmhouse.

Father Malloy

Although Masters never indicated the name of his model for this poem, he did reveal that it was based on a clergyman in Lewistown. In a 1927 article written for *The Commonweal,* he stated that the minister had been a friend of his father, Hardin W. Masters. The poet recalled him as a man who did not support the repressive forces who strove to impose their values on the community:

> With none of this did Father Malloy have anything to do. He was out at the parish maintaining a silence too significant to be understood by many. His boys and girls danced if they wanted to, and he was the amused spectator of their delight; the Sabbath being made for man and not man for the Sabbath, happiness and play were not denied to his flock on this day; and wine being good for the soul, his men and women could have it, avoiding only the forbidden sin of intemperence. Father Malloy neither compelling by threats, nor enticing by promises, nor bribing by economic advantages any to come to him, pursued his way in the confidence of an ancient divination of the human heart. The madness around him, which he could not exorcise, and which never appealed to him for help, had to go its way. ("Father Malloy," *The Commonweal,* Dec. 14, 1927, p. 812)

Lewis and Love assert that this poem was based on a "Father Thieber," but according to a booklet entitled *St. Mary's Church, Lewistown, Illinois 1865-1965* (Lewistown: Mid-County Press, 1965), p. 4, his correct name was Father Sebastian Thiebes, and he was pastor during 1884 and 1885. Burgess suggests that Father Michael J. Flynn, who was pastor at St. Mary's from 1891 to 1898, may have been the inspiration for the poem (letter to Hallwas, p. 5).

This poem is unusual because the character, Father Malloy, does not speak. Rather, some of the dead in Spoon River's community cemetery speak to him. Father Malloy is supposedly buried "over there," in the Catholic cemetery. Lewistown has a small Catholic cemetery, St. Mary's, located east of town, and it was started in 1879. No clergyman is buried there.

Peter the Flame, / *Peter the Rock:* Christ said to St. Peter, "you are Peter, and on this rock I will build my church" (Matthew 16:18). The Pope's authority as head of the Catholic Church is based on this famous passage. The name "Peter" is derived from the Latin word *petrus,* meaning "rock," and the succession of popes can be traced back to St. Peter, the bedrock or foundation of the church. Peter is not referred to as a "flame." However, in Hebrews 1:7 God's servants are described as "flames of fire."

Ami Green

Love asserts that this poem was based on Ami Severn (1847-1930), who "drove the hotel bus many years" in Lewistown and who later moved to Farmington. If that identification is correct, the references in the poem to being "hailed familiarly" and "loaded up" may be based on the poet's recollections of Severn in that occupation.

"a youth with hoary head and haggard eye": The speaker is recalling, not quite accurately, a line from Shelley's "Death" (1817) in which Misery is personified as "A Youth with hoary hair and haggard eye."

Calvin Campbell

Wrenn and Wrenn point out that the speaker's first name alludes to "the great exponent of theological determinism, John Calvin" (p. 53). Using plants to symbolize good and bad kinds of people, Calvin Campbell does view individuals as fated to be what they are.

arbutus: The speaker apparently has in mind trailing arbutus, a creeping plant that has fragrant pink or white flowers. It is viewed here as an attractive, desirable plant, in contrast to poison ivy.

dock-weed, / *Jimpson, dandelion or mullen:* Plants commonly viewed as weeds.

jessamine or wistaria: Woody, ornamental plants with lovely flowers.

Henry Layton

This poem apparently reflects Masters's awareness of the conflict-
ing personalities of his parents and his divided self. In *Across Spoon
River* he refers to his parents' marriage as "the union of conflicting
and irresistable forces" (p. 10), his father being easygoing and tolerant,
his mother being high-strung and intolerant. Later in the autobiog-
raphy he says of himself, "I have been two persons" (p. 399), and
he apparently never resolved his inner conflict.

Ippolit Konovaloff

Odessa: A seaport on the Black Sea, in the southwest part of the
Soviet Union.

Spencer: Herbert Spencer (1820-1903), the English philosopher
who asserted the evolution of life, mind, society, and morality.

Kant: Immanuel Kant (1724-1804), the great German philosopher
who was concerned with the nature and limits of knowledge.

Henry Phipps

The model for this poem was Lewistown banker Henry Phelps,
whose bank failed on January 9, 1894. He was superintendent of
the Sunday schools in Lewistown. See also the note to "Thomas
Rhodes."

My son the cashier of the bank, / Wedded to Rhodes' daughter:
Henry Willis Phelps, the son of banker Henry Phelps, was the cashier
in his father's bank, and he was married to Elizabeth Turner, a relative
of his father's partner, Moses Turner, according to Burgess, "*Spoon
River*: Politics and Poetry," p. 355.

*"the upright shall dwell in the land / But the years of the wicked
shall be shortened.":* Proverbs 2:21.

Harry Wilmans

Masters indicated that this poem was based on the experiences
of Henry Wilmans, a young man with whom he shared a room briefly
at a Chicago boardinghouse. As he said in *Across Spoon River,* "He
[Wilmans] went to the Phillipines as a soldier, and coming back to
Chicago called upon me and described to me a charge through the
swamps near Manila when a soldier at his side was killed" (p. 166).

Made a speech in Bindle's Opera House: After war was declared
in 1898, Masters's father made a patriotic speech to the people of
Lewistown, which the poet was probably recalling here: "and there
was my father on a drygoods box addressing the people, and calling

upon the young men to go forth and free Cuba from despotism and superstition" (*Across Spoon River*, p. 238). Regarding the opera house in Lewistown, see the note to "Nicholas Bindle."

Tagalogs: One of the peoples of the Philippines. The term is used here to mean Filipinos in general.

John Wasson

Masters indicated that this poem was inspired by his great-great-grandfather, John Wasson ("The Genesis of Spoon River," p. 39). Actually, he combined the experiences of his great-great-grandmother's two husbands—John Bryant, who died in the Revolutionary War, and John Wasson, who married her afterward and took his family to Tennessee. Wasson died there, however, and his wife later brought her family to Illinois. For information about John Wasson, see Burgess, "Ancestral Lore in *Spoon River Anthology*," pp. 190-96, and for brief discussions of the poem, see Hallwas, "Masters and the Pioneers," pp. 394-95, and the introduction to this edition.

Rebecca: See "Rebecca Wasson" and the first note to that poem.

Godwin James

This speaker's unusual name may allude to one or both of the following thinkers: William Godwin (1756-1836) and William James (1842-1910). Godwin was an English philosopher, novelist, and historian who believed in the perfectibility of humankind and wrote a kind of anarchistic utopian work called *Enquiry Concerning Political Justice* (1793). James was an American psychologist and philosopher who viewed the mind as an instrument in the struggle for survival in *The Principles of Psychology* (1890) and who analyzed religion in *The Varieties of Religious Experience* (1902).

Lyman King

Fate: The meaning of the term shifts in this poem, from an inevitable difficulty—which may seem to be avoidable—to death, the ultimate destiny of the individual.

Caroline Branson

Masters indicated that this poem and "Amelia Garrick" were based on Margaret George, an intellectual companion and sweetheart during his teenage years in Lewistown ("The Genesis of Spoon River," p. 45). See also the notes to "Amelia Garrick," "Julia Miller," and "Louise Smith." The love relationship between Masters and Margaret George is also depicted in fictional terms in the early chapters of his second novel, *Skeeters Kirby* (1923), and she is "Anne" in his autobiography, *Across Spoon River*. As those books and this poem reveal, the young lovers spent much time together outdoors. But in the autobiography Masters asserts that although they "indulged in amorous intimacies," Margaret "never yielded" (p. 101) to his sexual advances, so the poem apparently speculates on the disillusionment that would have occurred if they had proclaimed their love, gotten married, and then consummated their relationship.

"Caroline Branson" has two distinctive parts, spoken by different voices. The first half of the poem is Branson's memory of the intense love that led to disillusionment and a "pact of death." The second part is apparently a plea for life by the male child who was conceived through that relationship but died without being born when the lovers killed themselves. However, the star, soil, and "secret of the seed" imagery suggests that these lines were originally connected with "Mrs. Sibley" as the voice of her buried fetus.

Gazed at by Raphael and St. Francis: The unborn child who speaks in this part of the poem seems to be in a spiritual realm inhabited by such great figures as Raphael (1483-1520), the Italian painter, and St. Francis of Assisi (c. 1182-1226), the Italian founder of the Franciscan order. Perhaps the point here is that the child's potential for self-development or achievement, akin to that of such great figures as Raphael and St. Francis, went unrealized.

Save me, Shelley!: The speaker is perhaps appealing to Shelley (1792-1822) because the great British poet was so sensitive to the presence of the spiritual realm that underlies the natural world. Shelley had a large influence on Masters.

Anne Rutledge

The daughter of New Salem tavern keeper James Rutledge, Ann (1803-35) knew Lincoln, died of a "fever," and was later regarded by local people as the one true love of Lincoln's life. In "The Genesis of Spoon River" Masters discusses the background to the poem: "As I lived for years in the [Petersburg] neighborhood where this story of Lincoln's romance was one of the current legends, and was kept alive by the numerous Rutledges who lived there, it is not wonderful that it became a part of the twice-told tales of my formative years" (p. 51). "My grandmother, perhaps, believed the story of the love affair, for she took me a number of times to the grave of Ann Rutledge when we went to Concord church. It was in a country graveyard one mile south from the church, marked by a small rough headstone with the words Ann Rutledge carved on it, nothing else. It was not until 1890 that the grave was moved to Oakland Cemetery at Petersburg" (p. 52). The local legend was brought to the public by Lincoln's law partner William H. Herndon, first in an 1866 speech and later in his 1889 biography, *Abraham Lincoln,* which Masters read. As he later recalled, "in my studious days I read Herndon's "Life of Lincoln," as my father greatly admired it, and believed it thoroughly, and Herndon made much of the Lincoln romance" ("The Genesis of Spoon River," p. 52). The poet regarded the Lincoln-Rutledge romance as factual until scholars called the story into question during the 1920s. Masters himself later said, in *Lincoln, the Man,* that there was very little to justify the notion of a Lincoln-Rutledge romance (New York: Dodd, Mead, 1931, p. 47). Modern scholars continue to view the story as unsubstantiated.

However, the appearance of *Spoon River Anthology* did much to popularize the love story, and in 1921 a huge granite headstone with Masters's poem carved on it replaced the earlier marker (now the footstone) at the Rutledge grave in Petersburg's Oakland Cemetery. "Anne Rutledge" also became the most well-loved and often-re-printed epitaph in the *Anthology.* Readers of the book often asked Masters to autograph that page. For discussions of the poem and its background, see Burgess, "Masters and Some Mentors," pp. 180-82; John E. Hallwas, "The Lincoln-Rutledge Love Story," in *Western Illinois Heritage* (Macomb: Illinois Heritage Press, 1983), pp. 167-69; and the introduction to this edition.

The name "Ann Rutledge" was not spelled with an "e," as in the title and text of the poem, but Masters was apparently following the spelling used in Herndon's biography. In the *Reedy's Mirror* text, the title is "Anna Rutledge."

"With malice toward none, with charity for all.": A famous state-ment from the conclusion to Lincoln's Second Inaugural Address (1865).

Hamlet Micure

Like Shakespeare's famous tragic hero, this small-town Hamlet is afflicted with melancholy, or a pensive depression of spirit. Wrenn and Wrenn assert that the speaker's name is "a pseudonym" of Masters (p. 49), but that it is not the precise term. "Hamlet Micure" is a mask for the poet. See the notes below.

the little house: Lines 2-6 reflect the second house that the poet's family lived in at Petersburg. It had an oak tree and a swing in the yard. See *Across Spoon River,* pp. 25-26.

little Paul / Strangled from diphtheria: Masters indicated in *Across*

Spoon River that in this poem he reflected the death of his five-year-old brother Alex from diphtheria in September 1878 (pp. 28-29). He later wrote another poem on the same event, "In Memory of Alexander Dexter Masters," published in *The Harmony of Deeper Music,* p. 32.

a man in a dark cloak: Alfred, Lord Tennyson (1809-92), the author of "Tears, Idle Tears." The speaker sees him and little Paul in a vision.

Euripides: The great Greek tragedian of the fifth century B.C.

William H. Herndon

William H. Herndon (1818-91) was Lincoln's last law partner and his biographer. Later in his life Herndon lived on a farm six miles north of Springfield, where his house was on a bluff overlooking the Sangamon River. He occasionally tried cases with the poet's father, Hardin W. Masters, through a special legal partnership. Masters recalled seeing the old man around Petersburg. See *Across Spoon River,* p. 45, and *The Sangamon,* pp. 71-73. Herndon's biography influenced Masters, as Burgess points out in "Masters and Some Mentors," pp. 178-82.

a man arose from the soil like a fabled giant: Lincoln.

people: In *Reedy's Mirror,* Nov. 20, 1914, the word is "commonalty."

Vulcan of sovereign fires: In Roman mythology Vulcan was the god of fire, especially in its fearful aspects, and of metalworking. This phrase apparently refers to Lincoln's role in directing the Civil War, a conflict in which governmental sovereignty was at issue.

a child of Plutarch and Shakespeare: John Wilkes Booth (1838-65), who assassinated Lincoln, was a noted Shakespearian actor, and many of Shakespeare's plays were based on *Plutarch's Lives* (1579).

Rebecca Wasson

Masters indicated that this poem was based on his great-great-grandmother, Rebecca Wasson ("The Genesis of Spoon River," p. 39). However, it is probably also indebted to his memories of his grandmother, Lucinda (Young) Masters, who was an invalid during her last years. In *Across Spoon River* he depicts her as a bedridden figure looking out her window at falling leaves (p. 304). For information about Rebecca Wasson, whose first husband, John Bryant, fought in the Revolutionary War, see Burgess, "Ancestral Lore in *Spoon River Anthology,*" pp. 188-201, and for brief discussions of the poem, see Hallwas, "Masters and the Pioneers," pp. 395-98, and the introduction to this edition. See also "John Wasson" and the note to that poem.

I beheld you there by the bed: As the closing lines of the poem suggest, her husband's face appears to her as she is dying. She is finally reunited with him in death.

Rutherford McDowell

ambrotypes: Photographic positives made on glass, which were common in the mid-nineteenth century, when many old pioneers had their pictures taken.

Hannah Armstrong

This poem is based on an incident in Lincoln's life. Hannah Armstrong (1811-90) and her husband, Jack, befriended Lincoln when he moved to New Salem. After he was president and Jack had died, Lincoln discharged their ailing son William ("Duff") from military service. Hannah Armstrong did not have to travel to Washington, D.C., however, to obtain his discharge. See Chandler, p. 266, and the photographs that face pages 263 and 267. Masters refers to this as a "story told for years along the Sangamon" in *The Sangamon*, pp. 91-92, and he also discusses it in "Days in the Lincoln Country," pp. 786-87. His grandmother, Lucinda Masters, was a good friend of Hannah Armstrong, who later lived in the Sand Ridge district north of Petersburg and is buried in Petersburg's Oakland Cemetery.

James Garber: According to Chandler, Hannah Armstrong's neighbor, Jacob Garber, wrote the letter for her (p. 263).

Lucinda Matlock

In "The Genesis of Spoon River" (p. 39), Masters indicated that this well-known poem was based on his paternal grandmother, Lucinda Masters (1814-1910). She is described in *Across Spoon River* as a woman of vitality, simplicity, and good humor (pp. 6-8). See also *The Sangamon*, pp. 30-31. The account of meeting her husband at a dance (lines 1-5) was a story the old woman often told, according to Chandler, p. 259. Chandlerville and Winchester are small towns just east of the Illinois River in Cass and Scott counties, respectively. Lucinda Young and Squire Davis Masters were married at Manchester, Illinois, on March 6, 1834, and they remained together until his death seventy years later. They had eight children, several of whom preceded them in death. Squire Davis and Lucinda Masters are buried alongside the poet in Petersburg's Oakland Cemetery. Masters wrote a magazine article based on his grandmother's life:

"I Call Her Dorcas," *The Rotarian* 62 (May 1943): 8-10, 60. For information about Lucinda Masters and her family background, see Burgess, "Ancestral Lore in *Spoon River Anthology*," pp. 185-204, and for discussions of this poem, see Hallwas, "Masters and the Pioneers," pp. 391-92, and the introduction to this edition. See also "Davis Matlock," "Aaron Hatfield," and the notes to those poems. In *Reedy's Mirror,* June 26, 1914, this poem is simply entitled "Lucinda."

Davis Matlock

Masters indicated that his grandfather Squire Davis Masters (1812-1904) was the model for this poem ("The Genesis of Spoon River," p. 39). "Matlock" was the surname of his grandfather's mother. Squire Davis Masters was a kindly, dignified, religious farmer, and the poet idealized him as a man of simple piety, good will, hopefulness, and spiritual vision. See *Across Spoon River,* pp. 5-8; *The Sangamon,* pp. 22-23, 26-31; and "Days in the Lincoln Country," pp. 779-92. For additional information about him, see Burgess, "Edgar Lee Masters' Paternal Ancestry," pp. 48-52. Squire Davis Masters and his wife are buried alongside the poet in Petersburg's Oakland Cemetery. See also "Aaron Hatfield" and the note to that poem.

Herman Altman

This poem reflects the character and fate of John Peter Altgeld (1847-1902), the controversial reformist governor of Illinois in the 1890s. After he pardoned the surviving anarchists who were wrongfully convicted in the famous Haymarket Riot trial, Altgeld was viciously attacked in the press and failed to win reelection in 1896. Masters greatly admired him and wrote about him in "John Peter Altgeld," *The American Mercury* 4 (February 1925): 161-74, and in *The Tale of Chicago,* pp. 247-48, 257-59, 266-68, 345. See also, Ellen Coyne Masters, "Those People of Spoon River," *New York Times Book Review,* February 12, 1950, p. 5. The name "Altman," meaning "high man," reflects the speaker's high principles.

Jennie M'Grew

something black: Death. This is the last of several images of death in the poem.

Columbus Cheney

This weeping willow: This apparently refers to a weeping willow carved on the speaker's gravestone. That was a common gravestone symbol, which indicated sorrow.

Wallace Ferguson

Jean Rousseau / Was the silent music of all we saw or heard—:
Jean Jacques Rousseau (1712-78), the famous philosopher and author,
was born and raised in Geneva.

Marie Bateson

I can no more: The word "can" is being used here in an archaic
sense, to mean "know"—hence, "I know no more."

Tennessee Claflin Shope

This speaker is a namesake of Tennessee Claflin, Lady Cook (1845-
1923), who was a noted spiritual healer, reformer, and leader of the
suffragist movement. Masters did not characterize her in the poem,
but the speaker's assertion of "the sovereignty of my own soul"
suggests the kind of self-assertion typical of a reformer, and like
Claflin she displays an interest in spiritual healing—at least with
respect to herself. William L. Phillips has asserted that the poem
reflects Tennessee Mitchell (1874-1929), who had been the poet's
mistress in Chicago in 1909 and 1910 ("How Sherwood Anderson
Wrote *Winesburg, Ohio*," *American Literature* 23 [1951]: 17), but
there is little about the poem except the name "Tennessee" to support
that contention. However, as Kramer points out, Mitchell had been
named for Tennessee Claflin (p. 175). Rather, the poem is based on
Julia Brown (1866-1954), a friend of Masters who was interested in
eastern religions and who left Lewistown for Georgia in 1890 to
take a course in "mental science." The poet discusses her briefly in
Across Spoon River, p. 128. She is also the model for "Margaret
Fuller Slack."

the learned, like Rev. Peet, who read Greek: This refers to Rev.
Benjamin Y. George, a Presbyterian minister in Lewistown who was
very learned and had an excellent command of Greek. See the note
to "Rev. Abner Peet."

I asserted the sovereignty of my own soul: Julia Brown had been
influenced by Emerson, who had preached spiritual self-reliance.

Mary Baker G. Eddy: Mary Baker Eddy (1821-1910) was the
founder of the Christian Science Church and a pioneer in spiritual
healing.

the Bhagavad Gita: Literally, "the Song of the Blessed One." Part
of the sacred scriptures of India, it is a philosophical dialogue that
expresses pantheism.

Plymouth Rock Joe

The speaker's name refers to a kind of chicken, Plymouth Rock, and he views the people of Spoon River metaphorically as a barnyard full of chickens.

cock of the walk: The most important person in the group; also, a domineering person.

Immanuel Ehrenhardt

This poem mentions the kind of philosophical reading that excited Masters during his later teenage years and early adulthood in Lewistown. The speaker's first name means "God with us," an allusion to the immanent God posited by Spinoza. See the introduction to this edition.

Sir William Hamilton's lectures: Hamilton (1788-1856) was a noted Scottish philosopher whose volume of lectures was entitled *Metaphysics and Logic* (1858-60).

Dugald Stewart: A Scottish philosopher (1753-1828) whose chief interest was moral philosophy.

John Locke on the Understanding: The most influential work by the great English philosopher John Locke (1632-1704) was his *Essay Concerning Human Understanding* (1690).

Descartes: René Descartes (1596-1650), the great French philosopher and mathematician, who based his speculations on pure reason and posited a complete gulf between the material world and the mind.

Fichte: Johann Gottlieb Fichte (1762-1814), a German metaphysical philosopher who made the conscious ego the starting point for knowledge of the universe.

Schelling: Friedrich von Schelling (1775-1854), a German philosopher who viewed the ideal as a development of the real and asserted the unity of all existence.

Kant: Immanuel Kant (1724-1804), the great German philosopher who was concerned with the nature and limits of knowledge.

Schopenhauer—: Arthur Schopenhauer (1788-1860), a German philosopher whose works assert a very pessimistic view of the world.

Books I borrowed from old Judge Somers: The poem "Judge Somers" is based on Judge John Winter (1826-1906) of Lewistown, whose library was made available to Masters.

John Muir: Muir (1838-1914) was a noted American naturalist and writer of books and articles on nature. He may well have corresponded with Lewistown naturalist William S. Strode whose life is reflected in "William Jones."

Samuel Gardner

Lewis suggests that the model for this poem was William Jones (1835-1924), who owned the greenhouse in Lewistown. He is buried in Oak Hill Cemetery. See also the first note to "William Jones." For a brief discussion of "Samuel Gardner," see the introduction to this edition.

Dow Kritt

In a letter to Kimball Flaccus, Martha Viola Leeds of Lewistown commented that "this [Dow Kritt] was his real name and he always went barefoot or wore felt boots. He was about 5 feet in height and wore big brown curls and big brass earrings. Lived in a barn opposite the cemetery" (letter to Kimball Flaccus, November 16, 1952, Folder 1, Box 3, Flaccus-Masters Archive, Special Collections Division, Georgetown University Library). Chandler mentions that he was still living in Lewistown during the early 1920s and worked as a ditch digger (pp. 326-27).

William Jones

Masters indicated that this poem was based on "a naturalist and a devotee of Whitman" whom he knew in Lewistown ("The Genesis of Spoon River," p. 45). The poem's title in *Reedy's Mirror,* August 7, 1914, was "William Jones, Naturalist." The man was Dr. William S. Strode (1847-1934), a physician and amateur naturalist whom the poet briefly describes in *Across Spoon River,* p. 85. He was president of the Fulton County Scientific Society, of which Masters was the youngest member, and he later married Julia Brown, a friend and classmate of the poet. See Chandler, pp. 281-83, as well as Burgess, "Masters and Some Mentors," pp. 188-90. Fulton County sources include Heylin, p. 1130, and *Portrait and Biographical Album,* pp. 658-59. The name "William Jones" was that of a Lewistown resident who owned a greenhouse. See "Samuel Gardner" and the note to that poem.

Yeomans: In *Across Spoon River* Masters says that "he [Strode] was in correspondence with Yeomans, who was then editing the *Popular Science Monthly,* on matters of conchology and the flora of that part of Illinois" (p. 85). However, the man's name was "Youmans," either Edward Livingston Youmans (1821-87) or William Jay Youmans (1838-1901), who edited that journal successively.

Tyndall: John Tyndall (1820-93) was a noted British scientist, although he was chiefly a physicist rather than a biologist.

William Goode

In the deep woods near Miller's Ford: Miller's Ferry was located on the Sangamon River several miles north of Petersburg, and in 1922 Chandler pointed out that "the 'deep woods' of 'William Goode's' allusion still cover the hills on the right back of the Sangamon at this point" (p. 263).

J. Milton Miles

Burgess comments on this poem: "James Miles, b. 1822, a longtime friend of Squire Davis Masters, lived in an impressive house at the north edge of Petersburg, where the church bells certainly could have been heard. . . . The 'J. Milton' adds a wry literary touch, perhaps reflecting theological uncertainties that the presence of many sects could cause" (letter to Hallwas, p. 5). The name "J. Milton" clearly does allude to the great Puritan poet, whom Masters admired. The speaker's religious quandary stands in ironic contrast to the theological certainty of John Milton (1608-74).

Scholfield Huxley

As Narveson has pointed out, this poem was submitted to *Poetry* magazine in 1915, under a different title, "The Question," but Harriet Monroe did not publish it (p. 111). It subsequently appeared in the 1916 edition of *Spoon River Anthology*. The name "Scholfield Huxley" is apparently a composite of two notable last names: John Scholfield (1834-93), an Illinois lawyer and supreme court justice, and Thomas Henry Huxley (1825-95), the famous exponent of Darwin's theory of evolution. In *Across Spoon River* Masters mentions that he read Huxley while in Lewistown (p. 85), so the latter's humanism may be reflected in the poem. Spinoza's influence on "Scholfield Huxley" is briefly discussed in the introduction to this edition.

Willie Metcalf

According to Chandler, who was writing in the early 1920s, at Lewistown "a certain Charley Metcalf is pointed out as 'Willie Metcalf.' His occupation, and his place of residence as well, is a local livery stable. His talent for handling horses is well known" (p. 327). Thirty years later, in a letter to Kimball Flaccus, Martha Viola Leeds of Lewistown also commented on the model for this poem: "[His] true name was Charlie Metcalf. He loved horses and said he would walk to Havana if he could ride a horse back. The people of the town tormented him. The Doctor Meyers spoken of was Dr. Hull.

That part where it says, 'I lived in the livery stable, sleeping on the floor' is true. Also, where it says, 'Sometimes I talked with animals — even toads and snakes — anything that had an eye to look into' — was also true" (letter to Kimball Flaccus, November 16, 1952, Folder 1, Box 3, Flaccus-Masters Archive, Special Collections Division, Georgetown University Library). In a letter to Edwin P. Reese, Masters indicates that he knew Metcalf (July 27, 1925, Folder 1, Edgar Lee Masters Papers, Illinois State Historical Library). Metcalf (1865-1925) is buried in Lewistown's Oak Hill Cemetery. The influence of Spinoza on this poem is discussed in the introduction to this edition.

Willie Pennington

a tree sprang / From me, a mustard seed: This reflects the gospel parable in which a mustard seed grows into a tree (Matt. 13:31, Mark 4:31, Luke 13:19).

The Village Atheist

This poem reflects an aspect of Masters's intellectual life, his religious skepticism, discussed in the introduction to this edition. At Knox Academy Masters was nicknamed "the atheist." See *Across Spoon River,* pp. 60, 79-81, 85, 115. See also the brief discussion of Spinoza's influence on this poem in the introduction to this edition.

the Upanishads: Part of the ancient Vedic literature of India, these are speculative treatises concerned with humanity and the universe.

the Shadow: Death. This image evokes the famous line in Psalms 23:4, "the valley of the shadow of death," and like the Twenty-third Psalm, Masters's poem asserts a kind of spiritual triumph over death.

Alfonso Churchill

A recent history of Galesburg, where Masters attended school, provides information on the background to this poem: "In 'Alfonso Churchill' . . . the title itself combines the first name of Masters' influential Greek teacher, Professor Alfonso [Alphonso] Newcomer, and the last name of the principal of the Knox Academy, George Churchill, in which Masters was enrolled. The poem, however, chronicles Edgar Larkin, a self-taught astronomer who ran the observatory at the school and who educated not only the students at Knox but also the people of the town about discoveries of science and occasionally about the occult. (Though a bit too controversial for Galesburg, Larkin later became director of the Lowe Observatory.) It was Professor Larkin who became Masters's 'Professor Moon.' " See Jean C. Lee, *Prairies, Prayers, and Promises: An Illustrated His-*

tory of Galesburg (Northridge, Calif.: Windsor Publications, 1987), p. 59. Knox College historian Hermann Muelder also connects the poem with Professor Larkin (1847-1924), who taught at the college from 1888 to 1895, and he comments, "There is reason to believe that some of [the Knox students] laughed at his intensity." See *Missionaries and Muckrakers* (Urbana: University of Illinois Press, 1984), p. 192. See also the brief comments on the relationship of Spinoza's thought to this poem in the introduction to this edition.

Zilpha Marsh

the planchette: A small, usually heart-shaped board, which rests on two casters and—as a third vertical support—a pencil. Supposedly, when someone's fingers rest lightly on the board, it moves without conscious volition, causing the pencil to write a message. A planchette is sometimes used with a ouija board, on which the alphabet and various signs are written. In *Across Spoon River* Masters mentions that his friend Julia Brown often came over to operate a ouija board (p. 130), so an experience of hers may have inspired this poem. For information on her, see the notes to "Margaret Fuller Slack" and "Tennessee Claflin Shope."

"Charles Guiteau": Guiteau (1840-82) assassinated President Garfield in July 2, 1881, and was hanged a year later.

Mrs. Surrat: Mary E. Surratt (1820-65) was an alleged member of the conspiracy to assassinate Lincoln. She was convicted on slim evidence and hanged.

James Garber

There was a Jacob Garber in the Petersburg area, but whether this poem reflects his life is unknown. The name "James Garber" is used in the poem "Hannah Armstrong," where it clearly refers to Jacob Garber. See Chandler, p. 263.

Miller's Ford: Miller's Ferry, on the Sangamon River several miles north of Petersburg.

Lydia Humphrey

It was the vision, vision, vision of the poets / Democratized!: That is, the insight of poets, or those who saw deeply into the nature of reality, was made available to everyday people through the church.

Le Roy Goldman

Wrenn and Wrenn assert that this poem shows the poet's faith that his beloved grandmother, Lucinda Masters, will intercede for him and advocate his case with God, although Masters himself was not a Christian (p. 56). However, he expressed that view with respect to his grandfather, not his grandmother. A passage from *Across Spoon River* relates to this poem: "There were deaths about us; and altogether we lived in terror. The revivalist was flourishing on this soil; but somehow I never confessed my sins and took conversion and the church. . . . My grandfather's piety may have seemed sufficient to cover my Adam inheritance. I revered his religion, and found protection and sustenance in it. He seemed to be a good guardian for me against an angry God" (p. 32).

Gustav Richter

Caesar Borgia: Cesare Borgia (c. 1475-1507), an Italian military and political adventurer who is often regarded as the classic example of the unscrupulous prince of the Renaissance. The "Presence" in the speaker's dream apparently regarded this "flower" as a problem, or in other words, someone difficult to evaluate.

Arlo Will

door was open before you: In *Reedy's Mirror,* November 20, 1914, "open" is a verb in the past tense: "door was opened before you."

Captain Orlando Killion

Burgess suggests that this poem may reflect Thomas L. Harris (1816-58), a noted Mexican War veteran and U.S. congressman from Menard County, who was active in the Concord Church that Masters's grandparents attended. Burgess also points out that "Orlando" is "a name drawn from the Charlemagne legends, symbolizing a Christian warrior" (letter to Hallwas, p. 6). Masters mentions Harris in *The Sangamon,* pp. 54, 60, 62.

Jeremy Carlisle

See the brief discussion of this poem in the introduction to this edition.

Judson Stoddard

The influence of Spinoza on this poem is discussed in the introduction to this edition.

Russell Kincaid

This mythic poem is discussed in the introduction to this edition. *Miller's Ford:* Miller's Ferry, on the Sangamon River several miles north of Petersburg. The speaker seems to be looking north to the river from the approximate location of the Squire Davis Masters farm, so the landscape description is probably based on the poet's memory of that area.

And shoots of green whose delicate blossoms / Were sprinkled over the skeleton tangle: These lines are omitted in *Reedy's Mirror,* January 1, 1915.

Aaron Hatfield

Masters indicated that this poem celebrated his grandfather, Squire Davis Masters (1812-1904), whom he had often heard speak at the Concord Church north of Petersburg ("The Genesis of Spoon River," p. 39). A kindly, dignified, deeply religious man, he was idealized by Masters. For further information about him, see the note to "Davis Matlock." For discussions of this poem, see Hallwas, "Masters and the Pioneers," pp. 392-94, and the introduction to this edition. "Aaron Hatfield" was the name of a wealthy farmer whose land was adjacent to the Masters farm north of Petersburg.

Concord Church: The Concord Church, which served the Cumberland Presbyterian congregation to which Squire Davis Masters belonged, was three miles north of Petersburg. Masters describes it extensively in *The Sangamon,* pp. 121-29, and he also celebrates it in various poems, published and unpublished.

Atterbury: Atterberry, a village four miles west of the Masters farm, where the poet's family moved when he was very young.

O Pioneers: This phrase is probably borrowed from the title of Whitman's poem, "Pioneers! O Pioneers!" (1865), but Willa Cather had already borrowed it for the title of her novel that appeared in 1913, *O Pioneers!,* so Masters may have been recalling that.

the peasant of Galilee —: Christ.

the Comforter: the Holy Spirit.

tongues of flame: As Acts 2:3 reveals, tongues of flame descended upon the disciples at Pentecost, and that gift of the Holy Spirit united them as followers of Christ. That sacred event is reenacted in the congregation of pioneers at Concord Church.

Isaiah Beethoven

According to Masters, "Aaron Hatfield," "Russell Kincaid," "Elijah Browning," and this poem were written when he "was playing on the Victrola the Fifth Symphony of Beethoven" ("The Genesis of Spoon River," p. 51). By employing the name of the famous Old Testament prophet for the speaker's first name, Masters emphasized the spiritual and visionary aspects of the poem. "Isaiah Beethoven" is the most obviously contrived of all the names in *Spoon River Anthology*. See also the note to "Elijah Browning."

Bernadotte: A village on the Spoon River ten miles west of Lewistown, it was the site of a mill in the later nineteenth century.

Elijah Browning

The speaker's name was created by combining the name of the Old Testament prophet who ascended Mount Horeb, where God revealed Himself to him (I Kings 19:8-18), and Robert Browning (1812-89), one of Masters's favorite poets. This poem reveals the impact of Spinoza on Masters, as the introduction to this edition indicates. It was also influenced by Browning's "Sordello" (1840), and perhaps by his "Pauline" (1833) and "Paracelsus" (1825) as well, all of which are discussed in the introduction. The poem may also have been influenced by Browning's "Saul" (1855), which ends with an experience of rapture in which the speaker finds new life through contact with God. Like "Isaiah Beethoven" and the present poem, "Saul" has a kind of emotional development characterized by slowly rising intensity, which reveals the impact of music on its composition. See also the first note to "Isaiah Beethoven."

Webster Ford

"Webster Ford" was the pseudonym under which the *Spoon River Anthology* poems appeared in *Reedy's Mirror* until editor William Marion Reedy revealed that Masters was the author in "The Writer of Spoon River," *Reedy's Mirror,* November 20, 1914, p. 1. The name is a composite of the last names of two famous Renaissance dramatists, John Webster (c. 1575-1634) and John Ford (1586-c. 1640), but, as Reedy noted, "the poetry . . . was not like anything of Webster's or Ford's." For discussions of this important poem, see Hurt, pp. 428-29, and the introduction to this edition. The latter relates the poem to the Apollo and Daphne myth, the poet's struggle for self-realization, and the mythic-symbolic structure of the *Anthology.*

Delphic Apollo: Apollo was the Greek god of poetry, to which Masters had dedicated himself. In ancient Greece the famous Temple of Apollo was at Delphi, so references to "Delphic Apollo" abound in Greek literature.

Poor Mickey fell down in the water tower to his death: See "Mickey M'Grew" and the note to that poem.

Plutus: In Greek mythology Plutus was the god of wealth. The speaker is apparently saying that wealth would have made him less fearful to serve Apollo—that is, to be a poet. In *Reedy's Mirror,* January 15, 1915, the poem refers to "Pluto," the god of Hades, the lower world.

Avenged: In *Reedy's Mirror* the word is "Revenged."

O leaves of me: That is, the poems (or pages) of the *Anthology* are "leaves" dropped by the poet.

The Spooniad

"The Spooniad" was Masters's first attempt to create an effective conclusion to his series of Spoon River monologues. It appeared alone in the December 18, 1914, issue of *Reedy's Mirror,* and shortly afterward Masters sent a copy to H. L. Mencken, calling it "the epic binding together of the more than two hundred dramatic expressions of the microcosm" (letter to H. L. Mencken, January 4, 1914, in Folder 23, Box 3, Flaccus-Masters Archive, Special Collections Division, Georgetown University Library). Although several more epitaph-poems appeared after "The Spooniad," Masters was already looking forward to the book version of the *Anthology,* where the poem does appear at the end, accompanied by the explanatory note about Jonathan Swift Somers and the fragment's publication in *Reedy's Mirror.*

"The Spooniad" is a mock-heroic poem that treats a matter of little consequence—a small-town squabble over the legalization of liquor—in an elevated style. In a 1955 letter to Kimball Flaccus, British critic John Cowper Powys commented on the poem's literary relationships: "The 'Dunciad' of Alexander Pope (1728) must have put the word *Spooniad* into his [Masters's] head, & his 'Spooniad'... shows how he himself loved reading Homer, for he has wonderfully caught and caricatured here the very way Homer describes his battles & cries to the Muse to help him!" (letter to Kimball Flaccus, July 22, 1955, p. 1., in Folder 41, Box 13, Kimball Flaccus Papers, Dartmouth College Library). More recently, Herb Russell has pointed out that "The Spooniad" satirizes dullness ("prohibitionist killjoys") and ends with an unfinished narrative, as does the famous work by Pope. See "Edgar Lee Masters's 'Spooniad': A Source and Its Significance," *The Markham Review* 6 (1977): 27. Of course, the supposed author of "The Spooniad," Jonathan Swift Somers, is a namesake of another famous eighteenth-century satirist, so within the context of the *Anthology,* he is the appropriate figure to produce such a poem. For a discussion of "The Spooniad," see the introduction to this edition.

One apparent source for the poem relates to the climactic fight between "hog-eyed Allen" and "Bengal Mike." According to the Canton newspaper, a man named Allen was knocked unconscious in a liquor-related fight at Lewistown, although no temperance advocates were involved: "Lewistown whisky and two of its *devotees* had a melee on last Saturday night, in which one of the parties, by name of Allen, had his skull crushed by a blow from some club or instrument in the hands of a man named Moore. At last accounts Allen was still lying unconscious" ("From the County Seat," Canton *Fulton County Ledger,* September 3, 1885, p. 1).

When the poem appeared in *Reedy's Mirror* on December 18, 1914, it was preceded by an introduction written by William Marion Reedy. Because that introduction places the poem in the literary context of the *Anthology* and probably reflects information supplied by Masters, it is reprinted here:

What time Spoon River flourished, people read the epics — "The Iliad" as done by Mr. Pope or by Chapman, "Paradise Lost" by Mr. Milton — and imitated them, at least some few did. One of these was Jonathan Swift Somers. You will recall him as expressing himself and the anti-climax of his life in a flower from the Anthology, published along in September, thus [the text of "Jonathan Swift Somers" follows].

He did "The Spooniad," or started to do it, in twenty-four books, in blank verse. But he did not complete even the first book. The frustrate fragment was found among his papers and is here published. It is a strangely good work in which you anticipate that you are going to be taken into a burlesque, only to find that the work is wrought in a savage sincerity and flames up into a vivid bit of village homeric, terribly realistic and with the comic spirit hardened into irony. The epic echoes are faithfully preserved, even unto the catalogue, and the champion bad men — how like they are to Hector, Ajax, Achilles, taunting and bellowing in the fight. All the trouble about a woman too, it seems. "Was this the face that launched a thousand ships and burnt the topless towers of Ilium?" For Troy, read Spoon River. The more it changes in the world, the more it is the same thing. And Jonathan Swift Somers, with something of the patronymic Dean in his heart and in his ink, in his epic achieves something finer than "Mac Flecknoe" in that it is comic in an Aristophanic sense, with a burning, blasting scorn of men's littleness. The commonplace is pictured in a parody of the sublime, and yet for all the parody these people live and hate and rage and bleed real blood. Behold how life does fiddle as Jonathan Swift Somers' "Soul takes fire" from an unworthy altar. "The Spooniad" fragment is the very essence of genius gone awry, of a great soul in a small place, in conflagration, and Life fiddling in mockery over all. Mr. Masters' ironic pity, as expressed in trivial-gigantic creativeness, is here at its most splendid abandon — hear the laughter, see the tears! W.M.R.

Anarch hands: The hands of an anarchist. "Anarch" is also the personification of chaos in Milton's Christian epic *Paradise Lost.*

Sing, muse, that lit Chian's face with smiles: The poet is invoking the aid of the muse that inspired Homer when he composed *The Iliad.* According to tradition, Homer was born on the island of Chios and, hence, was "Chian."

Greeks and Trojans: An allusion to Homer's *Iliad,* the style of which is being imitated.

Scamander: A Trojan River.

Peleus' son: Achilles, the Greek hero of the Trojan War.

to lose Chryseis: The mistress of Achilles, who is stolen by Agamemnon. She is called Briseis in *The Iliad.*

Momus: In Greek mythology, the god of ridicule and mockery; also, according to Hesiod, Momus is the son of Night.

Thalia: In Greek mythology, the muse of comedy and pastoral poetry.

the hall of Nicholas Bindle: This hall where the liberals meet is based on Beadle's Opera House in Lewistown. See the first note to "Nicholas Bindle." The opera house is described in Chandler, pp. 327-28.

the son / Of Alcmene: In Greek mythology Heracles was the son of Alcmene by Zeus.

hog-eyed Allen: According to Flaccus, this figure is based on Sam Norman, "a big bully type of man" who lived at Bernadotte, and who was later shot to death (pp. 104-5). But see the newspaper account about the liquor-related fight at Lewistown, quoted above.

Apollo: The Greek god of prophecy — here portrayed as unable to foresee the outcome of the fight.

the town marshal . . . shot by Jack Maguire: This event is depicted in "The Town Marshal" and "Jack Maguire." See the notes to those poems.

Epilogue

The "Epilogue" was written for the 1916 edition of the *Anthology*. It is a rather confusing verse drama that attempts to place the world of Spoon River, and all of humanity, in a cosmic perspective, and it was influenced by the Walpurgis Night section of Goethe's *Faust*. For discussions of it, see Herb Russell, *"Spoon River's* 'Epilogue,' " *Midwestern Miscellany* 7 (1979): 34-39, and the introduction to this edition.

Beelzebub: A name for the devil.

Loki: In Old Norse mythology, Loki was the god of mischief, evil, and destruction.

Yogarindra: Burgess identifies this obscure figure: "Yogarindra, usually written 'Yoga-nidra,' is said to have been one of the aspects of the goddess Durga, i.e., delusion personified. Hindu mythology says Durga was attended by sorceresses called 'yogini.' Masters probably smoothed the name for metrical reasons" (letter to Hallwas, p. 6).

As if she were her Borgia to his Nero: As if she were as unscrupulous as he. Cesare Borgia (1475-1507) was an unscrupulous Italian prince, and Nero (37-68 A.D.) was the infamous Roman emperor who burned his city and persecuted Christians.

the Warden: God.

"Laocoön": In Greek legend, Laocoön was a priest of Apollo at Troy. He and his two sons were strangled by serpents that came out of the sea.

A Note on the Editor

JOHN E. HALLWAS is Professor of English at Western Illinois University, where he founded *Essays in Literature* in 1973. He received his Ph.D. in English from the University of Florida in 1972. The author of numerous scholarly articles on Illinois authors and history, Hallwas has written or edited a dozen books as well, including *Illinois Literature: The Nineteenth Century* and *Studies in Illinois Poetry*. He also coedits the Prairie State Books series at the University of Illinois Press and edits the journal *Western Illinois Regional Studies*.

Mr. Dooley in Peace and in War
Finley Peter Dunne

Life in Prairie Land
Eliza W. Farnham

Carl Sandburg
Harry Golden

The Sangamon
Edgar Lee Masters

American Years
Harold Sinclair

The Jungle
Upton Sinclair

Twenty Years at Hull-House
Jane Addams

They Broke the Prairie
Earnest Elmo Calkins

The Illinois
James Gray

The Valley of Shadows: Sangamon Sketches
Francis Grierson

The Precipice
Elia W. Peattie

Across Spoon River
Edgar Lee Masters

The Rivers of Eros
Cyrus Colter

Summer on the Lakes, in 1843
Margaret Fuller

Black Hawk: An Autobiography
Edited by Donald Jackson

You Know Me Al
Ring W. Lardner

Chicago Poems
Carl Sandburg

Bloody Williamson: A Chapter in American Lawlessness
Paul M. Angle

City of Discontent
Mark Harris

Wau-Bun: The "Early Day" in the North-West
Juliette M. Kinzie

Spoon River Anthology
Edgar Lee Masters

Studs Lonigan
James T. Farrell

True Love: A Comedy of the Affections
Edith Wyatt

Windy McPherson's Son
Sherwood Anderson

So Big
Edna Ferber

The Lemon Jelly Cake
Madeline Babcock Smith

UNIVERSITY OF ILLINOIS PRESS
1325 SOUTH OAK STREET
CHAMPAIGN, ILLINOIS 61820-6903
WWW.PRESS.UILLINOIS.EDU